FLOWERING
of the
BAMBOO

FLOWERING of the BAMBOO

William Triplett

WOODBINE HOUSE · 1985

Library of Congress Catalogue Card Number: 85-051266

ISBN: 0-933149-01-8

Book and Jacket Design: Sicklesmith & Egly
Illustration: G. Byron Peck

Manufactured in the United States of America

1 2 3 4 5 6 7 8 9 10

FOR A.M. — WITH LOVE

CONTENTS

ACKNOWLEDGMENTS

In a space as small as this it's impossible to name everyone who gave their time and help in researching and writing this book. Some appear in the story, and others don't. Between Tokyo and Washington, D.C., there are scores of people whose unconditional generosity I will forever remember, but can never repay.

Some contributions stand out: I am deeply indebted to Ann Marie Young-Schaeffer for her love and support that made it possible for me to start and finish this book. To Shigeo Motoike my special gratitude for his invaluable assistance from first to last. I am also grateful for the steadfast care Diana McGonigle and Terry Rosenberg used in preparing the final manuscript. To John Roberts, for making his extensive files available to me while in Japan, I also owe a debt.

My warmest regard and thanks to my editor Marshall Levin, whose absolute belief in the idea and unwavering commitment to the manuscript have made this book as much his as it is mine.

William Triplett
Washington, D.C.
July 1985

LIST OF NAMES AND PLACES

NAMES

JAMES ABRAMS *Reporter, Copley News Service*
YOSHIKO AKUZAWA *Clerk, Teikoku Bank*
KENICHI ASANO *Reporter, Kyodo News Service*
HENRY EATON *Chief of Public Safety Division Police Branch*
MAKOTO ENDO *Attorney for the Society to Save Hirasawa*
BYRON ENGLE *Administrator-in-Charge, Public Safety Division*
JIRŌ FUJITA *Chief of Detectives, Tokyo Metropolitan Police Board*
LIEUTENANT EUGENE HATTORI *Liaison and Interpreter,
   Public Safety Division*
TAKEHIKO HIRASAWA *Adopted son of Sadamichi Hirasawa*
SADAMICHI HIRASAWA *Japanese artist*
INSPECTOR TAMIGORŌ IGII *Detective, Tokyo Metropolitan Police Board*
MAJOR D.C. IMBODEN *Press and Publications Section of SCAP*
LT. GENERAL SHIRŌ ISHII *Commander, Regiment 731*
SHIRŌ ISHIZAKI *Tokyo District Court Judge*
ARTHUR KIMBERLING *Investigator, Public Safety Division*
HARRY KOBAYASHI *Liaison, Tokyo Metropolitan Police Board*
GEORGE M. KOSHI *Lawyer, Legal Section of SCAP*
SHIGERU MATSUI *Doctor*
KANAME MITSUMATSU *Acting Secretary General, Society
   to Save Hirasawa*
TETSURO MORIKAWA *Founder, Society to Save Hirasawa*
JOHNSON MUNROE *Investigator, Public Safety Division*
MASAKO MURATA *Deposits Clerk, Teikoku Bank*
ICHIYO MUTO *Writer, Pacific-Asia Resource Center*
KAZUHIKO NAGOYA *Columnist, The Daily Yomiuri*
SERGEANT HIDEO NARUCHI *Criminal Investigation Division,
   Tokyo Metropolitan Police Board*
YASUZŌ OGAWA *Manager, Nakai Branch of the Mitsubishi Bank*
MAJOR SAM PLEMMONS *Chief, Medical Section of SCAP*
SADANORI SHIMOYAMA *President, Japanese National Railroads*

KATSUO SHINMURA   *Member, Japan House of Representatives*
KYOSHI SUZUKI   *Detective, Tokyo Metropolitan Police Board*
HAJIME TAKAGI   *Tokyo District Procurator*
RIICHI TAKEUCHI   *Reporter,* Yomiuri Shimbun
TOKUKAZU TANAKA   *Teller, Teikoku Bank*
MASAMI TOMIZAWA   *Editor,* Yomiuri Shimbun
KEIICHI TSUNEKAWA   *Member, Society to Save Hirasawa*
YOSHIO YAMADA   *Attorney for Sadamichi Hirasawa*

PLACES

CHIBA   *City on eastern shore of Tokyo Bay*
HARBIN   *City in central Manchuria*
HOKKAIDŌ   *Japan's northern island*
HONSHŪ   *Japan's central island*
IKEBUKURO   *Northwestern district of Tokyo*
JIMBŌCHO   *Area near downtown Tokyo*
KHABAROVSK   *City in far eastern Soviet Union*
KOSUGE PRISON   *Located near Tokyo, Japan*
KYŪSHŪ   *Japan's southern island*
MANCHURIA   *Territory in northeast China*
MARUNOUCHI   *Central district in Tokyo*
MIYAGI PRISON   *High-security prison located in Sendai, Japan*
NAKANO   *Western district of Tokyo*
OTARU   *City located on the island of Hokkaido*
SAKURADAMON   *Area of downtown Tokyo near Imperial Palace*
SENDAI   *City located on Honshu island north of Tokyo*
SHIINAMACHI   *Area of northwest Tokyo*
SHIMBASHI   *Southern district of Tokyo*
SHINJUKU   *Western district of Tokyo*
SUGINAMI   *Area in western Tokyo*

U.S. OCCUPATION TERMS

G-1   *8th Army Intelligence*
GHQ MEDICAL SECTION   *Division of SCAP responsible for medical and health concerns of the Occupation*
INTERNATIONAL MILITARY TRIBUNAL (FAR EAST) (IMT)   *Court of law for war crimes trials*
LEGAL SECTION   *SCAP's legal division*
PRESS AND PUBLICATIONS SECTION   *Division of SCAP responsible for monitoring the Japanese press*
PUBLIC SAFETY DIVISION   *Branch of SCAP responsible for reform of Japanese police forces*
SCAP   *Supreme Commander for the Allied Powers*

"I am
the wound
and the
knife! . . .
the victim
and the
executioner!"

CHARLES BAUDELAIRE
Flowers of Evil

PART I
In Savage Light

July 1947

TWO STRANGERS *look out over the Sea of Japan on a hot afternoon, cooled by a sharp, salty breeze. One wears layered kimonos, the other a business suit. The train ferry they ride cuts a smooth wake from Hokkaidō, the northern island, to Honshū, the central island. The strangers are both in their fifties, and both politely regard one another. It is a short ride.*

The man in the suit carries a small bag, the other a large portfolio. When their interest in the seascape wanes, their interchange begins, a ritual as old and revered as Mount Fuji itself:

The bows, the greetings.

A reaching into pockets, a showing of smiles, and the customary exchange of namecards.

A moment of study, a set of nods, a careful pronunciation.

A proper introduction.

The man with the suit and the bag is a doctor. He is curious about this stranger, a painter, and the portfolio he carries. The artist says that he is delivering one of his watercolors to the Crown Prince, who has accepted the work as a special gift. The doctor notes the painter's clear, intelligent eyes and thinks, "What a gentle and modest man." They chat some more, until the ferry docks.

It is one of a thousand chance meetings this day across

Japan. Nothing unusual has distinguished it, and there is little that might trigger a recollection by either the doctor or the artist, except maybe for a cleaning out of one's wallet to inventory namecards. But when the two men part, perhaps never to see each other again, they are fatefully linked by this ferry crossing in ways that no one, not even they themselves, can begin to imagine.

The significance of the encounter remains unknown throughout the Japanese summer and fall and into the winter, and does not begin to take form until January of 1948, on a Monday. A Monday that taunts fact. A Monday that breaks open under a steel gray dawn streaked with wind and sleet.

TOKYO
January 26, 1948

THE NIGHT'S RAINS turn
icy and white at Monday's first light. The city lies in a muddy mass
and hulking U.S. Army trucks begin to fill the roads, grinding and
sliding across war-ravaged Tokyo. The Occupation is in its third
year and no termination date is in sight. People are rising, heaters
are being ignited, kettles are warming on the stove-fires. Outside,
the temperature holds near freezing and shows little promise of
climbing higher. A glassy film begins to form on the mud, over the
sidewalks, across the cinder lots, inside the bomb craters.

In western Tokyo, on the edge of the Shinjuku district, Tokukazu
Tanaka tries to keep warm. The bitter cold penetrates the walls of
his house, and his heater is weak and ineffectual. Tanaka, a slim
young man who looks younger than his nineteen years, is preparing
to go to his job at the Teikoku Bank in the northwest corner of the
city. He wears one of the two military-looking business suits he
owns. His breakfast is a pasty porridge made from potatoes distributed by the Military Government. White rice, which had been the
staple of his diet, has been in short supply and he is lucky to find
it on his table more than three times a week. Tanaka is fighting to
avoid the poverty gripping millions in the wreckage of postwar
Japan.

He looks outside and sees that the rain has turned to a mixture
of sleet and snow, a rarity in Tokyo. Tanaka leaves his house at
eight o'clock to catch his train to work and hopes that the Teikoku
Bank will close early because of the severe weather.

Nearer the Shiinamachi branch of the Teikoku Bank, Masako

Murata wakes up, puts on a gray jacket and trousers, eats a hasty breakfast, and leaves at eight-thirty for the bank, where she works as a deposits clerk. As she walks through the messy cold, she too wonders if she and her fellow workers will be allowed to leave early today.

In this residential section, people heading to work crowd the roads, and Miss Murata is packed among the throng that moves across the muddy ground. Occasionally an American jeep drives through, but these roads mainly belong to people on foot. It seems to her that the winter gloom this morning is absorbing all sound except the slogging of feet through the unpaved streets.

The Teikoku Bank sits on the corner of an intersection barely seventy yards from the Shiinamachi train station. Many markets and shops crowd the neighborhood, and the bank itself stands beside private homes and tall trees. Directly across the way rises the Nagasaki Shinto Shrine, remarkable for its lustrous dark wood and placement on high ground, overlooking the neighborhood.

This corner is one of the few in this area which survived the American bombings. Less than a hundred yards in any direction, other structures and other homes were not so lucky. Three years have passed and still they lie in ashes.

When Miss Murata arrives at the bank a few minutes before nine o'clock, she opens the sliding wooden panels, removes her shoes at the entrance, places them among several other pairs already there, puts on slippers, and goes to change into the blue uniform which the female employees wear. At nine-thirty sharp the bank opens for business, and as the day wears on, the sleet pelting against the ceramic-tile roof changes to rain, which continues into the late afternoon.

In the main section of the bank the employees are conducting business as usual. The heater is giving off ample warmth, and light from the overhead lamps fills the workspace. Clerks work amid papers and ledgers on the two rows of desks that lead back from the counter at the front entrance. Mr. Tanaka sits in a swivel chair at his desk in the front row. Miss Murata sits in her space behind

14

the front counter. In the back row of the main room, Mr. Ushiyama, the manager, and Mr. Yoshida, the assistant manager, work at their desks.

Removed from the banking section, in a side part of the building, the custodian, Mr. Takizawa, lives with his wife and their two children, a nineteen-year-old daughter and an eight-year-old son. The custodian is nearing his fiftieth birthday.

Elsewhere in the city it is neither an especially busy nor a remarkable day, aside from the weather. The police and fire departments are preoccupied with their normal routines, and the press is writing about the usual stories: the black market prices, the rising crime rate, the weak economy, the International Military Tribunal trying accused war criminals, the new, directives issued by the U.S. Occupation, the dismal sanitation conditions in Tokyo, and communist activity in Japan and abroad.

In the Teikoku Bank things proceed quietly and normally until around two o'clock, when the branch manager, Ushiyama, complains of a severe stomachache. He has had this pain for about a week now, but today it feels sharper than ever before. Dysentery and typhoid are rampant, claiming lives at an alarming rate throughout Japan. Ushiyama says he must go home.

No one says anything, but several think, "Poor Ushiyama-san, he's got one of the deadly diseases. Go home. Call the doctor. Pray. It could just be a stomachache. . . .but for a whole week?"

Mr. Yoshida, Ushiyama's assistant, supervises the last hour of business after Ushiyama leaves. At three o'clock the bank closes its doors for the day. The clerks begin to collate the transactions and tally the money. Ledgers open, cash piles up, receipts are stamped, and totals are recorded. There are only thirty deposits to check, and Miss Murata is confident that she can do them quickly, in ten minutes at most, she tells herself. No one hears the gentle rapping at the side door, except for the clerk who sits nearest to it and who goes to see who is there.

"Could I please see my friend," says the man outside. "I own a used-books store around the corner. I tried to get here before the bank closed, but the weather, and the time, well. . .but it's only a few minutes after closing, and I thought my friend would let me in to make a deposit for today."

The clerk says everyone is busy counting receipts, but he will check with the man's friend. The man says no, apologizes many times for imposing, and says, "Don't bother him, I'll come back tomorrow."

Bows. "Dōmo arigato." The man plods through the mud back to his store.

The clerk returns to his chair and resumes counting with everyone else. Some minutes later, another rapping comes. Yoshiko Akuzawa, a nineteen-year-old woman who has recently begun working for the bank, opens the side door and sees a rather thin, uniformed man with a pale complexion and a handsome oval face. He appears to be in his late forties, but she thinks he might be older because of the two brown spots on his left cheek. She has seen these age spots on older men before. He wears an armband bearing the official mark of the Metropolitan Office, City Hall of Tokyo, and he carries a small olive-drab bag with its strap slung over his left shoulder. His burnt-orange rubber boots are old and worn, but they are also surprisingly clean for such a sloppy day. According to Japanese custom, he presents his card:

JIRŌ YAMAGUCHI, MD
TOKYO METROPOLITAN OFFICE
WELFARE DEPT., WELFARE MINISTRY

The doctor asks to see the bank manager about an urgent mat-

16

ter. Miss Akuzawa, who had learned at an early age to be conscious of social vectors, notes the doctor's card and his armband, and politely asks him to enter through the front door. Yamaguchi rounds the bank and heads for the sliding panels, while the young woman readies a pair of slippers for him. After taking off his boots in the entrance, he steps into the slippers and walks into the bank. She says that the manager has gone home for the day with a terrible stomachache, but that the assistant manager will speak to him. Dr. Yamaguchi nods, *"Dōmo arigato."* No one takes special notice of the doctor's arrival since it is common for people to try to get into the bank right at closing time. Miss Akuzawa and the doctor walk to the back row of desks, passing Mr. Tanaka who sits working at his desk. Out of the corner of his eye, Tanaka sees a man in a brown coat with Miss Akuzawa, but he does not look up. Miss Murata does not focus on anything beyond her thirty deposits, which she has not yet finished processing.

Yoshida, the assistant manager, becomes deeply concerned when the doctor alerts him, in a very low voice, that the public well in front of a Mr. Aida's house, which is about five minutes away from the bank, has been responsible for a number of dysentery cases reported in Shiinamachi. In fact, the doctor continues, one of Aida's tenants was stricken today with dysentery, and this tenant had been in the bank today to make a deposit.

"How have you learned of this so quickly?" Yoshida asks.

"The doctor who saw the stricken man made a direct report to the Occupation authorities," Yamaguchi tells him. "I've been sent by Lieutenant Parker, who directs a disinfecting team with the Occupation. I have to inoculate everyone against dysentery, and I will also have to disinfect any items that have been handled today. Receipts, money, accounts, books. Everything. No one will be allowed to leave until I do, which will be when Lieutenant Parker and his team arrive to check my work. They will be here soon."

Poor Ushiyama-san. . .he must have it. . .

Yoshida understands the emergency. The doctor takes from his bag a small metal box and two bottles of pre-mixed solutions with English letters on their labels. The smaller bottle is marked "First Drug," and the much larger bottle, "Second Drug." Yamaguchi explains in detail how he has precipitated this extremely potent oral serum which the Allies have just developed through experiments using oil from palm trees.

"It's so powerful that it will make you absolutely immune from dysentery." he tells Yoshida. "Administering the vaccine will be a complicated procedure," the doctor continues, "because of its strength and relative newness. It has been carefully tested, but few people are familiar with it. The way you take the medicine is quite unusual."

The assistant manager considers asking for more reassuring details about the process, but Yamaguchi, in his solicitous way, anticipates Yoshida's questions before he can ask them.

"Why don't you bring me your teacups," Yamaguchi says.

Back at a desk in the front, Tanaka, the bank clerk, is finishing his collating. He does not see that all of the bank staff, including the custodian Takizawa and his wife and children, are standing around Yoshida's table. Yoshida calls him and Tanaka looks up, nods, and joins the group. Dr. Yamaguchi is measuring out the last drop of the first dose. Sixteen teacups, each belonging to one of the assembled employees, sit arrayed on a tray on the table. Yamaguchi takes his pipette and, holding it carefully, expertly, as if the pipette were a dagger in his hand, drips some of the liquid into each cup. Everyone takes his own cup. Little Yoshihiro Takizawa, the eight-year-old, uses both hands.

Before anyone drinks the medicine, Dr. Yamaguchi pronounces a solemn warning. This strong serum can cause great damage to the gums and to tooth enamel, therefore it must be swallowed in a specific manner. So saying, he dips the syringe into the liquid, squeezes up a measure, then drips the medicine onto his tongue, which he has placed over his lower front teeth and tucked under his lower lip. He tilts his head back and lets the medicine roll back into his throat.

18

The doctor looks at his wristwatch and raises his hand into the air, waiting. When he signals, they all lift their teacups and drip the liquid onto their tongues exactly as he has demonstrated.

Several people feel their mouths contracting from the bitterness. Yoshida says that it tastes like gin. There is barely enough serum in each dose to make it down their throats. Tanaka thinks that all of his medicine has stayed in his mouth. He thinks he should have some more, but feels certain that the doctor knows what he is doing. Yamaguchi announces that in sixty seconds he will administer another dose.

Miyako Akiyama, a twenty-three-year-old clerk who lives in the neighborhood, asks if she can have a gargle because the medicine has parched her throat. Yamaguchi says no, telling her that for the vaccine to be effective no one can drink anything for a full sixty seconds after taking the Second Drug, which he now pours generously into their cups. He checks his wristwatch as he pours, making certain to finish well before one minute has passed. Again he signals and they drink. This time they feel the liquid roll down their throats and into their stomachs. Tanaka feels confident now that he has been properly inoculated. The doctor says that they should now rinse out their mouths to make sure they have not hurt themselves from the medicine's potency. Fifteen minutes have passed since Dr. Yamaguchi introduced himself at the bank's side door.

The streets of Shiinamachi are already crowded with people heading for home. The darkness is deepening but not yet complete, which is normal here for a winter afternoon some minutes before four o'clock. The rain has lessened but the sharp chill has not eased. Soon another January evening in Tokyo will begin.

As the people rush past on the sidewalk, a young woman in a blue uniform crawls toward them. She inches through the cold muddy ground, desperate to stop anyone, but she can barely speak. Her agony is apparent. She is moaning, babbling. Two women see her and bend down to help.

"Please. . .at the liquor store. . .help me. . .I. . .my friend. . .get her. . .please. . . ."

She writhes, contorts. The women cannot tell if she is drunk or insane or both.

"The bank. . .it's awful. . .my friend!"

She cries out in delirium. One of the women runs to the corner liquor store, finds the friend, and tells her that something dreadful is happening. From the store they call the police. On the sidewalk, a crowd gathers around Miss Murata, who by now has begun to lose consciousness.

At the Mejiro police station, not far from the Teikoku Bank, a call has just come from the Shiinamachi district. Unsure of what has happened there, the policemen hurry through the neighborhood as ambulances race across the city to meet them.

The policemen arrive to find Miss Murata surrounded by a crowd, and then clear the way for the ambulance to rush her to Catholic International Hospital. Then the policemen turn to the bank and walk inside to an eerie scene.

There is a strange, unmolested calm. Nothing appears to have been disturbed. On a desk sit several stacks of money, almost three hundred thousand yen. Papers, books, and ledgers lie across several other desks, as if just moments ago people had been working on them. There is a tray of neatly arranged teacups, unwashed. Everything seems to be in its proper place, everything except for the bodies.

They are lying everywhere—in the panelled corridors, on the wooden floors, in the tiled bathroom, in the tatami-matted rooms. The most unsettling sight is a line of corpses near the water fountain, as if their last act was a desperate lunge for water. Almost all of them lie with their eyes still open. Blood and vomit trickle from their mouths.

"Some are still alive!"

Young Tanaka hears a rush of heavy clops. The ground is moving! He lies still but feels the ground shake. Boots. Footfall.

"This one's alive! What's your name?"

"Uhhhnnnnn. . . . ."

"What's your name?"

"Uhhhnnnnn. . . . ."

Tanaka is rising. Commotion. He is in the air.

"What's your name?"

"Uhhhnnnnn. . . ." He floats, into a bed, into a tiny room. He shakes. Coughing, spitting, combustion, motion. The room pitches, heaves. His ears split from a wailing siren. He sinks back into the. . . .

"What's your name. . . .your name. . . .your. . . . .?"

Four more victims are carried out to the waiting ambulances, engulfed in the swell of a growing crowd. Those nearest the front entrance push into the bank. They are neighborhood people come to offer help, in the Japanese way. As the police begin to remove the dead, some officers talk among themselves, calling this the worst case of food poisoning they have ever seen. Sixteen victims in all. The neighbors ask what can they do to help, and the police answer that, strangely, little is out of order. Somehow there is not much to clean. The neighbors say they will tidy up where they can. They start by washing the teacups.

Directly across from the moat around the Imperial Palace, in the press office of the headquarters of the Tokyo Metropolitan Police Board (MPB), a group of newspapermen stand around the stove trying to keep warm while chatting about the uneventful day. One reporter, Riichi Takeuchi, mentions the wailing ambulances that had zoomed past not long ago. He and the others wondered what all the noise had been about.

Takeuchi is a handsome young editor and writer in the group working a homicide beat for the *Yomiuri Shimbun,* one of the largest and oldest papers in Japan. He knows the workings of the MPB very well, and over time has developed good sources within the Criminal Investigation Division. The MPB has not issued a statement giving any reason for the fleet of ambulances, so the reporters think the police might not be involved. But they know that the MPB is not always forthcoming with explanations, particularly with details. One or two sirens would not have drawn too much attention, but so many. . . .

As the reporters talk about it, their curiosity increases. Competition among Japanese journalists for stories is keen, so none of the reporters yet dismisses the speculation about the sirens. Takeuchi feels a tap on his shoulder and someone whispers in his ear. He recognizes the voice as that of his colleague and friend, Sakari Shiratō, another *Yomiuri* reporter working a health beat.

"Over here," Shiratō whispers.

The two men step out of the circle. Takeuchi listens, and Shirató very quietly continues:

"You heard those ambulances?"

"Yes."

"The Teikoku Bank branch in Shiinamachi. Looks like the biggest case of food poisoning in years."

"When?"

"About an hour or two ago. The police are still up there. If we work fast we can get the scoop on this."

A booming voice interrupts:

"Takeuchi-san, *denwa!*"

Takeuchi excuses himself to pick up his telephone. Ono, his boss at the *Yomiuri,* asks if anyone has moved on those ambulances yet.

"Shirató-san just told me it's food poisoning at the Teikoku Bank. He's about to go there now."

"No. Keep him there. I want *you* to cover this. I've got a feeling it's not food poisoning."

They continue talking and Ono elaborates. Takeuchi hangs up and tells Shirató about the change in plans. He sends for another *Yomiuri* reporter and dispatches him immediately to Shiinamachi with orders to get inside the bank somehow.

"Phone back your report," Takeuchi instructs the reporter. "We're going to write this story tonight."

The other journalists are still talking. Takeuchi knows that his lead will become common knowledge any minute, and he also knows the risk of embarrassment he and Ono are taking by playing out this hunch instead of waiting for more solid information. The young editor casually sits down at his desk, consciously trying not to draw attention to himself, and begins composing a story about mass murder at the Teikoku Bank.

The main floor of the Catholic Hospital. Confusion. Ambulances race up to the entrance, one, two, five times. Six dying people are rushed inside. Delirium tremens. Nuns and doctors fight to save lives.

"What's your name?"

Policemen everywhere listen to the desperate rantings of the poison victims. In the ramblings they look for any sign, any clue.

"What happened?"

"Uhhnnnn. . . ."

Rubber hoses and stomach pumps. Fluids and bile rise and spew. The patients' heads roll from side to side. There is coughing, retching. The officers watch with concern—

"This one's going! "

A cry from another room. A frantic blur of hands and tubing, pumps and fears. A mad struggle to stop the dying, to cheat death, to hold it back for another hour.

"No!!!"

Chaos. Cursing and crying, running and racing, fighting over equipment and tactics. Two victims are slipping, sinking. One is in the clear now, and two more are improving. The policemen stand next to one, asking her questions, straining to hear.

"What did you eat?"

". . .drink. . ."

"What?"

". . .dysen. . .tery. . .doc. . .tor. . ."

"What happened?"

". . .med. . .uh. . .cine. . .medicine. . ."

"Medicine?"

". . .special. . .doc. . .tor. . ."

Another cry of agony, a guttural cry from the other room.

"Another one's going!"

The doctors go running in a rush of desperation, another sudden futile surge. Another corpse.

"What's happening here!?"

The policemen continue to move through the madness, asking questions. They piece together something about a special doctor, for dysentery, with medicine, and drinking. Suddenly, a cold reali-

zation hits them. This is not food poisoning; there has been no mention of food.

One policeman rushes back to the bank:

"There's been a mistake. Start looking for any evidence. Where are those teacups?"

For Jirō Fujita, head of the MPB's Criminal Investigation Division and chief of detectives, Tuesday, January 27, has been another long day in the Sakuradamon station. The disarray of police affairs resulting from the Occupation's plan to redesign the Japanese police system is causing constant problems. The inexperience of many of his men has resulted in numerous botched investigations. Worse, Chief Fujita knows, corruption is running high within the MPB. The newspapers also know it and continue to print damaging articles about it.

Fujita is athletic looking, a vestige of his college days in the judo club. As usual, he wears a dark, plain suit. Today the sleet has held off, which has made the assignment of cases simpler than yesterday, given that most policemen have only one means of transportation—their own feet. The lucky ones with bicycles are the envy of many, and those few who have access to a car are looked upon as demigods. Ironically though, travelling on foot often gets you there quicker than going either by bicycle or by car because of the miserable traffic and presiding chaos that choke the city's streets. However, the improved weather puts only one complicating factor out of Fujita's way. Disorganization and disrepute remain constant worries, and now this case—twelve people, including an eight-year-old child, dead inside the Teikoku Bank from some type of poison.

The coroners are not sure if it is cyanic silver, potassium cyanide, or prussic acid because they do not have enough of the substance to analyze with the appropriate tests. They would have had enough had the teacups—to Fujita's utter incredulity—not been washed clean by the neighbors. Fujita has learned that autopsies on the victims performed at Tokyo University and Keiō University suggest that the poison was potassium cyanide, but no one can be sure because the dosage was minimal, leaving the traces in the body almost undetectable.

In his report, which he has just released to every police station in the country, Chief Fujita has noted that the four people who survived the crime managed to tell the police important details of what happened. They all spoke of a doctor, dysentery, inoculation, and fainting. They told of the doctor's uniform, his equipment, his authority, his calm, even his warm smile and gracious warning. Fujita mentioned that an investigation of the bank's cash drawers and safe disclosed a missing sum of about one hundred sixty thousand yen along with a check which had been deposited that same day by someone named Toyoharu Gotō. Chief Fujita called attention to the crime's "tremendous repercussions" both for the public and the police force, and noted that the press is already denouncing the MPB.

As if the case itself were not difficult enough, Chief Fujita and his men are confronted by a larger, more obstructive reality. An aura of order hangs like a fine mist over Tokyo, but it only barely conceals the confusion roiling in the rubble and ashes of the city. One day's bombing alone had turned sixteen square miles of residential Tokyo into a raging inferno. On March 10, 1945, three hundred B-29s flew unmolested overhead and dropped their full arsenal of incendiaries on the city. The fires drove the temperatures to two thousand degrees Fahrenheit, melting roofs, buckling pavements, and sucking the air out of people's lungs even before singeing their flesh. Fujita is well aware that the city's wounds are still raw and open almost three years later, leaving all movement limited.

That the Mejiro officers got to the bank within twenty minutes was no small wonder. There are still many impassable roads, and the network of communication is limited. In the entire country there is only one telephone for every one hundred people. Almost a third of Tokyo's police stations still do not have direct telephone or telegraph contact with the other stations. Each station has as its motor pool the grand total of one car. The availability of taxis, buses, trams, and bicycles is changeable, undependable, yet often determines the intensity and daily assignment of MPB investigations. Fujita has come to live with this one more unpleasant fact. Crimes are sinister riddles, he learned long ago, which men think up for other men to solve. The answer, pursued, presents itself, even when chased on foot.

Fujita knows that the stakes are high for solving this robbery-murder. The Teikoku killings are not only gruesome, but a national shame. They exploit the feudal reverence for authority. Finding the culprit is crucial to salvaging whatever remnants of credibility or honor the MPB still has. He also knows that morale among his men is low, and the odds of cracking this case are slim. An order is given to cancel all vacations and leave, and every officer in Tokyo is mobilized for the investigation.

At the same time, the Japanese press is not only following the police investigation, but is doing a little investigating on its own. Some reporters are even posing as detectives.

A few blocks away from MPB Headquarters is the General Headquarters (GHQ) of the American Occupation. Inside the GHQ building are the offices of SCAP (Supreme Commander for the Allied Powers), headed by General Douglas MacArthur. SCAP resembles a large government bureaucracy staffed by soldiers and civilians. Everything from sewer repair to legal reform comes under SCAP's broad authority.

In a multi-storied office building, just across the street from General MacArthur's offices, officers of the Allied Occupation Public Safety Division (PSD) work at their assigned tasks. On the upper floor, Henry Eaton discharges his duties as chief of the PSD's police branch in Occupied Japan. One of the police branch's primary goals is to transform the entire Japanese police system from a feudal force into a democratic service. The man assigned to that task is Byron Engle, one of Eaton's Administrators-in-Charge. It is Engle's show, and for a country boy from Missouri, supervising the restructuring and reorganizing of a foreign nation's police force is worlds removed from where he began.

Byron Engle had started out as a meat packer at seventeen, then five years later joined the Kansas City Police Department as a patrolman. He worked his way up through the ranks until he became the second highest official in the K.C.P.D. He then attended the FBI Academy in Washington, D.C., where some months later he received a call from the War Department telling him that General MacArthur was looking for six police administrators to come to Japan to oversee the reorganization of that nation's police force. Engle was offered the job, accepted it, and in 1946 found himself in Tokyo working with other police administrators from locales as different as Los Angeles, Louisville, and Miami.

Engle and the others supervise a team of American investigators who have been brought over to help. Johnson Munroe, one of the investigators, is a newspaperman-turned-policeman from Nashville. A recent arrival in Engle's department, he has just completed his first assignment in Tokyo as an investigator with the International Prosecution Section of the International Military Tribunal, where his responsibilities had centered on assisting the prosecution in the trial of Hideki Tōjō, the Japanese Prime Minister convicted and hanged for war crimes.

Engle likes his job and does it well. On almost any evening he can look out his office window and see across the street into General MacArthur's office, where the legendary military man spends many late hours pacing the floor. Engle knows the weight on MacArthur's shoulders and watches the American *Shōgun* in his moments filled with pipe smoke and silence.

The police administrators and investigators do not intervene in Tokyo police investigations, unless asked to. As a matter of course, however, they do receive copies of all police reports. Engle, Munroe, and the others are busy today as most days, poring over policy changes and massive structural reforms. Japan's new Constitution, adopted last May, has been in effect for less than a year now. It is based on American democratic ideals and the protection of civil liberties. Yet Munroe and Engle realize that traditional Japanese police practices are still causing problems.

An American officer named Kimberling from the Public Safety Division walks into a Tokyo police station. His boss, Engle, has sent him to inspect the lock-ups. Kimberling talks with the Japanese station chief about the prisoner in the first cell. The prisoner watches them through the wooden bars.

"Why is this man here?"

"For stealing a kitchen knife."

"How long has he been here?"

"Two months."

"Two months for stealing a kitchen knife?"

"Yes."

"How long is his sentence?"

"He hasn't been sentenced."

"Why is he being held without a sentence?"

"He hasn't been tried yet."

"Why hasn't he been tried yet?"

"He hasn't confessed yet."

The more Byron Engle examines the situation, the more he knows that wholesale reform is necessary. The Japanese police encounter, he has learned, used to be a ritual of terror and subversion. Arrest was tantamount to conviction, and nearly ninety-eight percent of all arrests conveniently resulted in the suspect's confession. There were very few, if any, "unsolved" cases in Japanese police files, and people lived in constant fear of being stopped by a policeman.

Already the Occupation authorities have removed thousands upon thousands of people from Japanese public service because of their proven or suspected ultra-nationalist sentiment—the spiritual source, the Americans said, of Japan's bloodthirsty war. With these ideological undesirables purged, the Americans now are confident that democracy can begin to take root in the country and flourish. But the purging of the police departments has caused another and, in Engle's view, equally formidable problem. The ranks have been refilled with men who have little or no police work experience. Only certain officers know who is supposed to be doing what, and how or where. The lines of authority and responsibility are blurred, and among the Americans in Tokyo there is a feeling that the MPB still relies too heavily on the Occupation authorities for help. More strident critics call the police a silly band of puppets, incompetent and ineffectual without their former strong-arm tactics. Engle and his men are preparing to put the entire police force, numbering one hundred thousand officers, through intensive retraining. Among the subjects and skills to be taught for the first time in Japan are what a fingerprint is, how to lift one, and how to use it as evidence.

Near where Engle sits, Johnson "Jack" Munroe, who is spending most of his time just getting oriented to his new office, finds a copy of a Tokyo MPB report on his desk. It is about a bizarre bank robbery.

The snow is deep during winters in Otaru, a city on Hokkaidō island. In a dimly lit room inside a small wooden house, a painter stands at his easel, mixing pigments and thinking about his recent visit to his home in Tokyo. He had spent the early part of a Monday with one of his daughters and her husband in their downtown house.

30

Then, in the early afternoon he had taken the train back to his home where his wife and other daughter lived, but they were out. Only his daughter's American boyfriend had been there, and the two of them had played cards into the evening. The painter could never remember the American's name—Ely or Eddy—a GI who had met the artist's daughter at the Ginza Post Exchange where she worked. This American was a pleasant fellow, whatever his name was.

The artist also thinks about his work, and how proud he is to have a painting in the Imperial Palace. The Crown Prince of Japan accepted the piece as a gift from the artist last July. That honor alone is worth more than any sum that his other paintings might fetch. And he could use money. Before he left for Tokyo he could not even afford to pay his utility bill.

BANK ROBBER KILLS TWELVE WITH POISON
TOKYO POLICE SEEK POISON ROBBER
BANK ROBBER POISONS SIXTEEN IN DARING COUP—
TWELVE DIE

The headlines scream in bold type on the front page of every newspaper in Japan, from the *Mainichi* dailies to the *Yomiuri* papers to the *Nippon Times*. Everyone throughout the country is struck by the drama that has hit Tokyo like a bolt of lightning. Papers are selling faster than the presses can print them. While the entire nation reads with shocked fascination, one man in downtown Tokyo reads in horror. Yasuzō Ogawa, a middle-aged man who manages the Nakai branch of the Mitsubishi Bank, can hardly believe that he is reading about a scenario with which he is already familiar, except for the tragic ending.

On January 19, 1948, Ogawa and his staff at the Mitsubishi Bank wind up business after a normal day. Suddenly a uniformed man enters carrying a briefcase and wearing an armband of the Tokyo Metropolitan Office, and hands Ogawa his card.

Ogawa asks Dr. Jirō Yamaguchi what he wants. The doctor says that he has been sent to disinfect some money that has been deposited today by a known carrier of dysentery. Ogawa cannot imagine who this carrier of dysentery might be.

"Ōtani-san," Yamaguchi tells him. "A worker from a factory in the neighborhood here."

Ogawa has a clerk check the receipt books, and sure enough, a Mr. Ōtani has been in today and deposited 610 yen in postal orders.

Ogawa asks what should be done. Yamaguchi takes a bottle from his briefcase and drips a small amount of liquid onto the receiving book page and onto the postal orders. This accomplished, he bows and leaves.

Ogawa finishes reading the story about the Teikoku Bank killings and hurries to the nearby Marunouchi police station.

Aside from sketchy descriptions of the murderer from the survivors, Fujita has little to go on other than the namecard which the doctor left behind, perhaps as a sinister signature to his work. As a matter of routine, Fujita's men are checking out this Dr. Yamaguchi, if indeed there is a Jirō Yamaguchi who is employed now, or ever was employed, by the Metropolitan Office's Health Ministry. But Fujita holds little hope for this lead. His men are trying to trace the namecard back to the shop that printed it, but this second lead also has little promise. In Tokyo there seems to be a printer on every block. Almost every Japanese adult has a stock of personal namecards. In virtually every social or business meeting, people exchange their cards.

Not only has this crime struck in the middle of the most chaotic period in the history of the Tokyo police, and not only does the manner in which it was committed leave almost no clues behind, but it is a crime without precedent, a crime out of nowhere. It happens in daylight, in urban Tokyo, with hundreds of people walking past. It is executed with expert and chilling precision, and, completed, reseals itself like the closing of a surgical wound. It laughs at Fujita's claim that the police can protect the people, that Tokyo's police force knows its job and does it well.

The MPB is unable to haul in the usual suspects, the pool of repeat offenders, since the intellect and expertise required for this crime disqualify them. The police begin to wonder if the killer could have known that by pulling off such a cunning crime he would shift the public's attention away from his act and onto the police, that the public would condemn the police for their ineptitude and marvel at his barbaric genius. Was this a set-up? How long had it been planned? Who could have the expertise?

Fujita is aware of the foreboding air that has lodged itself inside the Sakuradamon station and is expanding like a dark cloud. One thing clear to him and to everyone is that either the police will solve the Teikoku case, or the twelve dead will haunt them forever. Shame is something no one forgets, and Fujita is acutely aware of this as he finds himself steering a search that has virtually nowhere to go.

Ogawa tries to explain. "Last week," he says, "a man came into our bank after closing, and he said he was a doctor and that a man infected with dysentery had been in the bank. He said a Lieutenant Porter or Parker sent him to disinfect the books and the money. I'm sure it's the same man." The officers at the Marunouchi station call MPB headquarters. They get Fujita on the Sakuradamon station line and relay what Ogawa has told them. Fujita leaves immediately for the Marunouchi station along with several of his men.

A persistent caller asks to speak with the officer in charge of the Teikoku investigation, but is told that Chief Fujita has just left. The caller asks to talk to any officer connected with the investigation. He wants to tell the officer something the police should know.

The man says he manages the Ebara branch of the Yasuda Bank here in Tokyo. Last November a man dressed like a doctor came into the bank and said that a typhus epidemic had broken out in the area and that he had been sent by the Occupation forces to inoculate everyone against infection. The manager says he agreed to cooperate, and then the doctor said he had to go out to his jeep to get his equipment and would be right back to perform the group vaccination. The doctor returned, gave everyone something to drink, and left. Nothing happened.

The caller says he never thought much about it until reading the paper this morning. The description of the Teikoku killings match what the manager remembers about the visit to his bank, except for one thing—the doctor's card did not identify him as Jirō Yamaguchi. The manager says he still has the card, which he pulls out as he speaks on the phone. It bears the name of Shigeru Matsui, M.D.

Chief Fujita listens carefully to Ogawa recount last week's incident at his branch of the Mitsubishi Bank. Ogawa says he feels sure he could identify the killer, but that he cannot really add anything to the description which the police already have. He says that a few of his clerks could serve as witnesses because they got a good look at the man when he first arrived. The police are grateful for the information, even if it does not amount to much.

Ogawa's testimony describes a definite rehearsal attempt, Fujita concludes. Such an elaborate crime would likely require practice. This revelation deepens the MPB's suspicion that the killer has a calculating intellect, and is possibly something of criminal genius.

Suddenly Ogawa recalls one more item. The doctor's armband was not like the one described in the Teikoku murders. It was not from the Metropolitan Office; rather, it had something written or painted on it about the Tokyo Epidemic Prevention Center.

Across town, at the Gokoku Temple, a Buddhist priest conducts the funeral service for the twelve dead. As the priest chants a ritual prayer, the family of mourners huddle against the cold.

When the news about this other rehearsal at the Yasuda Bank last November reaches Fujita and his men, the Yasuda manager, answering the same questions asked of Ogawa, tells them he is fairly certain that he and his employees would recognize the man if they saw him again, but no, they could not add anything to the description, except one point. The armband worn by the doctor was different from both the January 19 rehearsal and the Teikoku crime. It was not of the Metropolitan Office, nor from the Epidemic Prevention Department, but from some other agency, if it even was an agency. No one can really remember in detail. Health Office? Welfare Ministry? The manager tells them that the doctor, or whoever he was, gave strict instructions on how to drink the medicine, just as the Teikoku murderer did, and that the instructions matched the description he had read in the newspaper this morning. Also, he left a namecard.

Another one. The check-up on Dr. Jirō Yamaguchi's card has not yet been completed, but Fujita is convinced it will prove to be a fake. "Dr. Shigeru Matsui" this one reads. Disgusted at having nothing more solid in hand than this second, certainly bogus name-card, Fujita turns it over to his detectives for investigation. Another police routine, another step toward mockery.

Newspapers are being snatched as they reach the newsstands. Readers are hungry for new information about the Teikoku murders, almost forgetting about the squalor of occupied Tokyo. Even the black market prices, usually a focus of desperate interest to the Japanese, go virtually unnoticed next to headlines about the Teikoku investigation. Rumors about the crime are spreading across Japan like an epidemic. The mystery is grimly intriguing. People are torn between revulsion and respect—what a vicious crime, but what fearless daring, they think, worthy of the Samurai. And the consequences are major, national, mounting. An editorial in today's Yomiuri Shimbun *enjoins:*

> *The killer must be caught quickly, or the reputation of the Japanese police will be lost. People should realize that they are no longer under feudalistic rule and do not have to obey authorities unquestioningly.*

Within forty-eight hours of the crime the MPB has produced a number of witnesses, but no hard evidence. They have drawn certain conclusions about their quarry, most significantly their belief that more than one man is involved. A gang, all with sure hands and diabolical expertise. Two rehearsals, months of planning, and the mysterious Lieutenant Parker. Maybe the Americans could help, if Parker is a real person, and not some phantom, some killer's ruse. If the Parker lead proves solid, it will be the first unequivocal piece of evidence the MPB has. If. . . .

Two days later, Chief Fujita and his men are in a state of disbelief. The reports on their leads, few and unpromising as they believed them to be, have just come in, and for a crime so well planned and executed, there appear to be some remarkably stupid holes.

A Jirō Yamaguchi was indeed once employed by the Welfare Ministry in the fall of 1947, back when the disastrous typhoon struck. He remained for a month or so afterward in the Ministry until he was discharged for "improper conduct," the records show. The records do not show, however, a current address, but the police feel confident they can turn one up within a short time.

A printer in the Suginami ward on the west side of Tokyo recalls having printed twenty namecards with "Jirō Yamaguchi, M.D." on them for a man who fits the description of the killer.

Shigeru Matsui, the name on the card left at the Yasuda Bank rehearsal in November 1947, turns out to be an actual doctor, employed by the Welfare Ministry, and working in Sendai, a Japanese city only a few hours north of Tokyo.

No one says anything. Would a criminal genius be capable of the gross stupidity of leaving his own namecard at the scene? Could he have believed that anything so obvious would automatically be discounted? No one dares venture an opinion.

Fujita and his men believe that neither Yamaguchi or Matsui is the killer, but feel that one or possibly both of them might be able to offer important insight as to how their cards reached the scenes of this crime. The printer of Dr. Yamaguchi's cards would serve as another key witness, and he might even have an address for his customer. They agree that the printer seems the most promising lead. But then again, they wonder if maybe one of the doctors might actually be their man. It would be a bizarre twist if either Yamaguchi or Matsui turned out to be the killer, but after the strange series of events that has unfolded since the crime, nothing would be too surprising. Shocking maybe, but not surprising.

The investigation team divides into four subunits, each with a different angle to pursue. One investigates the robbery, one studies the unique methodology of the crime, one researches the availability in Tokyo of all forms of cyanide, and one checks out namecards.

Within each division the investigators are separated further into two groups, one for digging up evidence in the field, the other for processing and evaluating the evidence collected. The MPB is mobilizing, holding back no resources in solving these murders. Twenty thousand officers are involved in the investigation. In fact, the investigation of all other cases has been suspended.

Just answering the telephones in Tokyo's police stations keeps several hundred policemen busy on a full-time basis because the phones are ringing without let-up; people are calling to offer information. As the police begin tracking their new leads, a couple of calls capture their attention. Another bank manager is on the phone.

Did this guy practice in every bank in town?!

This manager says that he has just looked over a pile of checks cashed in his bank this morning, and one bears the name of Toyoharu Gotō. Among the stack of bills that the Teikoku killer took was a check bearing the same name. The manager maintains that he has positively identified the check as the stolen one. On the back of the check there is, he says, a signature and an address.

An officer from the Totsuka police station is on another line. He says they have detained someone who has two previous convictions for poisoning. A fifty-one-year-old former bank clerk who is the son of a physician. He does not match the physical description, but the officer believes this man is worth interrogating. The connections—knowledge of banking operations, access to drugs through his father, and experience with poisons—are too important to ignore. Chief Fujita agrees, and dispatches officers to the Totsuka station to interrogate the suspect, and to the bank to retrieve the check.

The Mejiro police station where the initial report of the crime was received, is designated as headquarters for the Teikoku investigation. After surveying the Mejiro operation, and after learning of all the new information, the Inspector-General of the MPB announces to the press that he feels "confident" that vital evidence will be secured "within two or three days" and an arrest will follow shortly.

After recovering from the poisoning and going home, Masako Murata and the three other bank employees who survived find themselves dogged by reporters who compete for their stories. The reporters want exclusive interviews and the scoop on when someone will identify one of the suspects as the killer.

One persistent journalist, Riichi Takeuchi of the *Yomiuri Shimbun,* focuses his efforts solely on Miss Murata because, he feels, she is the prettiest and most interesting of the survivors. He catches more than her passing attention, and the two of them begin spending time together.

Jack Munroe looked over the MPB report on his desk, remarked to himself that this was one hell of a crime, then passed the report on. The Public Safety men find the details very interesting, but they are too busy reorganizing the police system to do more than talk about the spectacular murder and robbery. They also are aware that they cannot yet place this crime in a context to understand it or judge it, since none of them, either before or after their arrival in Japan, had received any briefing whatsoever on what this country or its people are like.

Munroe has vivid memories of his own arrival at Haneda airport in the south of Tokyo a little over a year ago. He has not forgotten that first vision of scattered debris and desolation, and he can still remember the stabbing odors of dead fish and urine. Everywhere. His living quarters, which are inside one of three houses in a compound owned by the millionaire maker of Seiko watches, consist of one room with an Army cot, a small desk, an electric heater, and a frayed rug. Nothing at all like home in Nashville, but he had not come to Japan in search of luxury living.

Byron Engle also remembers his first impressions of Japanese society. What struck him most when he arrived two years ago was the feudal behavior of the Japanese, an example of which he had witnessed on his first day at work. While on a traffic observation tour with a colleague, he had seen an old man in kimonos and sandals urinate in the street. Suddenly a policeman had appeared and loudly remonstrated the old man, who quickly fell into submission as if the Emperor himself had chastised him. "Things have changed, the Americans are here, you can't do that anymore," the policeman had said, and then with his finger motioned for the old man to follow him. The two had walked about ten feet apart toward the *kōban*—a police box, a sort of mini-station—with the policeman leading. It had taken Engle several minutes to realize he had just seen an arrest. No handcuffs, no accusation; just a pointing of the finger.

Arthur Kimberling, working with Engle and Munroe, recalls his jolting introduction to Japanese society last year. His pals back in Louisville would never believe this one. The first day he arrived at his hotel he had noticed a large group of people outside, and he had thought that maybe they were waiting for him. Instead, he found out, this was a wedding reception waiting for the bride and groom. Kimberling had been on his way inside the hotel when the newly-weds arrived and, a moment later, appeared right behind him. Introductions were made by the bellhop, who was an attractive young woman. She then escorted Kimberling to his room, where he changed out of his clothes and into a robe to go for a bath. The woman took him down the hall to the bathroom and explained in broken English that he should scrub and rinse himself before getting into the wooden tub which was filled with very hot water. Kimberling nodded his thanks for her assistance, then waited for her to leave. She didn't. He made motions to take off his kimono, hoping that would signal to her his need for privacy, but she still did not move. Instead, she told him that she would wash him.

Kimberling, a modest man, politely protested, saying he would prefer to do it himself, then gently dismissed her. Finally alone, he washed, stepped into the tub, almost scalding himself, and stepped back out. Suddenly a door opened.

Kimberling turned, expecting to find the bellhop there and send her out again, when he saw a different woman walking toward him, smiling. It was the bride he had just met downstairs, and she was now, like himself, stark naked.

Kimberling leaped into the tub.

"Hello, Mr. Kimberling," the bride said and stepped into the tub from the other side. Within minutes the groom joined them. Kimberling was not sure whether the scalding water or his embarrassment turned his face red as he sat half-immersed with the newlyweds. That had been his introduction to Japanese custom, and to communal bathing.

Now, little more than a year later, the staff of the Public Safety Division has passed beyond these initial cultural shocks and has come to respect and even to incorporate Japanese customs in its work. Accordingly, the PSD authorities do not force new operations or procedures onto the MPB; instead, they try to introduce them, sensitive to preserving the ancient necessity of saving face for the Japanese police. The PSD officials, like Engle, Munroe, and Kimberling, know enough about Japan now to realize that the Teikoku crime is a colossal slap in the MPB's face. They are not surprised that Chief Fujita is asking for their assistance.

None of the PSD police branch staff, however, has mastered the language, and their illiteracy in Japanese is matched only by the MPB's feeble grasp of English. Fortunately, the U.S. Army has had the foresight to recruit interpreters and translators. Chief among these are the Niseis, the second-generation Japanese-Americans. Like most agencies of the Occupation, the PSD relies heavily on the

Niseis, many of whom are U.S. Army officers. One interpreter used often by the PSD is a young Lieutenant named Eugene Hattori, who is assigned to PSD and works as a liaison with the MPB. He is known around the office as a happy-go-lucky type, always with a smile, seldom troubled, and good at his job.

The MPB follows up its initial report of the Teikoku killings with a call to the PSD, asking if the PSD can help them locate a certain Lieutenant Parker. The PSD is glad to assist in this investigation. Lieutenant Eugene Hattori is assigned to the case as interpreter.

In January the winds are dry and cold in Sendai, and the trip from Tokyo is long, taking as much as six hours, depending on snow drifts. Several detectives from the namecard division of the investigation have come to Sendai in search of Dr. Matsui with hopes that something will come of this lead. They are aware that Dr. Matsui's card was probably stolen, or perhaps found on the street, before being used in the November rehearsal of the crime.

Before leaving Tokyo the detectives had learned that the printer could not remember very much about the man who had ordered twenty cards with "Jirō Yamaguchi" on them. Only when he read about the crime in the papers had he even remembered the man coming in. His records were poor, and he could not even guess how long ago the order for these cards had been placed. The MPB was also having no luck tracking the Dr. Yamaguchi who had been dismissed from the Welfare Ministry. The MPB's records and filing systems are in terrible disarray, a sad reality that has compounded the problems already posed by inexperienced people working in jobs they are not qualified to handle. Even Chief Fujita was not a career policeman. During his wartime military service, he had been trained as an administrator and could just as well have qualified for head of the Coast Guard or of a public school system, as for director of the Criminal Investigation Division. If the PSD officers would just hurry their revamping of the MPB's training programs and procedures, investigations like this one into the Teikoku murders might move a lot more smoothly.

Long, thin faced Dr. Matsui receives his callers very nervously. His face pale, his hands shaking, he can barely manage to keep his voice even. The detectives take note of this and do not inform Matsui of the reason for their visit.

"Doctor Shigeru Matsui?"

"Yes."

"Of the Welfare Ministry?"

"Yes."

"You live in Sendai?"

"Yes."

Sweat is visible on the doctor's brow; the detectives wait a moment.

"Have you been to Tokyo recently?"

"No."

"Sure?"

"Yes."

"Not last Monday, the twenty-sixth?"

"No."

"Can you prove it?"

"Yes. Why?"

"Have you heard about the Teikoku Bank murders?"

"Yes, I have."

"Is this your namecard?"

"Yes."

"Can you explain how it appeared at the bank?"

Dr. Matsui stiffens a moment, takes a short breath, then evens out his voice as he says, "No."

A lead is a lead is a lead, and up to now all leads have led nowhere. The MPB has been moving in almost every direction, spinning its wheels, but failing to get any real traction. Clues that seem full of possibilities end up empty, illusory.

Not one witness can say for certain that the ex-clerk and physician's son from Totsuka bears any resemblance to the killer. He is a good candidate for murder, with the requisite knowledge of and access to poisons, and with no alibi. But the witnesses remain firm, and the police let him go.

Some detectives go to the address on the back of the stolen check, 3661, 3-chome in Itabashi, and meet with similar frustration. No one named Toyoharu Gotō lives there, nor has any one ever heard that name before. The robbery division will hold the check and use it as evidence if an arrest is made. That division also intends to call in a graphology expert to see if any suspect's handwriting matches the signature on the check.

The namecard division has expanded to investigate the more than eighty namecards which the detectives brought back from their interview with Dr. Matsui in Sendai. Matsui had finally gained control of himself and had substantiated his claim that he had been nowhere near Tokyo on Monday, January 26th. The detectives determined his nervousness was just a case of the jitters, not uncommon in people suddenly called upon by the police. Matsui had offered one possible explanation—that the namecard which the detectives showed him was one of a batch of one hundred cards he had ordered last year. After checking, he found that, from the original batch of one hundred, only about ten of his namecards were left. Perhaps someone who had exchanged cards with him in the course of social custom had been responsible for his card's ill-timed appearance, he had suggested, and had started pulling out all the namecards that he had been given in the last year.

Weeks go by and each card acquires a face. All over Japan detectives knock on doors and ask,

44

"Is this your card?"

"Do you remember meeting a Dr. Matsui?"

"Do you have the card he gave you?"

Yes, this one still has Matsui's card. "Dōmo arigato."

Try this teacher, that journalist, this merchant, but maybe he doesn't have Matsui's card anymore. . .

Or maybe this driver. . .

Or this artist. . .

One by one the police track and check every card Matsui has given them. There are some, like the artist, who do not have Matsui's card anymore, but none of them match the killer's description, and all appear to have alibis. Suddenly, the police find themselves in the middle of a rather strange problem: Too many leads are presenting themselves.

On any day, anywhere in Japan, between ten to fifteen people walk into a police station and confess to the crime. The Teikoku killings have become an irresistibly sensational subject for the Japanese, and quickly both the press and the public have begun paying a sort of grim homage to the killer. The phantom doctor's exquisite premeditation has succeeded in impressing Japan and eliciting a sort of perverse veneration. It is the police, rather than the murderer, who are suffering the brunt of public reprobation.

Instead of helping the investigation, the confessors are slowing it down by tying up hundreds of officers who could be following up other more solid leads. Confessions no longer raise many eyebrows; according to the precinct log books, several hundred people—men, women, and even children—masterminded and executed the Teikoku Bank killings. Suspects and confessors continue to cram Japan's old and creaky police stations while the namecard search intensifies.

Detectives interrogate Shisuke Hibi, a convicted shoplifter who has been found with newspaper clippings of the Teikoku crime in his house. He looks like the killer, his alibi is weak. The police take his photograph, and show it to survivors of the crime who have come to the Mejiro station.

Not the man, they say.

Hibi is released.

Yoshitada Sakoma is brought in for questioning. He is thirty years old, but looks older. He has been arrested before and has several times escaped police custody. He is suspected of poisoning somebody in Beppu City in a manner that has made him a prime suspect in the eyes of the MPB for the Teikoku murders. He used the namecard of an official from the Osaka Sanitation Bureau, and Sakoma also knows medicines.

His photo is shown to survivors and witnesses.

Not him, they say.

The Saegi police arrest Kaneo Yamada, a man who looks the right age, and who has been posing as a doctor in his village to defraud people with his "cures." Yamada is released after witnesses say that he does not even remotely look like the killer.

Another has confessed. Norisada Fushimi is forty-four years old, and he says he robbed the bank because he desperately needed money. His gray hair matches the killer's description, and he is also the right height.

"Your face doesn't match the description."

"I am the man."

"How did you disguise yourself?"

"I am the man."

"Can't you hear? You don't look like him."

"I am the man."

"Where did you get the poison?"

"Cyanide?"

"Yes. Where did you get it?"

"I had it."

"Yes. Did you buy it?"

"I bought it."

"Impossible. Cyanide can't be bought."

"No?"

"It is restricted. Where did you get it?"

"I. . .don't know. . . ."
"Take him home."
"But I am. . . ."
"Take him home!"
A parade of faces.
A succession of head-shakes.

In the Mejiro headquarters the suspects file into the small room where the witnesses sit, then the suspects walk out. The pattern is familiar, the police know the routine. The same scene plays itself over and over again, like some film clip on a repeating loop, day after day after day.

Jirō Yamaguchi is found, but this Jirō Yamaguchi is not a doctor. He is the president of a local lumber company. Aside from not resembling the killer, he has a solid alibi. Mr. Yamaguchi is cleared, and the MPB presses on.

The namecard search begins to cut across divisional lines, and confusion erupts. No one can remember clearly who is to be held as a suspect and who is to be released. Opinions clash, tempers flare, and chaos ensues. From the top, an order comes down to start again on the cards, from the beginning. This time, the order instructs, divide the cards up among several detectives, and be sure at all costs to keep the individual investigations separate. Also, to ensure a fresh perspective some new detectives are assigned to the namecard division.

One of the new detectives is Tamigorō Igii. He flips through the namecards given to him, and notices one that looks vaguely familiar. He has seen this name before, he thinks, perhaps signed on a painting. Yes, Detective Igii recalls, the artist's work is not unknown to him. He flips through the other cards, checking to see if he might, by chance, recognize any others.

At the MPB's request, Byron Engle calls Captain H. F. Schwartz, who is assigned to the Adjutant General Section of General Headquarters (GHQ) of the Occupation. Captain Schwartz has access to all files of military personnel assigned to the Occupation, past and present. Engle asks Schwartz to check if anyone by the name of Parker appears on any personnel list. It would also be a help if somebody could determine what the specific assignment was for anyone who might appear on the list. Public health activities, for example. Schwartz says that the lists don't describe duties, they just name units.

A week or so later Engle gets a call back from Captain Schwartz, who tells the PSD administrator that the name of Parker turned up ten times. Captain Schwartz says that maybe four of these Parkers are still in Japan. The rest have already been reassigned elsewhere, either in Asia or back in the States. Engle turns the list over to Jack Munroe, who in turn notifies the MPB.

For the first time in Japanese police history, a composite drawing is made of a suspect. Police artists have taken the description of the Teikoku killer and have assembled a picture which most of the witnesses agree is a striking likeness of the criminal. The police artists' drawing is published in newspapers across Japan. Public response is staggering. A hundred phone calls come in each day from people saying they know of or have seen someone who looks just like the man in the drawing. No one can tell if the composite is helping or hindering the investigation. It is generating too many leads for the police to investigate properly; they can hardly keep pace with those already confessing to the crime.

In downtown Tokyo a popular radio broadcaster reads over the air a letter he composed to the Teikoku criminal.

Dear Murderer:

No matter how cleverly you may try to escape, the law is closing steadily upon you. Having committed a crime of such magnitude with superb coolness and self-possession, why don't you permit yourself a last heroic gesture for a climax? We beseech you to give yourself up by the end of this month. If you accept my request, I pledge to present you with 300,000 yen. With that money you can seek ways to support your family or you may offer the money to the families of your victims. If you are alone, you can pay the defense expenses and the like and I will faithfully carry out what you want done about the rest of the money. When you are gone, I shall never fail to put flowers before your tomb, treating you as a member of my family.

As the winter turns to spring, and summer nears, weariness sets in, and the leads, though still numerous, grow even more tenuous. To date, the procession of suspects has totalled an astounding twenty thousand—one for every policeman assigned to the investigation—and not a single one has yielded anything substantial. The crime itself, unprecedented in Japanese police annals, has been matched by an investigation of unprecedented scope, mobilizing a greater detective force than has ever been seen in all of Japan, perhaps in all of the Far East. Suspects have been questioned two, three, sometimes four times. Leads have been tracked and chased all across

Japan, and all have led to dead ends. The record of virtually every convict in the country has been thoroughly inspected to see if any one of them might be capable of orchestrating this crime.

The Method Division of the investigation has not been able to establish a definite profile for the man who could design such a cold-blooded plan for robbery. They are, however, convinced of one thing: This is the work of no ordinary criminal. The murderer is an expert, a professional. But their conviction poses another baffling question for which they can find no answer: If the killer is a professional, where did he get his expertise? He must have done some act similar to this one somewhere else. Why then is there no record of any crime at least remotely resembling the Teikoku murders, the poisonings, the technique?

Late Spring 1948

A room in Northwest Tokyo. Muffled sounds of trucks and jeeps passing outside. Afternoon light barely filters through the dark windows. Ten suited men, some standing, some sitting, surround a square-faced man who sits on a chair and looks straight ahead. One of the suited men holds up a photograph of a group of twenty men.

"Who's this one?"

"His name is ————."

"Did he work for you?"

"Yes."

"What section?"

"—— Section."

"In Manchuria?"

"Yes."

"For how long?"

"I don't remember."

They take turns with the questions. The man with the photograph pushes it again toward the seated man.

"Did he perform experiments?"

The man does not answer.

"Did he perform experiments?"

"I believe so."

"What kind?"

"That would have depended on which branch he was in."

"What branch was he in?"

"I don't remember."

"But there were experiments?"

"Yes."

"On humans?"

The man does not answer.

"On humans?"

"If you don't know that already, why am I here?"

The ten suited men stare at one another, then at the man who sits in the center of the circle they form. Are they just testing him or are they looking to confirm what is only suspicion?

"This one."

"Yes."

"What section?"

"Same as the last."

"So he performed experiments?"

"Not necessarily."

"Why not?"

"He may have assisted only."

"But he had access to the experiments?"

"Yes."

"What was the nature of these experiments?"

"They were of a scientific nature."

"Scientific?"

"Yes."

"Did they ever involve cyanide?"

"Yes."

This much they knew already. This knowledge had led to this meeting. It had surfaced, obscured and blurred by rumor, after a painstaking check into the activities of all units of the Imperial Army. Again they hold the photograph in front of the seated impassive man.

"This one."

"Yes."

"Was he ever involved in cyanide experiments?"

"There were very few of those."

A tall, thin man with glasses makes note of this.

"The few cyanide experiments...."

"Yes."

"Were they performed by officers?"

"Yes."

"Was this one an officer?"

"Yes."

"What rank?"

"Lieutenant Colonel, I believe."

"Any experience with cyanide?"

"Perhaps."

"Likely?"

"Yes."

"Any experience with a neutralizing substance?"

"Perhaps."

"Likely?"

"Yes."

"How old is he?"

"Now, maybe ————."

They remove the photograph and show the seated man a pencilled sketch of a face. They wait for his reaction. None comes.

"Did someone like this ever work for you?"

"Impossible to say."

"Why?"

"Because we were there for more than ten years, and thousands of people worked for me."

"You do not recognize this face?"

"No."

They return to the photograph. More questions, the same questions. The man in the chair gives the same answers. Nothing.

For almost a hundred and eighty days, from the northern tip of Hokkaidō to the southern extreme of Kyūshū, in every prefecture, in every ward, from city to village, house to house, policemen have questioned, searched, investigated, and questioned again for twelve to fourteen hours each day, and still they have nothing, no solid evidence, no solid clue. Discouraged and with deflated spirits, under relentless pressure from both the press and now the government, the MPB is facing another public embarrassment, another instance of professional disgrace: One thousand officers are about to be discharged for accepting bribes. The Tokyo MPB decides to pin any hopes of solving the Teikoku case on Dr. Matsui's memory, on the chance that he might recall something more in a second interview. Perhaps he will remember some new detail, some seemingly insignificant story relating to a namecard. Desperate for some new answers, the detectives continue their investigation as the rainy season descends on Japan.

A knock at the door interrupts the artist at the easel. He turns from his work, goes to the entrance, and admits a man who identifies himself as a detective from Tokyo. Tamigorō Igii is his name, he says. He asks the artist if he is Sadamichi Hirasawa, the painter. Hirasawa nods, and asks why a detective has come to see him again.

Inspector Igii explains his orders to investigate the namecards once again, and asks Hirasawa if he wouldn't mind answering some basic questions, just once more, for the sake of formality.

At Igii's suggestion they go to dinner. There the detective assumes an informal manner, hoping that Hirasawa might volunteer information in the course of a more casual conversation. In answer to one of the detective's indirect questions, Hirasawa says that he does not have a photograph of himself, as do most Japanese. Igii is disappointed because he hoped to carry a photo of Hirasawa back to Tokyo to show the witnesses, but he listens as Hirasawa continues. He answers a question that Igii has not asked. The painter tells the detective in considerable detail where he was last January 26th. He had spent the morning and early afternoon with his daughter and son-in-law in the Marunouchi district of Tokyo, then had taken a train to his other daughter's house where he spent the rest of the afternoon and evening playing cards with his daughter's boyfriend. Igii notes the willingness to supply an alibi before it is even requested.

Hirasawa also says that he regrets having lost Dr. Matsui's card because he seemed so nice, someone the painter would enjoy meeting again. A thief had some time ago picked his pocket, he explains, and had gotten his wallet, which held all the namecards Hirasawa had received.

The painter chats freely, and nothing particularly rouses serious suspicion in the detective, until the restaurant photographer wanders up to them and asks if they are ready for him to take the traditional dinner-table picture. Without hesitation Igii says yes, but the painter, while granting permission, shows a strange reluctance. As the photographer focuses and prepares to snap the picture, Hirasawa scrunches his face and looks away from the camera, as if trying to disguise or hide himself.

The next day, back in Tokyo, Igii files his report on his meeting with Hirasawa. He emphasizes the painter's strange behavior and actions. The detective feels certain that this suspect warrants further investigation and interrogation. Igii's bosses, however, disagree. They say that Hirasawa had been cleared months ago by the first team of detectives checking out the cards. They also tell Igii that Hirasawa does not match the physical description of the killer, and that the MPB has more promising leads than a watercolor artist whose character does not seem to fit the kind they are looking for.

Igii is adamant about his sense that something is strange with this suspect. He argues his case again, insisting that his hunch ought to be played out. When they tell him they need him on other good leads, Igii rejoins that *this* is a good lead.

After much debate and haggling, Igii's superiors relent, and the detective, with MPB authorization, commits himself to the exclusive pursuit of the artist.

Once at a near standstill, the Teikoku investigation gains new momentum from Igii's persistence, and during the next several weeks the case rolls toward a swift and portentous conclusion.

Nippon Times,

24 August 1948:

WELL-KNOWN ARTIST HELD AS POISON HOLDUP SUSPECT

Igii arrests Hirasawa and brings him down from Hokkaidō to Tokyo for interrogation. At Ueno station, where the train carrying the two men arrives, crowds gather to get a look at the latest suspect. Hirasawa, however, hides under a blanket. Back at MPB headquarters Igii's superiors realize that at this point there is only circumstantial evidence against the artist, and they feel that he will be cleared and released within forty-eight hours.

Riichi Takeuchi hears about the arrest before it hits the papers and races over to Hirasawa's Tokyo house where he meets the artist's wife for what he hopes will be an exclusive interview. She does not seem to understand why he has come. Takeuchi is pleased to see this reaction because it tells him he has the scoop. He informs her that her husband has been arrested for the Teikoku murders. She bursts out laughing.

She calls out to her daughter who is in the kitchen mending socks. The daughter comes into the room, and when her mother tells her that her father has been arrested for the Teikoku killings, the daughter bursts out laughing.

As the two women return to what they were doing, Takeuchi walks out, stunned and confused.

Nippon Times,

25 August:

MASS MURDER SUSPECT CLEARED; POLICE BAFFLED

The seven-month old question as to who perpetrated

the diabolical "poison holdup case" remained a baffling mystery today following the clearance of Sadamichi Hirasawa from suspicion.

Hopes entertained by police authorities, especially Inspector Igii, who made the arrest and went so far as saying that Hirasawa's guilt was "100 percent certain," fell dismally flat Monday evening when 11 persons who saw the Teikoku criminal could find no resemblance in the much-publicized latest suspect.

Although the "screening" was conducted under a tense atmosphere and all who saw Hirasawa were given ample time to make up their minds, not a single person charged the watercolor artist as being the Teikoku Bank criminal.

Six of them, in fact, were certain that he was not the man who committed the diabolical crime.

Inspector Horizaki of the 1st Criminal Investigation Section of the MPB yesterday expressed the hope of releasing Hirasawa from custody sometime the same evening. Officials of the Tokyo Prosecutor's Office said after cross-examining Hirasawa that two major points still need to be cleared up relative to Hirasawa's action at the time of the crime and subsequently. The first was said to be Hirasawa's alibi for January 26, and the other puzzling point, they said, was the suspect's construction of a new home and the fact he possessed 45,000 yen in cash at home, which he alleges to have been borrowed from a friend.

The next day the Attorney General's Office announces that when Hirasawa is cleared and released from suspicion, the judicial authorities may be sued for violating Hirasawa's civil rights. Despite having already been cleared by survivors and witnesses, Hirasawa remains in police custody. Criticism is mounting. The newly-established Civil Liberties Bureau and the Attorney General's Office in Tokyo publicly denounce Igii's remark that Hirasawa's guilt was

"100 percent certain" as a reckless statement of personal opinion which, they charge, was made in the absence of any evidence implicating the artist. They contend that the statement is slanderous to Hirasawa's reputation and prejudicial to the case. The MPB maintains that it has acted properly with respect to Hirasawa, although some authorities acknowledge that Inspector Igii may have been excessively eager when talking to the press.

At about two-thirty the following afternoon Hirasawa slashes his left wrist with the point of a pen while in his cell. Guards discover him and immediately rush him to the prison infirmary. They also discover, scrawled on the wall in fresh blood, "I am innocent."

Hirasawa survives. The MPB speculates that his near-suicide is the artist's attempt to escape the shame of discovery of crimes he may have committed separate from the Teikoku killings. The press ask what these other alleged crimes are and why the police are investigating them instead of the Teikoku killings, but the police refuse to disclose the nature of the new investigations.

The MPB transfers responsibility for continuing the interrogation of Hirasawa to the Tokyo District Procurator's office. Hajime Takagi, a procurator in his mid-thirties, takes charge of the suspect. Two days later the police change their theory on the suicide attempt, claiming that Hirasawa had tried to kill himself strictly to avoid divulging the source of his money. The artist's mysterious silence prevents the police from letting him go. The MPB also now claims that their investigation of his other suspected crimes will stop if Hirasawa will reveal where he got the money. Hirasawa's interrogators refuse to yield to the public criticism aimed at them, saying that until the source of the money is established, Hirasawa cannot be released from suspicion of the Teikoku killings.

As the interrogation forges on, the MPB turns up people who claim that Sadamichi Hirasawa once defrauded them or attempted to defraud them of money. The police, still under stiff harassment by the Civil Liberties Bureau and the press, declare that Hirasawa is under greater suspicion than before because in each case of fraud a bank had been either directly or indirectly involved.

On September 3, confronted with these new charges, Hirasawa admits that he had defrauded people, and had escaped arrest and prosecution each time.

Forty-eight hours later the Tokyo District Procurator's Office issues a statement explaining that Hirasawa is no longer being held in connection with the Teikoku killings, but rather on multiple charges of fraud. The legal amount of time alloted to detain Hirasawa on the original suspicion of murder has expired, but now, with the new charges, interrogators can continue pursuing the Teikoku connection without violating the new Codes of Criminal Procedure. Unnamed authorities in the Procurator's Office maintain that they are "eighty percent sure" that Hirasawa is the Teikoku murderer.

On September 7 Yoshio Yamada, Hirasawa's attorney and childhood friend, lodges a complaint that the police have violated the new codes by exploiting a semantic loophole regarding detention of a suspect. Yamada warns that a dangerous precedent is being set in this "vital test case" of civil rights and liberties.

On September 10 the MPB uncovers a new sum of money—eighty thousand yen—that Hirasawa deposited in a Tokyo bank three days after the Teikoku killings.

For the first time, Hirasawa answers his interrogators' questions on where he got the cash, explaining that an art patron had given it to him. The patron, however, denies giving Hirasawa any money at all. Hirasawa retreats into silence again, and handwriting experts begin comparing Hirasawa's script with that on the stolen check.

Two days later the MPB tells the press that investigators have disclosed yet more money, this time sixty-five thousand yen, which Hirasawa gave to his wife shortly after the crime. The police point out that the total amount of cash discovered in Hirasawa's possession matches the sum stolen from the bank. They push on with the question of how Hirasawa could have known enough about poisons to carry out such a crime.

On September 14 the MPB produces evidence that Hirasawa mixes potassium cyanide with copper materials to derive a light green pigment for his tempera paintings. He uses egg whites as a neutralizing agent for the toxic pigment, they say. The MPB also discovers that in this technique Hirasawa often uses a pipette similar to the one used in the Teikoku crime. The handwriting experts, however, still have not concluded that the writing on the check is Hirasawa's.

The next day two people, one a colleague of Hirasawa's, drop by MPB headquarters to level a new charge. Hirasawa, they say, has performed illegal abortions on at least ten women in the past. The police inform the press, and the press print the story. The two unnamed people also express their belief to reporters that Hirasawa's rights have not been violated by the police.

A week passes without word on the progress of the interrogations until September 26, when Chief Fujita tells the press that Hirasawa is on the brink of confessing the Teikoku killings. Two days later a riveted Japan reads:

MURDERER OF 12 CONFESSES CRIME / HIRASAWA ADMITS HE ADMINISTERED POISON TO BANK WORKERS; FAMILY STANDS BY HIM

This last article, appearing in the *Nippon Times* and bearing no byline, reports that at one o'clock the previous afternoon Hirasawa broke down and admitted to committing the Teikoku murders. District Procurator Hajime Takagi is credited with securing the suspect's confession. Chief Fujita says that his detectives are continuing to investigate Hirasawa to collect additional evidence to substantiate the confession. At present, Chief Fujita says, the MPB has only a few items to support Hirasawa's claim of guilt.

Hirasawa's attorney expresses his opinion that "the fact Hirasawa-san has confessed does not prove he actually committed the crime. It makes me feel sad to think that even today under a new constitution the police are still resorting to the methods of the last century in failing to prove actuality through objective evidence by trying to make a personal confession the basis of an indictment."

The article recounts the history of the crime, and also reveals two new details: Of the thousands of suspects the Tokyo police investigated, a mere three had ever been detained for questioning; and by the time of Hirasawa's confession, the MPB had already spent one hundred thousand yen more than its total annual budget on the Teikoku Bank investigation alone.

Almost all of the Japanese papers carry this same story. The *Nippon Times*, however, has one story that no one else could get. Earnest Hoberecht, a big American with a thick mustache and a veteran correspondent for United Press, along with his colleague Ian Mutsu, had managed the scoop of the year by getting an exclusive interview with Hirasawa almost immediately after he confessed. On the same day that the unsigned article on the confession is printed, their story appears on the front page of the paper under the following headline:

CONFESSED BANK SLAYER, SPEAKING IN ENGLISH PRAISES CHIEF PROSECUTOR

Sadamichi Hirasawa told as [sic] in an exclusive interview that he had confessed his guilt in the Teikoku Bank case and that the admission was made of his own free will.

Wiping tears from his eyes, the small 57-year-old artist said he felt relieved now that everything was over.

"I don't have adequate words to express the regret I have for committing such a horrible crime."

We talked with him for nearly an hour and saw no signs of his having received rough treatment at the hands of the police.

Hirasawa was emphatic in stating that police had treated him properly and had not employed third degree methods to obtain the confession.

Speaking in English, he described Chief Prosecutor Takagi as "highest class gentleman."

Our interview took place in a tiny room, 12 feet by 12 feet square, in the Metropolitan Police Building. It was the same room in which Hirasawa had undergone prolonged questioning. Hirasawa had been held more than a month while police checked the various angles of the many strange stories that he told.

Sometimes he smoked and we noticed that his hands were steady. His hair was closely clipped and greying. He had not shaved in several days.

His manner was delicate, almost feminine, and his voice was low and soft. When he came into the tiny room, he bowed politely. He seemed to be on the most friendly terms with the men who had been questioning.

He revealed that he had been writing poetry and said Takagi had been helping. Then he asked for a piece of paper and jotted down a copy of a poem he wrote last night.

He wrote the poem three times in our presence before it suited him and he signed it for us.

It concluded by expressing his desire that his soul might be "cleansed and saved by the great mercy of Buddha."

Sometimes smiling softly, sometimes crying, he said, "I was treated man-to-man, fairly. This treatment enabled me to bring out the best in my mind. I do not feel like making any statement in my defense at this time. But I can say that part of my motive was due to science."

We were unable to get him to explain this last statement which did not seem to us to be exactly clear. He sat there without answering.

Hirasawa did not seem to be afraid of the officials in the room and did not seem to be worried about his fate. His soft words, spoken in a low voice, conveyed an impression of profound relief, and, paradoxically, gratitude towards his prosecutors.

"At last I am able to sleep," he said.

The police and the public celebrate the solving of the Teikoku Bank crime by throwing a party. The chief of the MPB gives a short speech expressing gratitude that the murderer has been caught. Contributions for the party—over three hundred thousand yen—come in from hundreds of people and businesses. Public criticism follows, suggesting that the contributions had been coerced.

In October 1948, two months before his trial begins, Sadamichi Hirasawa recants his confession.

In early November, Riichi Takeuchi, the journalist, and Masako Murata, the poisoned woman who had crawled out of the Teikoku Bank in search of help, are married. The wedding ceremony is coordinated by Takeuchi's closest friend, one of Chief Fujita's principal deputies.

As 1949 arrives, Byron Engle's massive retraining program for the Japanese police gets underway. To the surprise and satisfaction of Engle's superiors in the Public Safety Division, the nation's entire force completes the intensive program in only two months.

From the day of his arrest until the conclusion of his trial, Sadamichi Hirasawa sits in prison for twenty-three months.

On July 25, 1950, the Tokyo District Court convicts Sadamichi Hirasawa of the poison-murder of twelve people and the attempted murder of four others while robbing the Teikoku Bank. His sentence for this bizarre and gruesome crime is death by hanging.

Immediately following the death sentence, Hirasawa's attorney files an appeal with the Tokyo High Court, but the artist's hopes of vindication are dashed in September 1951 when the High Court upholds the District Court's verdict. This first appeal rejected, Hirasawa's case ascends into the halls of Japan's Supreme Court. For the next three and a half years, the country waits to hear the final word on Japan's most celebrated criminal. During this time Hirasawa remains in Kosuge prison outside Tokyo, and the Allied Occupation of Japan comes to an end. As the Supreme Court reviews the case, the justices are presented with the arduous task of studying all the records of the crime and its investigation. Enough transcripts, files, and documents have piled up to fill a judge's chamber from floor to ceiling and from wall to wall.

In 1952, Hirasawa's wife divorces him in his fourth year of imprisonment, and his daughters dissociate themselves from their shamed father.

Finally, in the spring of 1955, Japan's Supreme Court rules that Hirasawa's arrest, detention, trial, conviction, and death sentence have all been proper and fair, in accordance with Japanese law. The painter is bound over to the Ministry of Justice for execution.

PART II
Port of Entry

COLUMBUS, OHIO
July 1978

O PENED IN front of my face
was the Sunday edition of the *Columbus Dispatch*. I was flipping
through the paper's middle section, about to finish my morning
coffee, when a headline caught my eye:

POISON CRIME 3 DECADES AGO IN TOKYO STILL
CREATES DOUBTS

The piece was datelined Tokyo, by James Abrams, for Copley
News Service. It concerned this crime involving an artist who dressed
up as a doctor, then with some ruse about dysentery, went into a
bank and poisoned sixteen people, twelve of whom died. The artist
had confessed to the crime, but had later retracted the confession,
saying the police had coerced it out of him by denying him sleep.
His conviction and death sentence had been appealed and upheld,
but even now, thirty years later, he had not yet been executed. I'd
heard of stays-of-execution, but thirty years was by any standard a
long stay.

The article pointed out that the *Guinness Book of World Records* listed this artist as having lived on death row longer than any
other convict in history. He was also the first artist ever to be
convicted of premeditated murder.

Abrams then recounted some of the intrigue behind the crime,
saying that many Japanese believed the painter had been framed.
There was no hard evidence to support any of the claims but, according to the piece, detectives were said to have been secretly

tracking former members of a Japanese Imperial Army unit, code-named "Ishii Company," which had allegedly conducted biological and chemical warfare experiments during World War II. The police were about to close in on one man who fit the description of the bank criminal, when the U.S. Army stepped in and said that Occupation authorities were holding all Ishii personnel under "special protection." The artist's supporters felt the term was deliberately vague because, they said, the Ishii Company was sharing the results of these secret wartime experiments with the Americans.

If the charges were true, the moral and political implications were serious. But what struck me most was the powerful image of a man in a bank, a man in uniform, in costume, dressed for the part, going through an elaborate act to poison people. This bizarre crime seemed orchestrated for the stage.

A month earlier I'd had my first play produced, and it occurred to me that here in this article were the makings of my next script. There was something peculiarly intriguing about this artist and his story. Controversial incidents often raised interest and speculation many years later, but only out of reflective curiosity. That an organized group of supporters had challenged and was still seriously challenging Sadamichi Hirasawa's conviction more than thirty years later indicated the deep and strange hold this crime continued to have on Japan. Was he guilty or innocent? Was he a criminal or a victim? The questions were rife with dramatic tension. If he was guilty, then according to Japanese law he should be dead; and if he was innocent, he should be free. Three decades after the crime he was both still alive and in prison, and that incongruity struck me.

I clipped the article out of the paper and finished my cold cup of coffee.

Two weeks later I was in Belgium working in the Brussels bureau of McGraw-Hill World News. I spent what spare time I had trying to find more information on Sadamichi Hirasawa and the Teikoku Bank crime, but I wasn't having much luck. Little material existed in English, save for some news clippings circa January 1948 when the robbery-murders ocurred. The few pieces of information

I had contradicted each other. Each version of events claimed to be factual, yet each had little, if any evidence to support its claim, and no two versions were alike. I began to wonder if I would ever find what I needed to accurately recreate the story.

I read about the postwar Occupation of Japan and researched the conflict that resulted from the clash of the Japanese and American cultures. The confusion and intrigue that marked the Teikoku killings and Hirasawa's conviction closely mirrored the confusion and intrigue of the Occupation period in postwar Japan.

I left Brussels for graduate school in Washington, D.C., carrying with me information far too sketchy to attempt a credible reconstruction of the Teikoku crime. Two years later, during the summer of 1980, while continuing to research Hirasawa's case, I discovered information about his confession that raised new questions. His explanation of how he manipulated the poison and dosage sounded awkward, unprofessional, not at all like the mastermind the indictment claimed him to be. On one side, it seemed that the prosecution had exaggerated any connection suggesting his guilt, and that the court had either ignored or omitted anything that pointed toward his innocence. Six people, four of whom had been poisoned at the bank and had seen the killer, told both the police and the press that Hirasawa was definitely not the Teikoku murderer. Apparently the prosecution was not troubled by this or by the fact that Hirasawa's confession was full of inconsistencies. On the other side, his own defense didn't seem bothered that Hirasawa's alibi was weak. I wanted to know why the whole thing was such a tangle of contradictions.

The *Bulletin of Concerned Asian Scholars* is an esoteric journal, the likes of which I'd never read before my research on the Teikoku crime began. An article in the October 1980 issue had caught my attention. The author, John W. Powell, had secured an array of U.S. Army documents through the Freedom of Information Act, and presented conclusive evidence of a rather ugly deal the U.S. Army had struck with some former Japanese military men in 1947. Powell showed that senior military and civilian officials in Tokyo and in Washington, D.C., had succeeded in covering up the deal.

As far as dirty ventures went, this one was fairly impressive. Not only were the Army's partners "Class A" war criminals, which had meant a guaranteed death sentence from the International Military Tribunal, but they were also responsible for the barbaric and scientific murder of American prisoners of war. The article said that the Army had known all of this in advance of the deal, and had decided that the information they could obtain was worth any risk, and any price.

Sometime in the late 1930s Japan had begun an intensive field program to develop germ warfare. Throughout Manchuria and in the various provinces of occupied China, Japan's 731 Regiment, which had been formed and commissioned for this top-secret program, built installations for research. From the day their work began and until the Russians invaded Manchuria in August 1945, this infamous 731 Regiment infected, dissected, bludgeoned, injected, poisoned, vivisected, and simply cut up people in the name of researching and developing bacteriological weapons. Most of the subjects for these experiments were Chinese, but occasionally an American or Soviet POW was mixed in with the others to see if Caucasians withstood germ-infection differently than Orientals. Major research was conducted on plague, cholera, anthrax, glanders, syphilis, and dysentery. A good deal of time was also devoted to pumping prisoner-subjects full of horse blood to see if it would work as a substitute for human blood. It didn't. After suffering horrible convulsions and seizures, each victim died.

After the war, rumors about Japan's biological warfare program surfaced. The Americans, a step ahead of the Soviets, caught up

70

with some senior officials of the 731 Regiment who were willing to sell the results of their experiments in order to avoid even a cameo appearance before the International Military Tribunal. The price was high—complete immunity and protection of all 731 personnel from any war crimes investigation or charges—but the U.S. Army bought it.

Powell quoted several Occupation-period documents that expressed grave concern over the crippling international embarrassment the United States would suffer if these secret negotiations with 731 were ever made public.

> It is recognized that by informing Ishii and his associates that the information to be obtained re BW [bacteriological warfare] will be retained in intelligence channels and will not be employed as war crimes evidence, this government may at a later date be seriously embarrassed. However, the Army Department and Air Force Members strongly believe that this information, particularly that which will finally be obtained from the Japanese with respect to the effect of BW on humans, is of such importance to the security of this country that the risk of subsequent embarrassment should be taken.

Some officials in Washington tried to withdraw the blanket immunity clause, but 731's stubborn leader and founder, a Lieutenant General Shirō Ishii, whose 731 Regiment was also known as the "Ishii Company," would not settle for anything less.

> Ishii states that if guaranteed immunity from "war crimes" in documentary form for himself, superiors and subordinates, he can describe programs in detail. Ishii claims to have extensive theoretical high-level knowledge including strategic and tactical use of BW on defense and offense, backed by some research on best BW agents

to employ by geographical areas of Far East, and the use of BW in cold climates.

So the Teikoku case wasn't just a story about a bank crime; it was the story of a war crime. While Josef Mengele, the SS doctor who conducted lethal experiments on prisoners in Auschwitz, was being declared at Nuremberg an enemy of humanity, General Shirō Ishii and his closest associates were brought to Fort Detrick, Maryland where they went to work for the U.S. Army Chemical Corps.

Of course, the Occupation could not tolerate anything that might expose this deal with the Ishii Company. Further documents revealed American fears that a Russian investigation of the same rumors the Americans had heard would blow the cover on everything. So would a Tokyo police investigation of former 731 personnel suspected in the Teikoku poisonings. Powell showed that the principal characters involved, from General MacArthur in Tokyo to senior officials in Washington, proceeded with extreme caution.

However, it should be kept in mind that there is a remote possibility that independent investigation conducted by the Soviets in the Mukden Area may have disclosed evidence that American prisoners of war were used for experimental purposes of a BW nature and that they lost their lives as a result of these experiments, and further, that such evidence may be introduced by the Soviet prosecutors in the course of cross-examination of certain of the major Japanese war criminals now on trial at Tokyo, particularly during the cross-examination of Umezu, Commander of the Kwantung Army from 1939 to 1944 of which army the Ishii BW group was a part. In addition, there is a strong possibility that the Soviet prosecutors will, in the course of cross-examination of Umezu, introduce evidence of experiments conducted on human beings by the Ishii BW group, which experiments do not

differ greatly from those for which this Government is
now prosecuting German scientists and medical doctors
at Nuremberg.

When the Russians, as feared, discovered 731's existence and
activities, they demanded the issue be brought into the International Military Tribunal, but not necessarily out of any moral out-
rage; they too were interested in the secret knowledge Ishii had to
offer. Shrewdly the Americans outmaneuvered the Russians in what
was one of the first bravura victories of the Cold War. The question,
however, of how close the Teikoku investigation got to the 731
Regiment remained unanswered.

After reading Powell's article, I saw the drama surrounding
Hirasawa in a new light. The story seemed to be writing itself,
emerging as fact, not as fiction, and with greater significance than
I had imagined.

Powell had gotten his documents from the National Archives
where nearly all Occupation records were held. Perhaps whatever
American connection or obstruction there was, or wasn't, in the
investigation of the Teikoku Bank murders was recorded in documents now kept in the Archives. Certainly it was the logical place
to start. Besides, the main building in downtown Washington was
less than fifteen minutes from my apartment.

I wandered into the massively columned entrance of the National Archives, found my way through the deep corridors into the
office of one of the main archivists, and learned that I'd come to
the wrong place. Everything I wanted to see, if it even existed, would

be at the Modern Military Field Branch thirty minutes away in suburban Maryland.

I made the drive in twenty minutes. I was impatient, anxious to rip through a few files and have all the 'answers tumble out at me. I imagined that all I had to do was walk in and say, "All you've got on the Teikoku Bank job, please." I was still unaware of the complexities of archival research. My thoughts focused on one thing: finding out if there was an American connection to the crime and investigation. If there was, maybe I could resolve some of the confusion and speculation, and see the story more clearly than anyone had before.

The building stood low but wide, like a one-story warehouse, over vast, well-kept grounds. Inside, a glass wall separated the reception area from the research room proper. There were three rows of five or six tables each, and every table had chairs for two. Less than a dozen people, most of them casually dressed, were in the room. I signed the visitor register, finished all the requisite procedures to apply for a researcher's permit, and waited for an archivist to assist me. As far as Washington bureaucracy went, the formalities here were rather simple. As I waited, I looked over some old news clippings I had collected about the crime and investigation. One claimed Hirasawa was a victim of the Ishii conspiracy. Another said Hirasawa was guilty because all the money in his possession matched the amount stolen from the bank. The next said he was not guilty by reason of insanity. Another pointed out the holes in his alibi.

Within a few minutes a tall man with a quiet voice introduced himself as Bill Lewis and asked if he could help me. I told him I was looking for information on the Teikoku Bank crime. He looked at me expectantly, waiting for more. I elaborated, hoping that some detail I mentioned might trigger a look of recognition in his eyes, that he might say, "Yes, I know exactly where that stuff is." Instead he stood silent, thinking a moment, then said that the records I was seeking could have been filed under a number of different classifications: G-2 Intelligence, the Legal Section of SCAP, the Army Surgeon General. It was not an auspicious beginning.

I spent the next year and a half going through cardboard box after cardboard box filled with musty old files and papers. The boxes held thirty-plus years of military bureaucracy, mostly routine memoranda about directives, new trends, food distribution, reforms, inventory lists, and so on in postwar Tokyo. My enthusiasm wore thinner and thinner. Even the Intelligence files had little of interest. I felt like I'd fallen out of the sky and into a pool overflowing with papers, most of them mildewed and mundane. I almost wished I was back in Ohio. Almost.

Discouragement set in after the first months and grew deeper each week. I was on the verge of giving up when early one morning in May of 1982 the phone rang. Through a wakening haze, I recognized the soft voice of Bill Lewis. "That box you wanted to look into has been screened," he said, "and there's something in it I think you'll want to see." I knew Lewis would never have called me if he'd only discovered something routine.

Twenty minutes later I was pulling into the Field Branch parking lot, wondering what he had turned up. Two weeks earlier I'd seen a list showing a box that I thought might be interesting. It had been logged under Record Group 331, Allied Operational and Occupation Headquarters, 1946-50, Public Safety Division (PSD), Assistant Chief of Staff, G-2, Supreme Commander Allied Powers (SCAP). On the basis of the Freedom of Information Act I had asked to see the box because the PSD had worked as an advisory team to the Tokyo police. I was told I'd have to wait because the contents were still classified and had not yet been through the preliminary screening process. I'd made the formal request that the contents of that box be declassified, but expected to find only more sheaves of reports on suspected communist activity.

Lewis' phone call, however, said the box held more than that. Suddenly the old hopes gripped me again. I was going to be the first person without a security clearance to see this file.

Lewis had the file pulled and waiting for me when I arrived. It was thicker than I had expected and there were bold black letters across it, spelling "Teikoku Bank Murder Crime." I opened it quickly and leafed through once without reading the pages. Forty documents were in that file.

The first was a letter, written by a Japanese man in Tokyo to someone in Nakano, translated into English and marked **CONFIDENTIAL** at the top. Right above the text the heading read: **INTELLIGENCE: SUSPECT OF TEIKOKU BANK MURDER CASE MENTIONED.**

Despite a promising start, however, the letter proved a disappointment. The writer had thought he'd seen the killer because a man answering the description printed in the newspapers had come to the writer's house asking for some sort of "medicine" which the tone of the letter suggested was illegal. The unidentified man appeared desperate, the writer noted, because he gave suspicious reasons for wanting this medicine. But the letter bore no date, and though it named the writer and the recipient, it did not identify them in any other way. There was no way of telling who the correspondents or the unidentified man were.

The folder also contained pieces on the background of the case, from press translations to an illustration of some of the medical equipment which survivors had described as the doctor's props. No actual equipment had been found on the scene, but the descriptions had been unequivocal.

Suddenly an envelope of police photographs fell out of the file. I picked it up, opened it, and found a picture of the Teikoku Bank, which I had never seen. It looked like a quaint little home in a quiet, wooded neighborhood, and not the bustling bank on the ground floor of some large office building as I had envisioned.

The envelope contained other pictures as well, and I looked at them now, one by one. The MPB photographer had taken a shot of each body where it fell. One framed a dead child who lay twisted with his mouth and eyes open. Another showed bodies contorted on the floor, vomit and blood trickling from the corners of their mouths. A third pictured ten cadavers laid out shoulder to shoulder in a tight line on the bank's floor.

There were several pictures without people in them. One was

76

of the bank's safe which was open and empty. Given that this crime
had been a robbery, this was certainly not peculiar. But the next
photograph was. It showed stacks of money lying on top of a desk
in the bank. I knew from reports I'd read that three hundred thousand
yen had been left behind by the killer, nearly twice the amount he
had taken with him from the scene of the crime.

I replaced the photographs, looking again at each one as I tucked
it back inside the envelope. These pictures, classified as "SECRET"
for over three decades, were more graphic and perhaps more valuable
than any other documents in this old and yellowing file, I thought.

The next document I picked up was a detailed, five-page report
issued the day after the crime by an officer named Jirō Fujita, chief
of the Tokyo MPB's Criminal Investigation Division. The report
identified each of the victims, instructed all police stations in Tokyo
about proceeding with the preliminary investigation, described the
criminal, and recounted the crime. Fujita's summary of the events
inside the bank showed that not even the police were immune to
a sort of perverse fascination with the genius of the crime:

> All the victims, wholly unsuspicious of the fiendish
> intention of the offender, whose perfect composure and
> plausible explanations as well as his armband from the
> Tokyo Metropolitan office having satisfied them to lay
> full credit in his words, formed a circle around him—a
> circle of poor victims sixteen in all.
> Then the devil opened his mouth and said. . . .

The next few documents gave me no new information, until
finally I reached the first document directly to involve the U.S.
Occupation authorities in the Teikoku Bank investigation.

A memorandum dated 20 February 1948 recorded a conference
held within the Public Safety Division at ten o'clock the previous
morning. Up to this point it appeared that the PSD officials had
been no more than observers. Now, however, Sergeant Naruchi of
the Tokyo MPB's Criminal Investigation Division came to ask Henry
Eaton of the PSD's police branch to help identify and locate two

American officers, a Lieutenant Hornet and a Lieutenant Parker, both of whom were believed to have been associated with typhus disinfecting teams in the Tokyo area. Parker had been named, Naruchi said, in the Teikoku killings, and Hornet, or something sounding like that, had been named in one of the rehearsals. Naruchi also asked for any information on Japanese citizens, particularly interpreters, who were either connected with or had knowledge of the work done by either Hornet or Parker.

According to the unsigned memo, the PSD checked out the two names for the MPB. No one named Hornet turned up on any official record, but almost twenty officers named Parker had been assigned in Tokyo during the Occupation. The names and current assignments of only ten of these Parkers were found, the memo reported, and of those perhaps four were still in Japan. There was nothing on record to indicate that any of them had been involved in health control activity.

Clearly, the Tokyo police were following any possible clue, and with good reason: If either Parker or Hornet was an actual person and not merely part of the ruse, he could be a vital link in locating the killer. The use of an American's name and the description of his duties seemed a little too real to have been invented. By the same token, nothing could be ruled out as beyond the imagination of a criminal genius.

The investigation began to narrow. Henry Eaton, the document further reported, found out that by 1946 all involvement of U.S. military personnel in local health operations had finished, and all disease prevention was now carried out exclusively by Japanese employees of each ward office in Tokyo. No Occupation personnel were connected with such health agencies at the time of the Teikoku Bank crime. The clear implication was that any connection between the killer and Occupation officials had been made before 1946.

The next document, however, provided new and contradictory information. It was another memo, dated later on the same day, from Jack Munroe to Byron Engle, and said that there had been a Lieutenant Parker working with a typhus control team in the Oji ward in Tokyo during March 1947. Munroe got the information from the chief of the Public Health and Welfare Section of the Tokyo Metropolitan Government (MG) who recalled Parker, but could not remember the man's first name. Neither could the chief's assistant, but he did remember hearing that this Parker had left Japan for Korea, and then had been reassigned to the States. The chief also mentioned that two MPB patrolmen had spoken to him three days earlier, and that he gave them the same information.

Two points struck me from this memo. First, MPB Sergeant Naruchi had told the Public Safety people that in one of the rehearsals the killer had mentioned Parker and something about typhus control in Oji. Second, according to Eaton's findings, all such activity involving U.S. personnel had ceased in 1946, yet the new information dated Parker's presence as March 1947. Why this discrepancy in the dates?

The next memo answered my question and revealed some new, disturbing facts. Munroe consulted records in GHQ's Medical Section on February 21 and three days later reported to Engle that he'd hit paydirt. The records hadn't been much help, but Munroe's discussion with office head Major Sam Plemmons certainly had. According to the report:

> . . .First Lt. Paul E. J. Parker, MC (Marine Corps), 0-1745617, 24th Corps (Korea) was assigned to the Tokyo area on several cases between 30 June 1946 and June 1947 to assist in various health control activities. The dates of these (temporary duty) periods are not reflected in the records of GHQ Medical Section. It was stated, however, that the above referred official was undoubtedly the "Lt. Parker" who was assigned on a typhus control team in Oji ward with the Tokyo MG in March 1947.

So Parker was for real, and a positive identification had been made. But there was no indication the lead was ever pursued beyond this point. There was not even any indication—as there had been concerning the relay of information—that the Tokyo police were ever advised of Parker's identity. Nor was there any explanation of why the dates of Parker's year-long duties were not included in the records, which had been thorough enough to note his full name and initials and his serial number. Nor was there an account for how Major Plemmons, with no available records, recalled the exact dates of Parker's tour of duty. The memo was not specific about who "stated" that this Parker was "undoubtedly" the man in question. Was it Major Plemmons, or somebody else? And what was it about Parker that made him so memorable?

The principal question, as it concerned the Teikoku case, was whether Sadamichi Hirasawa was ever connected with Paul E.J. Parker. I turned to the next document hoping that this link would be established and thus clear things up. Instead, I found something even more interesting—an American connection.

PUBLIC SAFETY DIVISION

4 March 1948
MEMORANDUM
SUBJECT: Teikoku Bank Robbery Investigation
    1. On 3 March Mr. Harry Kobayashi, Liaison for the MPB, related a request from Mr. Fujita, Chief of Detectives of the MPB, that the investigators of the PSD attempt to secure any information available pertaining to a group of former Japanese military personnel that were sent to Korea as *poisoners* during the war. It is believed that these persons were highly trained in preparation of various poisons and that a SCAP Section *is investigating them for possible war crimes.* (emphasis added)

BYRON ENGLE
Administrator in Charge
Police Branch

The wording was ambiguous in parts, and no names had been named, but the specifics were clear enough. The American officials of the PSD were aware of the existence of a special Japanese chemical warfare unit and that members of this unit were likely under investigation by Occupation authorities for war crimes.

Any possibility that this March 4 memo was unrelated to the 731 Regiment or to American knowledge of their probable involvement in the Teikoku crime was swiftly disqualified by the next document in the file. On March 11, 1948, a meeting took place between Chief Jirō Fujita of the MPB and Byron Engle, Jack Munroe, and Lieutenant Eugene H. Hattori of the Public Safety Division. A PSD secretary took the following notes:

> —Japanese people with gray hair were rushing to barber shops to have their hair dyed because of being stopped so many times by police for questioning in connection with case.
> —(The police) have new lead they hope will be productive of results. Checking former personnel who worked in the laboratory (Japanese Army) in Chiba *experimenting with prussic acid to be used as poison during the war. A corp* [sic] *was sent into Manchuria that used this poison on humans and animals successfully. Request made this information be kept secret for fear of prosecution by War Crimes Tribunal.* Japanese Army issued pamphlet on this subject that was issued to Japanese Army personnel. Modus operandi of the criminal who murdered the twelve people in this bank by the use of prussic poison was very similar to that as the training that developed from the Arsenal Laboratory. Information obtained by a detective who visited the bank reports that even in the language of the bank robber-murderer it is indicative that he was trained in this laboratory. As example he mentions "First Drug" and "Second Drug" in English that leads the police to believe that it is someone trained in the Arsenal Laboratory that was experimenting with prussic acid to be used in warfare.
> —The police further believe that they are on the right trail because the murderer drank from the same bottle that the employees from the bank drank from

knowing that due to fact that the poison had been precipitated and he could safely drink from the fluid that
was on top of the bottle.

—Told of the experiments in precipitation with
prussic acid using oil from Palm Tree's [sic].

—Further evidence that leads the police to believe
that the murderer was schooled at this arsenal laboratory
is because of the equipment he had with him that answers
description of equipment used at the laboratory. At the
close of the war when the laboratory was closed most of
the employees took equipment home, etc.

—Mr. Fujita stated that information as to personnel
who were at the lab when it was in operation was being
obtained from former Major Nonoyama and former Col.
Yokoyama.

—Mr. Fujita complained that he was having considerable difficulty with the press who were interfering with
the investigation and sought cooperation from this section in this matter. He complained particularly about the
Yomiuri Press. (emphasis added)

How much, if anything, the PSD people knew about the deal
that had been struck a year earlier with Ishii was unclear from the
document, but as of this meeting they now knew about the existence
of former soldiers who stood a good chance of entering the ranks of
Class A war criminals. I wondered why the Japanese police were
dealing with them so gingerly. Instead of threatening to throw them
to the Military Tribunal if they didn't cooperate, the MPB was
accepting their demands for secrecy. Worse, the American police
advisors were endorsing the MPB's acquiescence.

Later that same day Munroe typed up another report, this one
under the heading: "Civil Intelligence Section, G-2." Fujita had sin-
gled out the Yomiuri Shimbun's reporters because they had staked
out the homes of informers, and even had posed as detectives to get
former 731 members to talk. By one o'clock that afternoon, Munroe
wrote, Major D.C. Imboden of the Press and Publications Section

telegraphed all Japanese papers to keep the reporters clear of the investigation. Imboden further said that he was going to "communicate personally with the publisher of the *Yomiuri* about the problems his reporters were causing." Munroe's closing lines explained why, from mid-March until Sadamichi Hirasawa's arrest in August, there were so few articles in the Japanese newspapers with any new details of the Teikoku case:

> (Imboden) also said he would discuss the matter with Allied censorship authorities exercising control of Japanese publications and *request the censors co-operate in stopping publication of any article containing any reference to the police investigation of a Japanese Army Poison School being connected with the Teikoku case;* further he will request the censors to screen all articles pertaining to the Teikoku case on the basis of whether publication of the article will hinder apprehension of the culprit. (emphasis added)

The file held no further information about the investigation of the poisoners. Had the deal with 731 caused certain other records to be filed elsewhere, in more secure places? However, one significant and puzzling fact had been recorded: Graduates of the Japanese Army Poison School were officially shielded from the War Crimes Tribunal, presumably in the interest of securing other, more valuable information from them. Where did they get the leverage to force the Japanese police to accept and honor their demand for total secrecy? Why were the police willing to shield war criminals, instead of threatening to throw them to the International Military Tribunal? And why did the authorities in the Public Safety Division assist, rather than stop, the Japanese police in this?

I searched through the remainder of the file, looking for any documents on the arrest and interrogation of Hirasawa, but found none. All this evidence, I thought, and not one allegation connecting Hirasawa to the crime. There were only a few translated news stories on the painter's confession, which bore no mention of any of the foregoing details. Was Hirasawa ignorant of them, or had the censorship deleted them?

I closed the file, put it back in the labeled cardboard box, and headed out of the Modern Military Field Branch.

As I drove home, I felt as much disturbed by what the documents revealed as pleased at having discovered them. Allegations of the 731's involvement in the crime, for thirty years a matter of speculation, were now confirmed for the first time by Occupation records never before released to the public. The documents shed new light on previously dark areas, but the shadows they cast had not disappeared; they had only shifted. For example, Byron Engle's memo dated March 4 vaguely noted that "it is believed a certain SCAP section is investigating. . .for possible war crimes." Why was the SCAP Section not identified? The Legal Section of SCAP had dealt with Ishii, and the Legal Section also investigated war criminals. Was this the SCAP section "believed" to be "investigating"? How long did it take for the Legal Section to learn that the Tokyo police were poking around in something perilously close to the Ishii deal? The obfuscation, not only of the March 4 memo but of the greater American involvement, might very well have been accidental; it was also possible it might have been deliberate.

Over the year that passed since finding the documents, I'd discovered that many of the principals directly or indirectly involved in the investigation had died, and parts of the story had passed on with them. Only a PSD member could explain the ambiguities in the PSD memos. Only an MPB officer could answer questions about the curious actions taken by the police.

The telephone lines clicked, then buzzed through what sounded like echo chambers, then the phone at the other end started ringing.

"Hello."

"Mr. Hattori, please."

"Yes, speaking."

Eugene Hattori had a slow, measured voice, with just a trace of an accent, and he sounded to be in his late fifties. During the time he'd been with the Public Safety Division, he was a First Lieutenant, and so I guessed he'd been in his late twenties in those days. The odds were good, I had hoped, that he was still alive. Hattori had worked as a PSD liaison to the Tokyo police, and his name appeared on nearly all the documents concerning meetings about the Japanese poisoners. He would be that rare source of information for both the PSD and MPB sides of the story.

Hattori was not an easy find. I'd sent letters to him through the Veterans Administration, hoping they'd forward it to his last known address, but every letter had come back to me in the mail, stamped "unable to deliver." Locator ads in the *Army Times* had brought me no better luck.

There was a good chance he still lived in Japan. There was just as good a chance he lived in South America, Switzerland, or Ohio. I knew very little about him other than that he had worked in the Tokyo PSD offices during the Occupation and was a second generation Japanese-American. I had spent a long night in the Library of Congress poring over phone books, just to see if a Eugene Hattori was listed any place in the United States. It was a long shot and I knew it, but it was the only shot I could think of taking.

Three friends and I had rifled through the directories of thirty metropolitan areas, and somehow Eugene H. Hattori had turned up in the greater Los Angeles phone book. Now I had him on the line.

"I'm calling about the Teikoku Bank murders," I told him. Mr. Hattori said yes, he remembered the incident and had worked closely with the Public Safety Division and the Tokyo MPB on the case.

I asked if he would mind answering some questions about the investigation.

There was a slight pause and I could hear him draw his breath, before saying, "I can talk about it only in, ah, certain parameters."

I asked why.

Very politely he explained that there were "too many people still alive in Japan" whose reputations would be "damaged" if he were to "talk openly."

I asked what he meant but he would not elaborate. So we talked about my research, his time in Tokyo, and the files concerning the crime I'd found in the National Archives. My tone was casual in hopes that he might feel comfortable enough to say something more about his previous remark. I mentioned that I would like to go to Tokyo someday and see what records, if any, are left there.

"Oh, I'm sure the Tokyo police still have something on it," Mr. Hattori said, "but I'll tell you right now, there's one file in Japan that, even if it still exists, you'll *never* see."

Was he serious?

I asked him which file he was referring to, and again he would not elaborate, but before we finished talking Mr. Hattori agreed to an interview through the mail. I hung up the phone, unsure whether I should be pleased or worried that this old crime in Japan was suddenly assuming a new life in America.

The next day I drafted twelve questions to send to him. Some were innocent, others loaded.

> 1. What was your rank, citizenship status, and official capacity in the U.S. Army during 1948?
> 2. Briefly describe your background and how you came to Tokyo at that time.
> 3. What was your general impression of the crime, the investigation, and the MPB?
> 4. What was the Japanese (in particular, Tokyo) judicial system like in 1948–1949? Was it then still operating under the Meiji Constitution or the Allied Constitution?

5. Who was your immediate superior?

6. Did you know anyone in GHQ's Legal Section?

7. Did you ever have any contact with the editor of the *Yomiuri Shimbun* in 1948?

8. Ever hear the name Evan J. Parker or Paul E.J. Parker, 1st Lieutenant, Marine Corps?

9. On the phone you mentioned you could only talk within certain "parameters" about the case because of certain people who are still alive in Japan. Is this a professional or personal commitment you wish to honor with these people? Does anyone else know to the same extent the obviously sensitive information you hold, or are you the only one?

10. What was your opinion of Byron Engle as a Police Administrator?

11. Do you believe Hirasawa is the Teigin killer?

12. Was he fairly tried?

A month passed and I received no answer. When two months passed, I began to wonder if maybe he hadn't received my questions. After three months and no word, I called.

A woman answered and, after asking me who I was, said that Mr. Hattori wasn't available. I inquired if he ever had received my letter. She said that she was sure he had and that, if she wasn't mistaken, he had just mailed me his reply the other day.

A few days later I found a letter from Gene Hattori in my mailbox. He answered my twelve questions as follows:

Dear Mr. Triplett:
Sorry but I don't think I can be of any help.
Sincerely,
Eugene Hattori

That was it, all of it. It took him three months to write one cheap sentence, and on a full-sized sheet of paper yet. I couldn't believe he was closing the door. What was so threatening to him? What was he hiding?

Three months later I flew to Los Angeles. He wouldn't see me. I called him, but he refused to talk. I told him that I was continuing to write the Teikoku crime story and wanted to give him the chance to comment about his involvement in the investigation and to explain why the PSD cooperated with the Tokyo police in keeping the poison school a secret.

Very anxiously he told me, "Whatever gets printed, I'm sure there's no fraud or defamation."

Who said anything about fraud or defamation? I just want to know what happened.

We talked for only a few seconds more, until he hung up on me. I couldn't tell if he was actually afraid or if his loyalties ran deep, or both. He had said nothing and he had said a lot. Something stank, and we both knew it.

I spent the next year, 1984, ransacking every possible source, from transcripts of Hirasawa's confession supplied to me by his supporters in Japan, to press reports, to the Archives again. I checked out every name that appeared anywhere in connection with the Teikoku story, got addresses for all I could find, mailed off letters, and got back a lot of envelopes marked "Deceased" or "Address Unknown." Many of the letters I sent to Japan never came back. Hattori's comments continued to irritate me. He could clear up so much of this, I thought, but he wasn't talking. Maybe, as Hattori suggested, the answers were still in Japan.

Tokyo's Narita Airport was bright and clean, looking as modern and western as any airport in America. I was surprised that there was nothing remarkably foreign or surprising about the place. Even the Muzak sounded familiar. After clearing customs, I stopped to change some money, then passed through the sliding glass doors to where a huge crowd of people stood waiting. I was tired from the seventeen-hour trip and started to scan the sea of faces in search of the people who had come to meet me, when it suddenly hit me that I didn't know who to look for because I had never met them. I was feeling deflated and weary, when I saw a pair of hands holding up a huge rectangular piece of cardboard above the crowd. On it were neatly painted English letters that read:

THE SOCIETY TO SAVE HIRASAWA
WELCOMES
WILLIAM TRIPLETT

It looked like a giant namecard.

Holding up the sign was a solid-looking young man in his late twenties. He had black hair, a warm smile, and wore a dark suit with a dark overcoat. Having no idea of proper Japanese greetings, I awkwardly held out my hand and stood ready to bow. He put down the sign, shook my hand, paused a moment, then carefully said, "Good. . .trip?"

Yes, I said, and asked his name. He didn't understand me, so I pointed to myself and said my name. He smiled, pointed to himself, and said, "Takehiko Hirasawa."

I hadn't expected the leader of the Society himself, who was also the twenty-five-year-old adopted son of the convicted painter, to greet me at the airport. We were joined by another Society member whose slow but reliable English finished the introduction.

The three of us boarded a train for downtown Tokyo, which lay about an hour to the west. As we rode toward the city, I stared out the window at a series of neon flashes sweeping past in a pearl-black night. Nothing seemed recognizable, not the silhouetted shapes, not the faces, not even the time. It could have been any year, I thought. This was not the familiar-looking airport. The travel, jet lag, and a growing feeling of alienation were finally taking their toll on me. The landscape was a blur of concrete and wood held together by neon tubing, clotheslines, and railroad tracks. Even the ubiquitous Coca Cola billboards looked strange.

We passed inside the city limits and the night exploded into millions of blinking and bursting lights. A tape of official directions crackled through the train's PA system. Suitcases came off the overhead racks. Bodies filled the aisles. When we stepped onto the platform the air tasted like it had a cold foil wrapper on it.

About twenty-four hours later I was situated in a small room in a small house in Shinagawa-ku, a prefecture at the southern end of Tokyo. The predominant feeling I had was one of compression: Not only did I have one month to reconstruct thirty-seven years of history, but also I kept bumping my head on the tops of doorways (and I am not a tall man; five feet ten inches on a good day). My room was spare but adequate, with floor mats, a table and chair, some bookshelves, a space heater, and a mattress under several layers of sleeping bags and blankets. I prepared materials for my first meeting. Takehiko Hirasawa, who had met me at the airport, and other officials of the Society to Save Hirasawa were expecting me at Takehiko's house in about an hour. I left early, to allow myself time to get lost.

Asagaya was a quiet but elegant neighborhood, sort of suburban yet full of shops and cafes and strollers. Takehiko met me at the train station and was accompanied by Keiichi Tsunekawa, the gray-haired Society member who had translated for me at the airport. Tsunekawa agreed to act as interpreter during our interviews.

The entrance of Takehiko's house was narrow and dark, and as I walked in I smelled the rich odor of fine wood. We took off our shoes, put on slippers, then stepped up from the foyer onto the main floor of the corridor. Takehiko's mother, a fragile looking woman with a soft, gentle face, appeared and greeted us with a warm smile. She ushered us into the sitting room, where I discovered the source of the deep wood smell.

Along three walls wooden bookcases rose almost to the ceiling. Takehiko joked that he was afraid the house was going to tip forward because there were so many books here in the front room of the house. A color television, a space heater, a sofa, two chairs, and a coffee table filled nearly all the remaining space. On the only side of the room that was not lined with bookcases was an open sliding panel that revealed a beautifully carved wooden shrine that the Japanese traditionally build for the dead. Amid carefully arranged flowers and pieces of incense on the shrine was a photograph of a man wearing ceremonial kimonos. I looked once again around the room and noticed that a different photograph of the same man— Tetsuro Morikawa, who was a famous Japanese writer, the founder of the Society to Save Hirasawa, and Takehiko's real father—stood on nearly every bookshelf.

Morikawa formed the Society in 1962 and was elected its Secretary General. The Society, with about two thousand supporters, petitioned Japan's Ministry of Justice with thousands of pages arguing that Hirasawa could not be the Teikoku killer. Morikawa staged reenactments of the crime to prove that Hirasawa could not have reached the bank at the time the prosecution claimed he had. He and Society members drove around downtown Tokyo calling through megaphones encouraging the public to join their struggle against the "false charges" against Hirasawa. Morikawa held exhibitions of Hirasawa's paintings, including the works that the artist continued to paint while in prison. The Society filed sixteen appeals for retrial and four appeals for pardon. All had been rejected.

Some years ago, when Hirasawa's health began to fail, Morikawa became concerned about what might happen in the event of the artist's death. He knew that the Japanese courts allow surviving family members to continue pleading a deceased man's case. With none of Hirasawa's blood relatives willing to pursue an appeal on his behalf, the possibility of his vindication would die with him. Morikawa thought about it, and took his own son Takhiko aside one day and asked him if he would accept legal adoption by Hirasawa. Takehiko, who had been aware of his father's commitment to freeing Hirasawa and who had come to share his father's beliefs, agreed.

At first Morikawa was pleased by his son's decision. But after the adoption was completed, something changed. Morikawa began to fall silent, began withdrawing from his family, no longer sat with them at meals. He stayed more and more in bed stricken by some strange and profound sadness. Takehiko was certain his father was ill and tried repeatedly to discover what ailed him.

Finally Morikawa spoke. Tearfully, he said that his fervent desire to see Hirasawa released had cost him his own son. He felt that he had lost Takehiko, that he had given away his own child, and he felt terribly ashamed. Takehiko assured his father that these feelings were unfounded and that, in Takehiko's view, the adoption was actually a way of getting closer to *him,* to Morikawa, his real father. It was a way of embracing his father's beliefs and of guaranteeing that his father's work would continue.

In a short time the trauma passed, and the family celebrated a sense of renewed union, until about a year later when Morikawa took to bed again. This time, however, the symptoms were neither depression nor shame. He had contracted a liver disease, and in the fall of 1983 Morikawa died.

I pulled out my notes and papers as Takehiko pulled down worn copies of his father's writings from the shelves. Mrs. Morikawa came back into the room with a bamboo tray of cups and coffee. As I thanked her, Takehiko set up a portable tape recorder.

I wanted to know how things happened from the start. If I could determine exactly where all the confusion began, I might be able to discover some answers. I started by asking Takehiko what interested his real father in the Teikoku Bank crime.

He said that when the crime occurred in 1948 his father was still a student. Not until 1953, when Morikawa was an investigative reporter covering the Japanese courts, did he come upon the history of the Teikoku case. In Japan it had come to be known as *Teigin jiken,* a sort of hybrid term derived from *Teikoku* (Imperial), *Ginko* (Bank), and *jiken* (incident). Morikawa had become familiar with cases in which it appeared the accused was falsely charged, and as he learned more about the Teigin incident, he began to consider it the most extreme case of uncorroborated allegations he had ever encountered. From the beginning of his inquiry he believed the case against Hirasawa was at best weak. As he researched more deeply, he became utterly convinced that the artist was innocent.

Hirasawa's was not the only case Morikawa was working on at the time. He was in constant touch with other convicts whom he believed had been framed, but as his doubts about the Teigin affair grew increasingly heavy, he found himself consumed by his research. Morikawa secured records from the Public Procurator's Office and began to make voluminous copies of court records regarding the case.

As we talked, the door swung open and Mrs. Morikawa politely escorted a man into the room. He looked to be in his late forties, with thick black hair, plastic-frame glasses, and a dark green jacket of heavy cloth. Takehiko introduced him as Kaname Mitsumatsu, the man who had replaced Takehiko as acting Secretary General of the Society. Mitsumatsu has been a member of the Society for twenty years. He bowed, sat down, and lit a cigarette. Mrs. Morikawa withdrew to get Mr. Mitsumatsu a cup of coffee. Mitsumatsu apologized for being late and asked us to continue.

I knew that very few people in Japan knew of the existence of the 731 Regiment before, during, or after the war. Even within the Imperial Army, hardly anyone outside of Ishii's employ knew what was going on inside the 731 installations, all of them euphemistically called Water Purification Units. Details of Ishii and 731 were still a secret in postwar Japan, but Morikawa had somehow discovered that the MPB suspected 731 Regiment personnel in connection with the Teikoku murders. I asked Takehiko if his father had seen any official records that proved this.

He said that he and his father were never certain precisely how the MPB came to suspect 731 involvement, and that no one had ever seen any sort of records to prove that the Japanese police were tracking 731 people. Word had it that the MPB "just knew" of Ishii's activities, and in turn, everybody "just knew that the MPB knew." Takehiko said this without affectation. It was my first lesson in what proof meant in the Japanese lexicon.

I said I had brought with me some documents from GHQ that might be of help to the Society. Tsunekawa didn't even have to finish translating my sentence. The Japanese still know the meaning of GHQ, and when I reached into my file, the three Society officials quietly tensed and leaned forward. Tsunekawa kept translating, but their attention was on the papers in my hands.

I first pointed out the document recording the meeting between Byron Engle and Jirō Fujita on the MPB's investigation of poisoners trained by the Imperial Army, and the ensuing press interference. As soon as Tsunekawa finished explaining what the document contained, Mitsumatsu and Takehiko immediately conversed, nodded their heads, and said *hai* (yes) several times. Tsunekawa, eyebrows raised, asked what else I had.

I showed them the document on censoring the *Yomiuri Shimbun,* and then pulled out the fully detailed report that Chief Fujita filed the day after the crime. The three of them were beside themselves with excitement. GHQ documents. Tsunekawa couldn't translate fast enough. He could barely handle the military jargon but tried to convey the memorandum's general content. As he sometimes paused and groped for a word, Takehiko and Mitsumatsu waited anxiously but politely.

Ah. . .
Hai.
Choto. . .
Hai.
Ah. . .
Hai. . .
Choto. . .

Takehiko said they were excited because his father had wondered for years just what files the Occupation had concerning the

Teikoku affair and, more specifically, had wondered whether the files would corroborate the Society's claims. Morikawa had died not knowing. Takehiko pointed across the room to the open sliding panel to his father's shrine and said, "At least he is here in spirit, and now he knows."

The Society knew that the name of Parker had been used during the robbery, but they had no specifics indicating that this Parker had indeed existed. I showed them the Public Safety document positively identifying Marine Corps Lt. Paul Parker, and Takehiko scrambled to find a note pad. Not only did it identify him as an American officer, but as one discharging the exact duties the killer had said Parker was involved in. Tsunekawa translated, Takehiko scribbled, and Mitsumatsu nodded gravely.

When they finished with the Parker document they went back again to the previous ones, and Takehiko continued scribbling. Tsunekawa said that Takehiko had forgotten to take notes on the other documents because their content had surprised him so much.

I realized from their reactions that these documents were the first pieces of hard evidence to confirm what had only been speculation and hearsay up to this point. Certain specifics, such as Paul Parker's name, the location and existence of the poison school, and the MPB's investigation of the school's graduates, had never before come to light in such incontrovertible terms.

I had come to Japan to learn about the Teikoku mystery from the Japanese side, not fully realizing to what extent I had brought with me the historical complement—the American side.

We continued. I still wanted to know what specifically convinced Takehiko's father of Hirasawa's innocence. In my research on Morikawa, I'd found out that *his* father, Takehiko's grandfather, had been executed in Manchuria by the Chinese communists after being denounced as a rebel trying to incite students to revolt against Mao Tse-Tung. Morikawa claimed that his father had been falsely accused and had in effect been assassinated but could never prove it. Was Morikawa's defense of Hirasawa based on authentic concerns for justice supported by facts, or on finding another martyr? My eye

95

fell on one of the many photographs of Morikawa. He seemed such a kind looking man, with a serene, almost feminine aura about him. How much had his biases filtered the light in which he had studied the crime?

Takehiko explained that, after reading through all the court records and poring over volumes of testimony, Morikawa believed that there was no material evidence in the prosecution's case to link Hirasawa to the crime. Morikawa was even doubtful about the signature on the confession, alleging that it didn't even remotely resemble the artist's.

Morikawa found sixty-two records of interrogation in which, supposedly, Hirasawa was to have confessed little by little. The records of the first fifty-nine sessions were chaotic and contradictory, particularly regarding the use of cyanide, but the sixtieth interrogation brought a dramatic, and baffling, change. Suddenly in that sixtieth session, Hirasawa's confession proceeded logically from first to last. The sixty-first and sixty-second sessions were almost verbatim repeats, with only a minor departure here and there. Morikawa looked over all the records again, and decided that Hirasawa's confession had been the product of fifty-nine rehearsals.

Takehiko remembered that on the day of his father's death his mother had received a threatening phone call from a man saying that soon she and her son would join her husband if they didn't leave the Teikoku case alone. Just then Mrs. Morikawa entered with more coffee for everyone. We stood, bowed, and thanked her. She had put on an apron, and I could smell something cooking, something exotic wafting down the corridor from the kitchen.

We turned our attention to Hirasawa's alibi. If Morikawa was right, then Hirasawa's alibi must have been legitimate, truthful, but problems lay there, too, because the alibi had never been corroborated. Takehiko recounted the artist's version. Hirasawa had spent the early part of January 26, 1948 with one of his daughters and her husband in downtown Tokyo. About two o'clock that afternoon, he left them and caught a train, he said, to Nakano in west Tokyo where another of his daughters lived. He arrived but his daughter was not home. Only her boyfriend, an American sergeant named Wayne Ely or Wayne Eddy (Hirasawa was never sure of the correct name), was in the house. Hirasawa said that he and the American played cards into the evening.

This U.S. Army sergeant, Ely or Eddy, never appeared at Hirasawa's trial to corroborate the artist's alibi. By the time Yoshio Yamada, Hirasawa's attorney, wanted to subpoena the American, Ely or Eddy had already been rotated back to the States. Yamada had submitted to the court the gate-pass Ely/Eddy had used to leave his Army base on January 26 as evidence, but the court rejected it. The Society maintained that Yamada had originally tried to get the American to testify in the early stages of the trial when Ely/Eddy was still in Japan, but somewhere somebody interfered and prevented the American soldier from appearing. It didn't sound like an unwarranted accusation, in light of the Society's larger theory that elements of GHQ colluded with the Tokyo police to frame Hirasawa. When the Society's current attorney, Makoto Endo, inquired at the Procurator's Office if the gate pass was still in their possession, he was told that all exhibits not admitted as material evidence had been destroyed.

More than a year before coming to Japan I had put ads in newspapers across America for both Wayne Eddy and Wayne Ely, but never received a response. I'd even tried the phone books the same way I'd succeeded in locating Hattori, but this time I had no luck. I was having a hard time understanding how such a crucial factor— the *only* material witness for the defense—could be so elusive. How could Hirasawa have been so indeterminate in recalling the name of the man who could have secured his freedom, who could have saved his life?

I then asked Takehiko about Hideo Naruchi, who was an MPB officer working on the Teikoku case from the start and who, according to Takehiko's father, believed Hirasawa was innocent. Takehiko said that when the Japanese newspapers published the namecard of Dr. Shigeru Matsui, the card used at the rehearsal in November 1947, Naruchi started to receive unsigned letters that

Matsui was the Teikoku criminal. Additional unsigned letters arrived, claiming that Matsui had killed about two hundred fifty Indonesians by lethal injection during his wartime assignment in Java, where he had served as chief of the Public Sanitary Department, Health Administration for the Imperial Army. The letters, from places across Japan, identified the writer only as a former subordinate of Matsui in occupied Java.

If these claims were true, Naruchi had enough damaging information on Matsui to pressure him, even arrest him, before questioning him. When the MPB confronted Matsui in Sendai the doctor started to quake and sweat. He was sure that they had come to take him to the International Military Tribunal on a war crimes charge. Then, when the detectives said they wanted to talk to him about the Teikoku crime, the doctor regained his composure and said that although he didn't know anything about it, he'd be glad to cooperate.

Naruchi immediately pressed Matsui about the Java killings. Matsui buckled and pleaded desperately for Naruchi not to publicize them. They were an accident, he said. He had meant to inject everyone with a typhus vaccine, but instead had shot them with tetanus bacteria. Two hundred and fifty times. Naruchi asked him where he had been on January 26, and Matsui somehow articulated, reportedly through tears, a letter-perfect alibi. The details of the doctor's alibi were never made known. All that was ever published was the MPB's certainty that, based on Matsui's story, he had been far from Tokyo on the day of the Teikoku murders.

Naruchi apparently accepted Matsui's alibi, believing in the first place that a criminal as methodical as the Teikoku killer would hardly leave his own namecard at the scene of a rehearsal. But if Matsui hadn't committed the Teikoku killings himself, it seemed clear that he knew things or perhaps knew people who could blow the case wide open, and Naruchi was after whatever information Matsui might possess. He had the right background. His card was in the bank. More than that, though, was the curious fact that shortly before the Teikoku crime a man had entered the pharmacy of the Tohoku University Hospital in Sendai and asked for some prussic acid to kill some fish in his pond at home. The man identified himself as Dr. Shigeru Matsui. By coincidence the pharmacist on duty knew the real Dr. Matsui, and so knew that this man was an impostor. The pharmacist told the fake doctor he could not dispense prussic acid without a prescription, and the man left. After the Teikoku crime, when the description of the killer was published in the newspapers, the pharmacist told the police what happened and said the impostor's looks matched those mentioned in the papers.

Naruchi tried to press Matsui on these points, but Matsui was ready. He boldly laid down a condition, saying that if guaranteed he wouldn't be taken before the Tribunal, he would help all he could.

Naruchi, thought about it, demurred, then agreed. Matsui immediately took out his wallet and started removing dozens of namecards he'd received during the past month. Perhaps someone he'd met, he said, and exchanged cards with, had used his namecard.

Takehiko stopped. I waited for him to resume, but he didn't.

"And?" I asked.

"And what?" he said.

"That's it? That's all Naruchi got?"

"I don't understand."

"Matsui was afraid of a war crimes trial, he knew what poisons were about, and he was linked to someone seeking prussic acid in his name before the crime, and all he could offer was namecards?!"

"Hai."

"Who the hell was Matsui to bargain for anything when all Naruchi had to say was that he'd throw him to the IMT if he didn't talk?" I asked.

They still didn't understand. To them it was simple: Naruchi confronted Matsui, Matsui maneuvered, they made a deal, and Naruchi honored his end of it. Why Naruchi felt compelled to bargain with Matsui struck me as incomprehensible. Matsui was accused of war crimes, of murder. As I saw it, Naruchi held all the cards. None of this struck Takehiko, Mitsumatsu, or Tsunekawa as odd. That Matsui got off with tossing out no more than namecards didn't seem strange to them either. Unless I missed something, or something got lost in translation, Naruchi was taken for a one-way ride by Matsui. Maybe Takehiko was too jaded to react anymore, or maybe a Japanese sense of fatalism, the belief that events are foretold and cannot be altered by the individual, was at work here. I thought it was the Society's aim to overturn Hirasawa's conviction. They were a strange group, these three men—independent enough in their thinking to fight the system, but still directed by old codes of honor not to question why certain things happen. I was confused.

After leaving Takehiko's house, as I stood on the platform waiting for my train, I reflected on how much information there was to mull over and unravel. I'd come to Japan to interview sources, yet with my first interview I'd learned more about the case, but understood less. In order to understand the mystery of the crime I would have to understand the Japanese character more fully.

The next day I was walking to meet Kazuhiko Nagoya, keen observer of Japanese life and veteran columnist for *The Daily Yomiuri*, the English language edition of the *Yomiuri Shimbun*, one of Japan's largest and oldest newspapers. On my way to the meeting I noticed that the cash I'd changed at the airport was almost gone, so I stopped into a bank to change some more. While waiting, I looked around the inside of the bank. It was full of desks and computers, couches and counters, people and recorded music. Everything there reminded me of banks back home. I remarked to myself how impossible it would be to commit such a crime as the Teikoku killings today in Japan. Unlike the Teikoku Bank, this bank was large and staffed by many people, and I doubted that the Teigin ruse could ever work in Japan again. So much had changed. Then as the teller handed me my money, I noticed a tray of teacups sitting on a table behind him. Perhaps not as much had changed as I'd thought.

I headed back up the street toward the *Yomiuri* offices. On one side of the street lay the Imperial grounds, marked by traditional pointed roofs and massively elegant evergreens. On the other side was downtown Tokyo, with its modern high-rises, office buildings, and sprawling boulevards. Cars and trucks stood bumper to bumper, inching forward in the jammed traffic lanes. As busy a quarter of the city as this was, it was remarkably quiet. No horns, no yelling. Presently I entered the *Yomiuri* building and looked around the big and breezy foyer.

Nagoya, a diminutive older man in a dark blue suit and heavy glasses, greeted me and took me to the eighth floor tearoom where we could talk. He and I had exchanged letters over four years, and I had looked forward to meeting him. During the past few years, Nagoya had written articles about the Teikoku crime and was continuing to explore the impact of the crime and of Hirasawa's death row status on Japanese public opinion.

We stepped into the tearoom, and I froze. The tables and chairs looked like they belonged in a doll's house. Everything was set so low to the floor that ground clearance was only eight inches or so. I self-consciously folded myself into a chair as Nagoya also took a seat. He lit the first of what would be a chain of pungent cigarettes, ordered drinks for both of us, then began telling me about life in Japan during wartime.

When the Imperial Army held Japan in its fist Nagoya was a teenager, and passionately pro-American. He didn't tell many people, other than his family, about his sentiments. He hated Japan's militarists and rejoiced at the Allies' victory. When the Occupation came, Nagoya was eager to use his knowledge of English and go to work for the Americans.

He was pleased to see democracy come to Japan, but, like many of his countrymen, he knew it wouldn't be an easy transition. He spoke of untold numbers of unprovoked attacks by GIs on Japanese citizens during the postwar Occupation. American arrogance toward the defeated people accounted for each attack, he said, and it was often difficult to endure the pain and insult. By and large, though, Japan endured and evolved, and Nagoya was happy to see things like the advent of women's suffrage and the return of free speech.

Not all Japanese embraced the Occupation as Nagoya had, he pointed out. The older generations, with deeper roots in feudalism, resisted. Nagoya's own family didn't share his enthusiasm for the

Occupation. It was a controversial time colored by mixed emotions and powerful cultural conflicts. The occupiers were rich, the occupied were poor; some Japanese loved the Americans, others hated them; half the Occupation officials wanted to make Japan a true democracy with rights for everyone, Nagoya maintained, and the other half only wanted a bulwark against communism. The Japanese character was under a great strain.

I asked Nagoya how the Occupation figured into the Teigin incident.

"I don't think the Occupation had any responsibility for Hirasawa, but indirectly it contributed to Hirasawa's arrest by stopping the police investigation of the 731 Regiment."

I asked what proof he had of this.

"Sergeant Hideo Naruchi was quoted as saying it. I didn't always think Hirasawa was innocent. In fact at first I thought he was guilty. Then I read some stories about the case. The police were very excited because such a mass murder on this scale had never happened before in Japan. The Japanese police were known to torture people, particularly murder suspects, and many times they would get a confession."

Then he cited the familiar reasons for Hirasawa's innocence—the artist's inexperience with poison which was inconsistent with the survivors' recollections of such precise procedures and sophisticated technique, characteristic of an experienced poisoner, an expert. I asked if he thought there had been a conspiracy in the arrest and conviction of Hirasawa.

"No, I don't believe there was a conspiracy against him. I think the police needed an arrest. They had their prestige at stake. But I don't think the police planned a conspiracy either. I think they really believed Hirasawa was guilty."

The evidence supporting that belief was, of course, the artist's unexplained cash reserves and his refusal to divulge their source. As Nagoya talked, it became more and more evident to me that cultural forces had influenced the disposition of facts. Perceptions and beliefs are functions of the environment. If the MPB officers *wanted* Hirasawa to be guilty, as Nagoya contended, then they could believe he was guilty, even with evidence contradicting that belief, even with six witnesses saying he was not the killer.

Nagoya maintained that Hirasawa has not been executed because the authorities, despite what they say, are not sure of his guilt. The fact that he's still alive, he said, supports that assertion. I understood that to mean the Justice Ministry normally doesn't tarry in executing death row convicts. Nagoya added that, having followed the case for twenty years, he has concluded that the Japanese public does not want Hirasawa to be executed. From the succession of Justice Ministers to the people in the streets, either tacitly or vocally, Hirasawa's guilt is still in question. This collective doubt, however, has not been sufficient to win him a retrial during three decades.

"There is in Japan a very agreeable relationship between the people and the government, much more than in the U.S.," Nagoya explained. "The Japanese do not interfere with government action because there are vestiges of feudalism in Japan that still play a strong role in Japanese regard of authority.

"The authorities won't release Hirasawa because their prestige is at stake, and people are too busy with their own lives and their jobs to take up Hirasawa's side. Most Japanese think that if a man is convicted, then that's all that matters. It doesn't matter to them if he's guilty or innocent."

As we continued talking, he confirmed several more of my impressions about Japanese society. I was beginning to realize that the cultural context of the crime played a larger role than I'd originally suspected.

A few days after my meeting with Nagoya, the Society opened

a three-day exhibition of Hirasawa's paintings. Takehiko rented space in a narrow concrete building almost ten stories tall and with a steep, narrow staircase and no elevàtor. When I entered the exhibition, people stood in a wedge of a room thick with cigarette smoke. Fluorescent fixtures glared overhead and a space heater provided ample warmth. Men and women were whispering their comments as they looked at the works that covered the walls and at the few paintings propped up on the floor. I was interested in seeing what Hirasawa revealed about himself in his art.

While in prison Hirasawa has been prolific, painting more than thirteen hundred watercolors, all of which have been entrusted to the Society. He had quit painting regularly in the late 1970s, and a year passed in which he produced no new pictures at all. He then started to paint again, but sporadically, and now completes maybe four pictures a year. The forty or so pieces displayed here were selected from significant periods of the artist's last thirty years.

Bleak winter scenes dominated the pictures painted during the mid-1950s when Hirasawa's death sentence was upheld by the Supreme Court. One ominous nightscape painted in heavy gray and black tones stood out with its dead moon floating over a country house. There were a pair of paintings which looked to me like metaphorical self-portraits: One entitled "Flower in Hell" was a child-like painting of a flower engulfed by flames; another was a scene of Mt. Fuji covered in snow and majestically stolid amid a raging tempest.

Bright and colorful outdoor scenes of fields and clouds, all done from memory years after the artist had seen anything outside the prison walls, marked the pieces from the early 1970s. Presumably Hirasawa had resigned himself to his fate then and, despite his impending execution, had found the impulse to celebrate life and nature again. These more celebrant works, however, were not rendered as skillfully as the darker, earlier paintings.

Other pictures also caught my eye. There was a large tempera painting of a sunset over cherry blossoms that was strikingly expressive in its mood and suffusion of colors. And finally, a literal self-portrait of the white-bearded painter in kimonos and a cap. Next to the self-portrait were photographs of Hirasawa. My eyes switched from the portrait to the pictures, and I thought about what Masako Murata, the woman who crawled out of the bank for help, had written to me:

> Hirasawa is not the killer. The killer had a round face. Very round like an egg. I saw Hirasawa in the interrogation room and the first thing I noticed was how square his face was. He is not the man. I told the police he is not the man.

In every photograph I saw that solid square jaw. In the portrait, there were the same sharp corners around the mouth, the same square face.

The size of the crowd had swollen, the space in the room seemed to have diminished, I found myself feeling claustrophobic. How many times had Hirasawa had this same feeling over three decades in his cell, I asked myself.

My interpreter and I left the exhibition and crossed the street to a restaurant where the Society planned a formal dinner. I had been invited to attend. A strong smell of ginger hung in the air and austere Japanese melodies played as a slippered hostess led us to a large room where several Society members were already waiting for us. We removed our shoes and walked softly into the room, onto the tatami mats made from barley reeds.

The setting was traditional Japanese, from the silk cushions that designated where we should sit to the paper lanterns in the corners. The tables were arranged in a large U, and a Society member directed me to the head of the table, dead center. "Guest of honor," my interpreter said.

Soon more people arrived and every cushion was occupied, except for Takehiko's. Waitresses delivered lacquer bowls all around, then disappeared. A moment later they returned, setting a warm ceramic bottle of sake in front of everyone, then cups, and more bowls, and finally the food arrived, in separate dishes, one by one. Sushi, tempura, rice. No one touched anything.

A quarter of an hour passed, and no one moved. Some people talked quietly among themselves, but most remained silent. They sat still, as if sculpted, looking forward, waiting. I didn't expect that we would start eating without Takehiko, but I thought there would be drinking and talking and laughing until he arrived. Wrong.

Another ten minutes passed, and the decorum had grown unbearable. I was starved, but if anyone felt as I did, no one betrayed any sign.

Finally Takehiko appeared, and a ripple of relief ran through the room. I *knew* they were hungry!

As we ate I asked why each of them had joined the Society. The misfortune that strikes one person, they believed, could easily strike another, and so, as one member told me, "I regard someone else's troubles, like Mr. Hirasawa's, as my own."

One moment rushes into the next and the next and so on and every moment is marked by something done. Blank spaces mean wasted time and time moves so fast. Why were these people sitting so quietly? Why didn't they at least start a little of the festivities, such as some pre-dinner small talk?

Because in Japan you don't start anything until the party is complete. Because in Japan waiting is not wasting time, but using time. Because in the west they think time is linear and that it leaves you behind. Because over here they think time is circular and that you're never released from it. The Emperor reigns in twelve-year cycles; the President serves in terms; the dinner guest waits interminably, and so, it seems, does the convict.

Jim Abrams, the author of the original article I'd read in the *Columbus Dispatch* seven years earlier, was still in Tokyo and now working for the Associated Press. I called him and he agreed to meet me for lunch at the Foreign Correspondents Club of Japan. I was interested to hear what more he might have learned about the Tei-koku affair.

The FCCJ sits on the top floor of the Yurakucho Denki Building, which stands a few blocks east of the algae-covered moat around the Imperial Palace, and a few blocks north of the Ginza, one of the largest shopping districts in the world. At twenty stories Yurakucho Denki is one of the tallest structures in Tokyo, a city often shaken by earthquakes. From the Club one gets spectacular views of the city because of the floor-to-ceiling glass that wraps the building.

Abrams was fortyish, a light middleweight wearing a blue sport coat. His hair was gray, and his deep-set blue eyes, behind plastic-frame glasses, gave him a gentle look.

He'd come to Japan in the 1960s as an exchange student from Indiana University and was struck by how the Japanese still abided by regimented social order. He'd known something about Japanese culture before arriving, but was still jolted when Japanese students lined up and shouted out "Good morning!" to the professors at the start of every class.

The insularity of Japanese society intimidated Abrams back then, and, according to him, still does to a lesser degree. Many foreign correspondents complain how Japanese sources always give information and stories to the Japanese press first. Abrams told me that the foreign correspondents, often kept at bay by primary sources, get stories mostly by reading them in the domestic papers first, then following up on them. The home town of course loves the home team, but that arrangement wasn't without disadvantages for the very people it was designed to favor, even in Tokyo.

Abrams explained that because many Japanese reporters know they have the scoop and are essentially being fed the news, there is little incentive for them to check facts or to probe beyond what's told to them. The result is often a story weak on corroborating evidence. Abrams didn't say that the domestic press is a mouthpiece for the authorities, but the implication, as I saw it, was clear: Anyone controlling the release of information could easily exploit the

Japanese media by releasing only the information he wanted known, confident that the domestic reporters would not pursue him or pressure him for additional revelations.

Because of this peculiarly insular and restrictive arrangement, the Japanese reporters tend, according to Abrams, to become somewhat zealous when given free rein in covering any sensational story. Abrams maintained that the papers have a way of convicting a suspect in the public eye long before the suspect is even tried. He described the case of a Japan Air Lines pilot who ditched his jet in Tokyo Bay some years ago. The plane had been full of passengers. The Japanese papers crucified the pilot long before the investigation of the accident concluded. Editors showed little compunction about printing damaging stories about the pilot that were based only on rumor and gossip. One of the first insults the papers flung was dropping the deferential term *san* after the man's name, an act of severe denigration. Abrams said that the pilot was nearly insane from the damning publicity, and that the stories continued to appear until a civil liberties group protested on his behalf.

Had Hirasawa been a victim of this same sort of reporting? Had the insular relationship between the Japanese newsmen and their official sources hurt the artist?

Abrams maintained that saving face remains as powerful a social force in Japan today as it was during the reign of feudalism, and that it accounts for much frustration not only for foreign correspondents but for the local reporters as well on occasion. Politicians and policemen are particularly difficult to get statements from because of the constant public scrutiny that follows them. It is not uncommon, he said, for officials to publicly defend a mistaken position simply because that was their initial position, taken before the public eye, and so, while they may privately concede the tenuousness or inaccuracy of their position, they will never admit their error publicly. To do so could irreparably damage their prestige. There is a powerful sense of fatalism that still holds parts of Japanese society hostage.

Had Igii's statement that he was "100 percent sure of Hirasawa's guilt" established the MPB's public position, in effect sealing Hirasawa's conviction from the day his remark hit the front pages across Japan?

I asked about the relationship between the Justice Ministry and the press in general. Abrams explained that of all the Japanese governmental offices, the Justice Ministry is one of the last feudal strongholds. The Ministry is intensely secretive, and its officials like to do things their way. When I asked him what he meant by that, he handed me a copy of one of his articles, which was carried by the AP wire on the morning of August 20, 1982:

> Tokyo—Morning is said to be a disquieting time on Death Row in Japan...
>
> Unlike in the United States, where public controversy and frantic legal maneuvering surrounds [*sic*] each execution, Japan prefers to carry out its death sentences behind closed doors. The public is never informed of executions, and even some inmates don't know about their date with the hangman until the guard stops at their cell.
>
> (Jirō Ishiki, a well-known writer, said that the] secrecy surrounding executions is...one reason there is almost no public debate in Japan on the morality or effectiveness of the death penalty...
>
> The Justice Ministry denies that it tries to enforce the law in secret...
>
> Akira Kyohara, of the (Justice Ministry's) correction bureau, said authorities decide on a case-by-case basis, according to the prisoner's "mental state," whether to tell him or her when the trap door will fall. The situation is similar for family members, who may be allowed last visits but at times learn of the execution only when told to come and collect the remains.
>
> ...Details of executions are not publicly disclosed, but (Ministry authorities consider) a recent account pieced together by the Asahi Shimbun, a leading daily, (to be) generally accurate.
>
> ...The prisoner is led into the gallows room, where

a Buddhist priest says a few words of parting and offers prayers. In the corner, a candle and incense are burning. If the prisoner so requests, he is given candy or a last cigarette.

He is then handcuffed from behind, and blindfolded with a white cloth. A curtain opens. A white rope noose is placed around his neck. His feet are tied and at a signal from the prison official the floor beneath him is opened, sending him hurtling into an underground chamber. . .

I asked Abrams if he had ever gotten a statement from the Justice Ministry on the Hirasawa case explaining why the Justice Minister had not ordered the artist's execution within six months after the verdict, as required by Japanese law. He answered that the Ministry is normally difficult to get any answer from, but they were uncommonly silent about Hirasawa. (The entire month I was in Tokyo I tried to get a statement from the Ministry but was never granted an interview.) Abrams recalled that the Ministry claimed that Hirasawa had not yet been executed because the Society kept filing appeals on his behalf. Justice Ministers have told the press they don't want to execute someone whose appeal is on file.

That didn't make sense, however, because for the seven years between Hirasawa's final verdict in 1955 and the Society's creation in 1962 no appeal of any kind was filed on Hirasawa's case. Privately, Abrams told me, the word around the Ministry was that they won't execute the artist because they're unwilling to gamble with the uncertainties in the case. If Hirasawa were ever found innocent after the execution, that would result in a devastating and permanent loss of face for the Justice Ministry and for Japan's legal system itself. This was now even more of a possibility, Abrams explained, because of a few recent cases of death row inmates who had been freed after appeals courts ruled that the police had obtained "questionable" confessions.

Abrams then cited a rather astounding statistic. During its history the Japanese Procurator's Office, according to Justice Ministry records, has averaged between a ninety-eight and ninety-nine percent conviction rate on all cases brought to trial. He said the prosecutors have such a high record because they rarely bring a case to trial that they're not positive they'll win. In almost three out of four cases the suspect brought to trial has confessed to the crime for which he has been charged.

Shōko no o, or roughly translated, "king of evidence," is the term Japanese judges, prosecutors, and policemen have used to describe the confession. It has been the premium of any investigation, and has been wielded as the most damning piece of evidence, even though it has not been reliable in many instances. In Japan, when the poor are falsely accused they often confess because they have no money to pay for the ensuing legal battle. Also, entering a guilty plea frequently results in a lighter sentence.

There is, however, a powerfully unique character of the Japanese confession. *Okami,* the ancient and high Japanese regard for authority, determines how Japanese people perceive the law and how they should react to it. Professor Uematsu Tadashi described this unique perception in a round-table discussion entitled *What is Confession? Trials and the Credibility of Confessions,* the transcript of which was published in the March 1954 issue of *Sekai* magazine.

> Compared with other people Japanese characteristically make confessions easily. Seldom are Japanese suspects able to maintain their own contentions to the last. Not completely free of their feudal consciousness, they cannot maintain their own point of view in the presence of superiors.

Similarly, in his book *Conspiracy at Matsukawa,* Chalmers Johnson provides a thoughtful and exhaustive analysis of the Japanese confession from an American perspective. One of two traditional theories on confession in Japan is that the feudal character predisposes the Japanese citizen to give authorities the answers they want. The other stems from the Justice Ministry's formal role as the judicial representative of the Emperor. This second theory holds that the institutional and highly bureaucratic structure of the Justice Ministry, backed by the belief in Imperial superiority and infallibility accounts for zealous prosecutors—also deemed agents of the Emperor—worrying about losing face if they should lose a case. Johnson points out that, since authority figures can never be perceived as acting wrongly, the prosecutor can't be seen backing down once major steps are taken. Accordingly, many prosecutors pressure arrested suspects to confess.

Johnson observes that neither theory can effectively be advanced over the other. The fact is, in Japan, the two theories are interdependent. Values (the first) and praxis (the second) form an organic and, in this instance, unjust whole.

Other Japanese factors contributing to confession are, in Johnson's parlance, the "detention reaction," and the unfamiliarity of a new and dishonorable context. The Japanese are sharply aware that arrest or detention is serious business. Suspects often succumb to a sense of consuming despair and loss, and confess from having sunk into despondency. Japanese heritage is built upon loyalty to the group, and the Japanese define themselves in relation to their position in a society premised upon mutual dependence and cooperation. So when someone finds himself in an unfamiliar context, such as in the interrogation room, his reflex sense of compliance leads him to allow his interrogators to define his new status for him. To do otherwise requires him to draw on his own choices and perceptions, which he has been taught not to do.

Otoya Miyagi, another participant in the *What is Confession?* round-table discussion, said Japanese people, when taken into custody, will confess for various reasons, ranging from wishing to avoid a scene to yielding to a sense of inferiority. But no matter what the reason, it's always linked to the old Japanese regard of authority as unimpeachable.

The confession didn't achieve its status in Japan as the result of some conscious conspiracy against the accused. The judicial system had been remodelled in 1889 on the European, or Continental, system, in which the accused bore a good part of the burden of proof, and wherein pretrial investigation and testimony determined the bulk of the ultimate trial. A defendant had virtually no hope of declaring certain evidence inadmissible because his rights didn't include such an ability to object. Juries were not used by the court. Sole discretionary power lay with the judge, and prior to Occupation reforms the procurator had the power to detain a suspect for as long as he desired. The result was often sustained detention on a lesser charge (such as fraud) while police investigated a far more serious charge (such as murder and robbery). Because detention could go on indefinitely, and because third degree interrogation and torture by the police were common in prewar and wartime Japan, and because of the way Japanese people are conditioned to cooperate, confessions were easy to get. And the more confessions the police got, the less they were inclined to investigate. Why bother, they figured, if somebody was eventually going to say he did it?

Still, there wasn't any hard rule. The Japanese also confess because they are guilty. Hirasawa showed all the signs of having given a courtesy confession: He accounted for why he did it, but never for how. Yet he'd also had a lot of money in his possession, which he couldn't explain.

The cultural context of the Teikoku affair was becoming more clear. I was beginning to better understand the relationship of the Japanese press to official sources and the significance of Hirasawa's confession in the broader reality of Occupied Japan. I wanted more information on these points and preferably from a native, rather than an American. I chose to talk to a former *Yomiuri Shimbun* reporter, one of the few living principals of the Teikoku affair.

Riichi Takeuchi was the first journalist to act on the suspicion

113

that what had happened inside the Teikoku Bank was not food poisoning but murder. During the Occupation Takeuchi was well-known throughout Japan and well-respected by his colleagues as one of the best senior reporters on the homicide beat. After covering the Teikoku mass murder-robbery for the *Yomiuri,* he had married one of the four survivors of the crime.

In the thirty-seven years that have passed since the Teigin incident, the press has only recently begun to leave Mrs. Takeuchi, the former Masako Murata, alone. She has given interview after interview until exhausted. The interviews have made it more difficult, rather than easier, for her to talk about her brush with near death. She still agrees to discuss it, but no longer in person. The distance offered by letters allowed her to write me a thorough account of her memories of January 26, 1948. She apologized for not being able to talk with me when I got to Tokyo, but her husband agreed to a personal interview.

Takeuchi met me and my interpreter at the *Yomiuri* building where, although Takeuchi retired years ago, he remains a popular and respected figure. He was sharply dressed in a conservative but stylish suit with an elegant silk tie. He had gray hair, looked to be in his late fifties, and had a surprisingly youthful smile.

After introductions and an exchange of namecards, we went to the fifth floor where we sat in a room barely large enough to hold the small table and five chairs.

Takeuchi's enthusiasm and charm surprised me. I figured that he, like his wife, had been over this terrain so many times that it was now tiresome to discuss it. But he carried on in such an energetic, bright manner that I could have been convinced he was speaking about the Teikoku Bank case for the first time. His sense of humor about the confused and botched investigation was balanced by a deep sensitivity towards his wife's terrifying experience.

His sources in the MPB confirmed for him that the police were at a loss in the beginning of the investigation because the *modus operandi* of the crime was so unusual. The first conclusions the MPB drew were that the culprit was an expert killer, but an amateur

114

thief. He'd left stacks of bills in plain view and had taken a comparatively small sum.

Takeuchi then confirmed that, when the Matsui namecard turned up, the police questioned Dr. Matsui and discovered that he'd been in Java during the war, that he'd killed people by injection, and that he was afraid of war crimes prosecution. Takeuchi neither interviewed Matsui nor saw any police reports on the Matsui interrogation; his information came again from his sources inside the homicide division. I asked Takeuchi if he had known the MPB was secretly investigating 731 personnel. He said yes, that he'd even seen some written police reports, but those reports had not been, nor probably ever would be, available to the public.

Takeuchi was still struck by how Hirasawa's wife and daughter laughed loudly when he told them the artist had been arrested for the crime. He felt that if there were even a remote possibility that Hirasawa was guilty, his family would have been at least concerned, if not distraught. He was also convinced of the criminal's expertise, especially when the survivors told him that the killer had timed everything to the second by constantly referring to his watch while distributing the poison.

After Hirasawa confessed, the more Takeuchi reflected on the whole case, the more odd it seemed to him. From covering the investigation he knew the police had pursued every lead in good faith, but with the pursuit of Hirasawa, he contended they had undergone a sort of personality change. They'd gone from observing proper procedures to doing a sloppy job. Takeuchi remembered how eager the police were to solve the Teikoku crime because of the enormous challenge it posed both to their abilities and to their integrity.

Takeuchi had been the first journalist to maintain publicly that Hirasawa was falsely charged. During his time covering homicide he'd developed a very good relationship with then Chief of Detectives, Jirō Fujita. So good, in fact, that Fujita's right-hand man coordinated Takeuchi's wedding. Normally, Takeuchi felt, the MPB did good police work, but with the Teikoku affair something had gone wrong, something that he couldn't precisely identify.

I asked him if he knew for certain that Hirasawa's attempts to explain his sudden possession of large sums of money soon after the murders had proved untrue. Takeuchi nodded and informed me that his own research had disclosed that Hirasawa suffered "psychological problems." I'd known that Hirasawa's mental state had always been a source of debate, but I'd never heard reference to any specific disorder. Takeuchi's own investigation had discovered that Hirasawa had once been bitten by a rabid dog and had received improper medical treatment for the bite. A poorly administered serum or the disease of rabies itself had impaired his mind. Takeuchi explained that no one could determine whether the artist's self-incriminating actions were prompted by illness, eccentricity, or guilt.

About Hirasawa's money Takeuchi had his own theory. Because of dire financial straits, Hirasawa had anonymously painted and sold pornographic pictures for quick cash, a common practice for starving artists during the postwar period. For Hirasawa, proving this claim would have meant producing the graphic pictures in court, in public, thus permanently destroying his reputation as an artist. Takeuchi said it made perfect sense for Hirasawa to choose a death sentence over such personal and professional dishonor.

I asked if Takeuchi knew about Hideo Naruchi's encounter with Dr. Matsui, and he began explaining at length that Naruchi was never part of the murder investigation, but was involved only in the robbery side of the investigation. Rumors had floated that Naruchi was pressured to leave the 731 Regiment investigation alone but they weren't true. Equally false, Takeuchi emphasized, were rumors that *Yomiuri* people had been ordered to back off from the investigation.

I almost pulled out my document that said *Yomiuri* people *had* been ordered to stay away, but I decided against it. Instead I let him continue without contradiction to see what more he would say. I said only one word.

"*Hanto?*" (Really?)

The censoring, he said, had just been gossip.

When I asked if he thought the truth about the crime would ever be known, he replied sadly, with an echo of fatalism, "I don't think so, but at this point it really doesn't matter, does it?"

We concluded and said goodbye. During the elevator ride down I stared at the floor and wondered why Takeuchi had left me with several contradictions. If there had been censorship of the press in 1948, wouldn't a *Yomiuri* journalist be the first to know about it, and squawk about it? Was Takeuchi unreliable, or was my GHQ document? And what about Naruchi? What exactly did he do in this investigation? What was his level of credibility? I walked out willing to pay any price to get just *two* people to tell me the same version of the Teikoku story.

Mr. Masami Tomizawa had been with the *Yomiuri Shimbun* for sixteen years, first as a reporter and now as a senior editor. He was going to arrange an appointment for me with Yoshiko Akuzawa, the clerk who had given slippers to the killer. Today was the time set for the interview.

My interpreter and I met Tomizawa in the same room where I had spoken with Riichi Takeuchi a couple of days earlier. Tomizawa began by apologizing for not having reached me before my arrival. Miss Akuzawa, he said, could not be found. She had moved and had left no forwarding address. Years of publicity, Tomizawa surmised, had driven her into seclusion. Again he apologized and suggested we go for tea. Perhaps I would settle for talking with him, he said.

In the parking garage, he spoke to a dispatcher who called a car for us. Tomizawa said that in Japan working for a newspaper basically got you two things—a nice phone and a nice car. A black sedan pulled up, and a uniformed driver with white gloves stepped out to open the doors for us. We climbed in, and the sedan sped away toward the Palace Hotel, a modern mid-rise near the Imperial grounds. The driver aggressively cut through the traffic, and ten minutes later deposited us at the hotel door. On the tenth floor was the tea room, lushly carpeted in shades of blue. We sat at one of the marble tables near the spectacular windows that looked out over the commercial district of Tokyo on one side and the Imperial Palace moat and forest on the other.

Tomizawa ordered tea, which was served to us in fine bone china with a sterling cream and sugar set. The Japanese know how to apologize, I thought. Tomizawa then eased himself back in his chair and asked if I'd become sufficiently confused with the Teikoku case yet.

I told him that I'd been confused sufficiently before I came to Tokyo, and was beginning to understand why so few Japanese journalists had ever dug into the case. He smiled.

I was still trying to figure out why Takeuchi had said there had never been any censorship of the press in the Teikoku affair. Tomizawa knew Takeuchi as a *Yomiuri* colleague, so I asked him about it, and Tomizawa responded indirectly at first.

In Japan, he said, news is disseminated through official announcements which are very similar to other press releases except that in Japan these official announcements tend to be more formal, more wordy, and more vague. According to Tomizawa, the reporter goes to his inside sources to get the specifics. The inside source, however, requires greater effort, time, and patience to develop in Japan than it would in America. Tomizawa added that this applied not only to Japanese journalists, but to businessmen as well. Foreigners who expect to develop a network of local contacts in Tokyo within a month or two often are frustrated when these contacts do not develop. The private source grows out of what Japanese journalists call "the personal relationship," a connection that may take a year or more of shared dinners and drinks to cultivate. Its fundamental principles are fealty and, of course, honor.

Tomizawa then answered my question about censorship more directly. It was possible, he explained, that Takeuchi would not divulge to me the fullness of what he knew because he was honoring a commitment to a personal relationship. He also said it was possible that Takeuchi may have only heard by rumor that GHQ had imposed censorship, and Takeuchi, with a strong reputation for integrity, would never speak about something for which his only support was a rumor.

The personal relationship with its insular formality epitomizes Japanese custom. And as custom serves to define and reinforce the character of a culture, it can also serve as a barrier to those who are not born into it. One hundred years after Commodore Perry sailed into Tokyo Bay, Japan is still repelling the intruder.

The personal relationship is a Japanese tradition, but it's now being questioned by a new generation of journalists. Tomizawa said younger reporters who are complaining of the old ways are trying to establish less restrictive relationships with their sources. For a long time the escape from the bind of honor has been the composite story. Tomizawa described how a reporter who gets a hot tip through his relationship but can't write about it will go to several sources to confirm separate parts of the original lead. The reporter writes the story as a composite of various opinions that may not add up to the original lead, but at least he gets to write the story.

"GHQ and the Occupation cast a shadow over everything," Tomizawa continued, alluding to the U.S. Army deal with Ishii and the 731 Regiment. "If I were going to investigate the Teikoku incident, I'd need at least two years just to study the Japanese end of it."

He had seen the documents I had brought and was waiting for the final translations to come through so that the *Yomiuri* could run stories about them.

"The Teikoku incident is one of the most peculiar and unusual crimes that ever happened in Japan," Tomizawa went on. "The question of who is the real criminal has never been solved, and now the documents. They are the only thing new on the case in thirty years."

119

A few minutes later he paid the bill, and we left. On our way back to his office, we drove through the Imperial Palace grounds. We wound through thick greenery and passed rank after rank of uniformed guards. Our chauffeur drove slowly over the hilly ground. Tomizawa told me that the *Yomiuri* had clearance to get closer to the Palace than the public could. I wondered what personal relationship his paper had with the Emperor.

Tomizawa's explanation of the personal relationship echoed Jim Abrams' observations about the Japanese press and its exclusive relationship with official sources. The press itself was a powerful force, occupying a station of high authority in the country. In 1985, circulation of the *Yomiuri* newspapers alone was eighteen million. I wanted to learn more about the specific relationship between the press and the police, and how that relationship affected the Teikoku story.

Kenichi Asano, a crime reporter with Kyodo News Service (Japan's largest wire service) for thirteen years and author of *The Crime of Criminal Reporting,* was an affable man with a very friendly face. As a student he'd opposed the Vietnam War, and had been active in anti-government demonstrations. At thirty-six, Asano had a reputation as an individualist, which in many quarters of Japan is still derided as egotistical.

We met in a restaurant near the southern curve of the Japanese National Railroads (JNR) loop and talked at length about the role of the press in Occupied Japan.

"In Japan," Asano told me, "nobody wants to be an enemy of the mass media because the mass media have such vast power. All the big people in Japan are very friendly with the mass media because

The Teikoku (Imperial) Bank, scene of the bizarre murder and robbery, as it appeared in 1948. Note the dirt roads surrounding the building.

The Teikoku Bank building as it appears today. The original (Shiinamachi) branch of the Teikoku Bank closed shortly after the murder-robbery.

Inside the Teikoku Bank after the crime, with teacups arranged on a tray and stacks of money on top of a desk. The money, left in plain view, totalled approximately 300,000 yen, almost twice the amount taken by the killer.

Behind a counter inside the bank.

Body of a bank employee lying in the washroom. After drinking the "Second Drug," this victim tried to reach the faucet.

Poison victims lying in the bank hallway. Note the teacup on the floor.

Bodies lying in a hall, inside the bank. The poison victims made a desperate rush for water. Note the overturned teacup and the police chalk outlines on the floor.

Bodies of the custodian and his family as found by police.

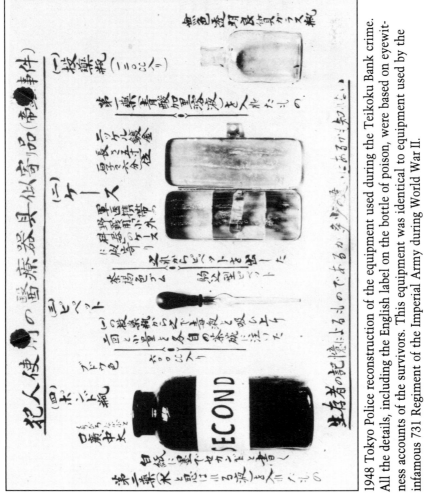

1948 Tokyo Police reconstruction of the equipment used during the Teikoku Bank crime. All the details, including the English label on the bottle of poison, were based on eyewitness accounts of the survivors. This equipment was identical to equipment used by the infamous 731 Regiment of the Imperial Army during World War II.

Bodies of the custodian's family arranged by Tokyo Police at the bank. The child in the foreground was eight years old.

Ten poison victims arranged by Tokyo Police at the Teikoku Bank. Six other bank employees were taken by ambulance to a hospital, four of whom survived.

Composite drawing of the killer prepared by Tokyo Police, based on eyewitness accounts. First composite drawing of a crime suspect ever used in Japan. Hirasawa's hair was cut by Tokyo Police to match this picture.

Sadamichi Hirasawa at his trial in 1949.

Retouched photograph of Hirasawa after years in Miyagi Prison in Sendai, Japan. Now 93 years old, Hirasawa has sat longer on death row than any other convict in history.

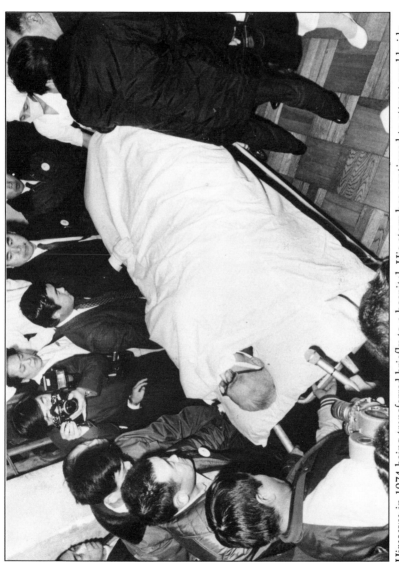

Hirasawa in 1974 being transferred briefly to a hospital. His story has continued to attract worldwide attention.

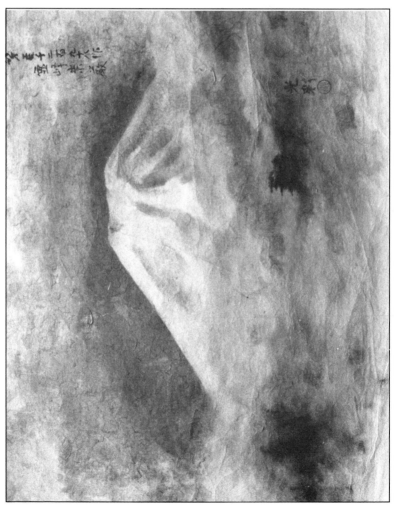

One of the more than 1,300 watercolor paintings completed by Hirasawa during his over 30 years on death row.

they believe you can't get anything if you fight with the press. 'Be patient,' they say when the press gets angry at them, 'this will pass, like a typhoon, and people will forget.'"

Asano maintained, as Abrams had, that journalists write about suspects in a crime as though they've already been convicted and sentenced. He recited a list of incidents in which reporters had dug into a suspect's past and had found damning rumors or gossip, which were usually irrelevant to the investigation, but which made for gaudy headlines. Asano exhibited an exceptional command of names, dates, and places as documentation. In the eyes of a people as acutely sensitive to their image in society as the Japanese are, embarrassing publicity tends to convict a suspect long before the court reaches its verdict. He concluded that the press basically issues a mass media endorsement of the position taken by the police, regardless of the facts in the case.

What Asano said supported my own feelings about how Hirasawa had been treated by the Japanese media after his arrest. Many of the headlines on the Teikoku case were based on unsubstantiated charges.

Asano hadn't studied the Hirasawa case for his book, but he had studied the general issue of Japanese crime reportage during the Occupation.

"The Occupation gave Japan freedom of the press, but the press had no idea what that meant, because during the war all papers were strictly controlled by the authorities. The press was not part of democratization. The three biggest newspapers—the *Asahi, Mainichi,* and *Yomiuri*—are still publishing under the same names they had during the years of military rule. And many of the older reporters and editors from back then are still with them. In Germany the Nazi-controlled papers were totally dismantled by the Allies. But not so in Japan."

He explained that Japan's criminal code allows the media to print a suspect's name prior to indictment under three conditions: if it's in the public interest, if it's newsworthy, and if it's true. The Occupation built these conditions into the code so that the media could have access to police information, which before the war had never been available to anyone but the police and the Imperial Army. The Occupation assumed that the press existed as a public instrument and would serve the public interest first. Asáno believed that over the years the press has served the public for the most part, but in the area of reporting crime, he concluded that the media most often abuse this access, wielding it against the public.

"All this is really a violation of civil liberties," he said, "and the role of the journalist is to monitor civil liberties. In Japan, to see your name and picture in the paper or on TV in connection with anything dishonorable is worse than conviction. Japanese people believe in the police, and the national sentiment knows that it means a lot to be arrested. If the police make an arrest, then the man must be guilty."

I thought once more of Detective Igii's remark to the press. "I am 100 percent certain of Hirasawa's guilt." Hirasawa slashed his wrist with a pen and wrote "I am innocent" in blood on his cell wall. Was he trying to escape shame? Or guilt?

The Occupation had introduced freedom of the press without delineating what responsibility such freedom entails, Asano said. The wholesale transfer of the American First Amendment to Japan was meant to promote certain civil liberties as the press could promote and even defend them. However, there was one fundamental and crucial cultural difference. Implicit in America's adoption of the First Amendment was an inherent distrust of authority, the fear that government can be self-serving and corrupt, that it can exploit people and deny them independence. The Japanese people never shared such a distrust for their Imperial government. Only recently has the abuse of power become a concern at all. The concept of a free press was placed in the lap of a nation holding an inherent distrust not for the government, but rather for anyone who did not conform to either the government's or the society's wishes. Thus, the concept of a free press in Japan was first wielded *against* the individual.

It's not difficult to make a case that the artist's trial was conducted in the papers. A review of headlines from the 1948 editions of the *Nippon Times* follows:

25 August
MASS MURDER SUSPECT CLEARED; POLICE BAFFLED

26 August
MURDER SUSPECT'S ARREST RAISES CIVIL RIGHTS ISSUE

27 August
SUSPECT HELD IN TOKYO ATTEMPTS SUICIDE IN CELL BY SEVERING ARTERY WITH PEN POINT

29 August
SUSPECT REFUSES TO REVEAL SOURCE OF MONEY

3 September
4 FRAUD VICTIMS IDENTIFY ARTIST

5 September
HIRASAWA HELD ON FRAUD CHARGES; AUTHORITIES STILL PINNING HIGH HOPES ON LINKING ARTIST WITH CASE

7 September
TOKYO SUSPECT'S INDICTMENT (FOR FRAUD) CONSTITUTES VITAL TEST CASE

10 September
PAST ACTIVITIES OF ARTIST BARED

12 September
NEW EVIDENCE IS FOUND IN HIRASAWA CASE/POLICE UNEARTH MORE FUNDS OWNED BY TEIKOKU SUSPECT

14 September
POISON SEEN USED IN MIXING COLORS—PRESENCE OF CYANIDE IN TEMPERA MAY PIN ARTIST

15 September
HIRASAWA FACES ABORTION CHARGE

26 September
POLICE CLARIFY HIRASAWA CASE; DECLARE TEIKOKU SUSPECT IS ON THE POINT OF MAKING A VITAL CONFESSION

28 September
MURDERER OF 12 CONFESSES. . .

All of these headlines caused Hirasawa public disgrace, all were supplied by official MPB (police) sources, and all were reported and printed *prior* to his indictment. In an ironic reversal, on September 30 the press printed an article citing specific civil liberties violations in the treatment of Hirasawa. The violations had been documented in a Civil Liberties Bureau report which was translated from the original Japanese into English and delivered to SCAP's Legal Section. The report reads:

CIVIL LIBERTIES COMMITTEE URGES JUDICIAL AUTHORITIES TO RECONSIDER

(Tokyo Minpo-30 Sept 48)

The following points are called to the attention of judicial authorities:
1. Hirazawa [sic] *should be released because he had not been indicted as the Teikoku bank criminal within 10 days after detention.* (Art. 8, Item 5 of Provisional Code of Criminal Procedure.)
2. Hirasawa had been forced to pose as the offender for the purpose of taking pictures. (Violation of Art.

35 of the Constitution, Art. 144 of the code of Criminal
Procedure and Art. 7 of the Provisional Code of Criminal Procedure.)
    3. Compelling the suspect to make unfavorable
statements. (Violation of Art. 38 of the Constitution,
Art. 10 of the Provisional Code of Criminal Procedure.)
    *Procurator Takaki [sic, Takagi] and 2 or 3 assistants
have questioned Hirazawa for 12 or 13 hours a day. Con-
sequently, he is virtually half-insane and there is apprehension that he may confess to imaginative crimes.*
    4. A warrant of detention was not issued within the
specified period after arrest. (Art. 8, Provisional Code.)
    5. *Defamation of the suspect himself, his family and
relatives.* (Art. 144 of the Code of Criminal Procedure
and Art. 230 of the Criminal Code.)
    6. Restrictions in the right of defense: A guard had
been placed while Hirazawa was being interviewed by
Mr. Yamada, his defense counsel. (emphasis added)

The Civil Liberties Bureau issued the report as a public statement urging the judicial authorities to reconsider what they were
doing to Hirasawa because of the "many mistakes committed" in
the investigation and interrogation. Characteristically, the Justice
Ministry never even responded to the Bureau's report, and the Legal
Section of SCAP simply filed it away among their internal copies
of Japanese press translations. Two months later Hirasawa went to
trial. No response, redress, or further review of the Civil liberties
violations ever occurred.

Kazuhiko Nagoya, the *Yomiuri* columnist, had said that the
Japanese were too busy with their own lives to take up Hirasawa's
cause. It seemed that he was right about the present-day Japanese
public, but it didn't fully explain the attitude of the public in 1948.

The history of democracy, due process, and civil rights in Japan
is a short one. For centuries all Japanese were raised to believe that
life's ultimate glory was to die for the Emperor, and the militarists
exploited that belief during the war. As Japan began losing the war,

the leaders at home blamed the public, saying that their weak devotion to the Emperor was undermining the spiritual resolve of the Imperial Army. The Japanese people had been trained to accept the slow, systematic destruction of Japan—the fire bombings and strafings, the wholesale slaughter of men, women, and children that culminated in the atomic incineration of two cities—as their own fault. It's hard to imagine anyone climbing out of that rubble to protest the civil liberties violations of any one man.

In the fall of 1978 Tetsuro Morikawa of the Society to Save Hirasawa wrote to Makoto Endo, an attorney, to see if he would take up the Society's concerns in court. Endo was familiar with the Hirasawa case because of the publicity it had generated over the years. Endo, however, was not sympathetic. From the little he knew he felt that Hirasawa was guilty. All the publicity about the crime, the conviction, and the stays of execution had done nothing to change his opinion. If anything, it had only strengthened his belief in the artist's guilt.

Morikawa attached some of his writings about the Teikoku Bank crime to his letter. Endo read all of them, and though they did not change his mind, they did pique his curiosity. He did some research on his own, and to his surprise came to believe in Hirasawa's innocence.

Endo, a harried man, agreed to inform me about the role he and some of the legal procedures have played in the Teikoku affair. His office was near Shimbashi on the south end of the city. Takehiko Hirasawa met my interpreter and me by the black locomotive which stands on the edge of Shimbashi Square. We hurried through the streets until we found Endo's building.

A mimeograph machine cranked loudly as we entered Endo's

office, and I could hear a man's deep voice booming from somewhere inside the partitioned room. We walked around a wall of bookshelves, and there stood a middle-aged man wearing a white headband, baggy pants, and a rumpled white shirt with its tail out as he regaled the air.

Books lined every wall from floor to ceiling, and a steel desk lay buried under stacks and avalanches of papers and files. Endo shouted something to us, and bowed. We bowed also.

He yanked off his headband and threw it aside, then heavily motioned us toward a sofa near his desk. He hauled a chair up, reached into his pocket, withdrew his namecard, pushed it at me, then flung himself back in his chair, holding his head in his hands. He barked out something which I assumed was the Japanese equivalent of "Shoot."

I wanted to know why there had been no retrial for Hirasawa.

Hearing my question, Endo lunged forward. Hirasawa's case was the first he had known to last so long without an execution. The main problem with the Hirasawa case, he said, from a legal viewpoint, was the remote possibility of a retrial. Historically the chances for a retrial in Japan have been so hopelessly small that the appeal option has been commonly referred to as "The Closed Door." From 1949 to 1970 Japan's Supreme Court reversed only approximately one percent of lower court verdicts. Recently, though, Endo pointed out, a few cases have gained retrials because evidence was adduced to show that the courts had convicted the wrong person. The press has publicized these cases, which in turn has influenced public opinion. As a result, there has been a very slow but discernible loosening of the grip that *okami* (high regard for authority) has on the country. "The Justice Ministry," Endo said, "is very, very stubborn, but things are changing with the people. And the Ministry can no longer ignore it."

Endo closed his eyes, and his head bobbed from side to side as he raced through his answer. When he finished talking he leaned so far back in his chair that I thought he would slide down and slip off the front.

Everything in Hirasawa's case, Endo continued, hinged on new evidence. "I am confident that the GHQ documents you have brought will qualify as such," he told me. It was an auspicious time for them to arrive, he said, because he was preparing for an unprecedented move in the history of Japanese law, and the more support he had, the better were his chances of succeeding. Endo explained that he planned to invoke an obscure Japanese law which prescribed a thirty-year statute of limitations on a death sentence. This law required that if after thirty years a condemned prisoner has not been executed, he is to be released. The wording of the law, however, was vague, and Endo said he anticipated trouble from the Justice Ministry over their interpretation. If the law applied according to Endo's interpretation, Hirasawa would either have to be released by May 7, 1985—the thirtieth anniversary of his death sentence—or he would have to be executed.

Endo didn't believe that the Ministry would execute Hirasawa. The attorney's concern lay in how the Ministry would manage to circumvent the law without taking any new action and keep Hirasawa in prison. Suddenly, Endo fell quiet, introspective. I knew he had to return to business, and I had another appointment. I left him with Takehiko, the two of them sitting in silence. The mimeograph had stopped churning some time ago, but none of us had noticed.

Back in my room, I read Masako Murata Takeuchi's letter once again, the one about the events of January 26, 1948.

She was still going through that day's thirty deposit documents when the killer arrived at the bank. She didn't see what time it was when he entered, but business had closed at 3:00 P.M. as usual, and she had immediately begun counting. She was certain, she said, that the thirty documents would have taken her no more than ten minutes, which put the murderer's arrival somewhere between 3:00 and 3:10 that afternoon. The prosecution had claimed Hirasawa had entered the bank at 3:15 after walking directly there from Ikebukuro station.

When the killer distributed the poison, she wrote, she looked at him and thought that he looked to be in his mid-forties. Later, when she saw Hirasawa, she thought he was much too old. Also, she remembered, his face was too square. She said that she told this to the police, but somehow her statement was passed over and ignored.

Another survivor, Mr. Tokukazu Tanaka—the teller who had sat at his desk in the rear of the Teikoku Bank that Monday morning and who had been summoned forward to join the group of employees standing with Dr. Yamaguchi—had drunk both the first and second drug.

Tomizawa from the *Yomiuri* had tried several times to reach Tanaka for me. The first call was answered by Tanaka's wife, who said that her husband had already talked too much about the crime, and that she wished the press would leave him alone. When Tomizawa asked her to please tell her husband that he had called, she said no. A day later Tomizawa called again, and again Mrs. Tanaka answered. She barely stayed on the line long enough to say no before hanging up. Determined to hear the answer from Tanaka himself, Tomizawa tried yet again, and this time Tanaka answered the phone. The *Yomiuri* journalist said that he was calling on behalf of an American journalist who wanted to talk to him about the Teikoku crime. Tanaka agreed to meet me for an interview.

Tomizawa and his driver picked up my interpreter and me around seven o'clock. It was a January night that had turned strangely warm, like a spring evening, with the air damp and heavy from rainfall. As we drove toward the Shinjuku district where Tanaka lived, I thought of the other two survivors—Yoshiko Akuzawa, who could not be found, and Takejio Yoshida, the assistant manager, who had recently celebrated his eightieth birthday and whose memory was too feeble to recall the events of more than thirty years ago.

It was unlikely that either of them would offer much of significance, even if I could see them, since neither had spoken publicly about the Teikoku incident in years.

We were no longer on the big avenues. The car swung through narrower streets, deep into the twists and bends of residential Shinjuku. The houses looked older, a striking contrast to the modern facades of downtown Tokyo. We squeezed past poles and pedestrians as the car jerked through turns that did not look wide enough for a bicycle to pass through. I was getting worried, but the driver looked impassive. Bored, almost.

We were lost. We stopped at a grocer's outdoor market, and Tomizawa asked the owner where Tanaka-san lived.

"Who?"

"Tanaka-san."

"Never heard of him."

"The Teigin *jiken* survivor."

"Ah, *Tanaka-san!* Just that way. You can walk it easily."

He pointed behind us to a one-way street that we had just driven through. We got out of the car and began walking. Along the way I asked my interpreter how common it was in Japan for people in a neighborhood to know where everyone in that neighborhood lives. Very common, she said, because people in Japan do not often move from their original community. Mobility here is very limited.

The housing area resembled a concrete compound, with not a centimeter of wasted space. Everything, including the trees and bushes, looked sculpted. Tomizawa checked the address he had, then pushed open the big steel gate and led us to the front door.

When Tomizawa knocked, I wondered if Tanaka's wife would come out and tell us to go away, and thought I wouldn't blame her if she did. The publicity had been overwhelming and disruptive, but I did hope Tanaka himself would greet us.

Mrs. Tanaka opened the door and smiled pleasantly. She invited us to come inside where slippers waited for us, then she took us into the parlor where Tanaka was sitting. We passed by floor screens bearing painted landscapes and a dining table of fine oiled wood, then entered an adjoining room where chairs and a coffee table had

130

been set for us. Almost before we had taken our seats, Mrs. Tanaka disappeared and returned, bringing us green tea and sweets. Protocol had been established. Guests were guests, no matter how unwanted.

Mr. Tanaka had thin hair, a firm jaw, and spoke in a soft voice. He wore a tan pullover, dark pants, and eyeglasses. As we talked, he seemed perfectly at ease discussing the fact of his near death. Calmly he reenacted the distribution and consumption of the poison. He folded his tongue between his lower teeth and lip, as the killer had instructed. He also described drinking a small first dose and a larger second dose, both dispensed from bottles with English labels.

Only once during his description of the poisoning did he show any sign of dread. After the second dose one woman went for a drink of water. Suddenly Tanaka felt faint, and he wanted water, too. He remembers seeing Miyako Akiyama, the twenty-three-year-old clerk, lying on the floor as he went past. "I knew I should check on her but my mind was only telling me that she was an obstacle to the water. I rinsed my mouth and tried to get back to her, but that's when I lost consciousness."

As Tanaka spoke, I had an odd but definite sense that he was studying me with unusual care. It made me self-conscious, but I said nothing about it. I asked him if he had ever felt suspicious about the doctor in any way.

He said there had been absolutely no reason to suspect the doctor of anything. He was so perfect in his appearance of authority. Everything, down to demonstrating how to drink the liquid, had been executed with such definite expertise.

Tanaka remembered lying on the floor of the bank and suddenly becoming aware of boots banging around him, and then people were asking his name. Everything seemed like a hallucination until maybe ten o'clock that night, when he awoke to find himself surrounded by police in a strange room. At the time, he didn't realize he was in a hospital. When he asked the police why they were there, he recalled, they told him they were more interested in why *he* was there.

After many weeks of recovery Tanaka returned to work at the

Teikoku Bank. The police and the press, however, made constant claims on his time. For two months he spent more hours looking at suspects than he did working. Each suspect was presented individually to him. Tanaka never saw a line-up.

News of Hirasawa's arrest reached Tokyo even before Hirasawa did. Tanaka remembered that while the painter was riding the train down from Hokkaidō with Inspector Igii, an ambitious reporter came to Tanaka's house and asked the survivor to come with him to Ueno train station to look at Hirasawa before the police could organize an official identification of the suspect. Tanaka agreed and went to the station with the reporter. When the train arrived, however, Hirasawa hid himself under heavy blankets despite the hot August weather, so Tanaka could not see his face. His first look at Hirasawa was the next day in Sakuradamon police station, at the behest of the MPB.

At first glance, Tanaka told me, he thought he had seen Hirasawa before but couldn't be sure. Then, as he looked more closely, his initial doubts faded and he came to believe that Hirasawa was indeed the man who had tried to kill him seven months earlier in the Teikoku Bank. He remains convinced of it.

I asked what he had thought after these second and third looks at Hirasawa. I mentioned that the former Miss Murata firmly believed that he was not the killer. Tanaka paused for a moment, seeming to study something in the distance, then said, "That's a hard question. All four of us (survivors) gave different descriptions of the killer. There was never full agreement on what he looked like, but everyone saw him from a different angle."

Amazing. How could the police have assembled a uniform description of the man with four separate accounts of his looks? Apparently, detectives took as many similar points as possible and extrapolated one image from them. In a way I was using the same technique to reconstruct a picture of the whole affair.

The MPB had relied heavily on visual identification of suspects up to the point of Hirasawa's arrest. Three times Tanaka saw Hirasawa, and by the third he was convinced that Hirasawa was the murderer. Masako Murata saw Hirasawa an equal number of times, and swore that he wasn't the Teikoku killer. Who was accurate? Whose memory of that Monday, of that face, was keener?

In the years that have come and gone, Tanaka has referred to January 26, 1948 as his second birthday, as the day when he was "reborn." He still prays for the other three victims who survived, and for the twelve who did not.

I looked at Tanaka and saw little to suggest that anything unusual had ever happened to him. He spoke Hirasawa's name without any evident malice or anger, and betrayed not the slightest hint that he felt Hirasawa should be executed. At times I thought he might have been speaking of the mailman, instead of the man who had almost killed him. I looked more closely and I realized that Tanaka's scars were beneath his calm, soft-spoken exterior. At the start of the interview I had thought I was imagining things, but now I was certain that he had been furtively and intently studying me, Tomizawa, and my interpreter. I asked him about it.

Tanaka flushed with embarrassment, and shyly looked down. Ever since the crime, he said, he had become "quite unconsciously, very aware of meeting people—their physical features, the way they act and speak," so that he would remember them in specific ways and in clear detail. He apologized for making us feel uncomfortable.

After explaining that we fully understood, we rose to leave. In the entrance we put on our shoes and thanked the Tanakas for allowing us into their home. It was understandable that people who were *not* at the crime would have different opinions of what had happened, but it was strange, I thought, that no one who *had* been there—even among the survivors I had interviewed—noticed common details about the killer's appearance.

At the Tanaka's doorway I noticed I'd forgotten my coat, which hung on a wall peg down the hallway. I did not want to impose further on Mrs. Tanaka, so I walked back inside to get it myself. Suddenly everyone stood rigid. Tomizawa and my interpreter called out frantically to me to come back. The Tanakas were horrified. I grabbed my coat and rushed back to the entrance, hoping somebody would tell me what I'd done.

When I reached the entrance and saw the slippers there, I realized I'd committed a serious transgression. I'd walked into their home with my shoes on. I fumbled through several apologies, and the Tanakas assured me it was all right. I felt horribly clumsy as we left.

Out on the street, the irony of this incident struck me. The killer at the bank had meticulously followed each social custom and none of his victims had looked at him more than casually, but if he had walked into the bank with his boots on, his victims would have remembered every detail about him.

In 1948 Mr. Shuji Takada was chief of the Kyodo wire in the Sakuradamon police station. When I met him at the Foreign Press Center in January 1985, he told me that he had taken part in an unusual and unpublicized scene. The police, he said, had called him in to witness Sadamichi Hirasawa's confession. Takada explained that the police asked for his presence because they feared people might think the confession had been forced, so he was summoned as an impartial observer. Hirasawa had walked into the interrogation room very calmly, occasionally smiling, even laughing. Takada concluded there was no reason to suspect coercion.

When I told Tomizawa of the *Yomiuri* about Takada's having witnessed the confession, he said he had never heard of such a thing. To Tomizawa's knowledge the police had never called any reporter to witness any suspect's confession. Tomizawa was impressed by what he called Takada's "good fortune."

Takada was convinced, and remained convinced, of Hirasawa's guilt. I asked what made him so sure, and he, like the police and procurators, cited the money in Hirasawa's possession. When I suggested that while it was indeed a strong point, it was hardly conclusive, especially in a case built on circumstantial evidence, Takada gave me new information. Hirasawa's past, he said, had been rife with criminal behavior, and fraud was not his only offense on record.

I asked him for specifics, but Takada would not, or could not, give me a simple answer. He said he had learned from the MPB that Hirasawa once wrote a postcard under an assumed name and mailed it to the Tokyo police about a year before the Teikoku killings. In the card Hirasawa identified himself as a thief who had attempted to rob the home of one Sadamichi Hirasawa, but had been caught in the act by the artist who, instead of turning him over to the police, gave him a lecture on goodness. The artist then let him go, making no claim against him. Hirasawa, the postcard concluded, was a good and just man.

It was a curious piece of information, I thought. But for what earthly reason would Hirasawa, who supposedly was planning the intricacies of the Teikoku crime, draw any sort of attention to himself? And why would he write to the police of all people? If intended as a diversion, it only made him seem a more likely suspect. What did Takada's theory mean? That Hirasawa was telling the MPB, "I'm a good man, so don't suspect me if twelve people turn up dead in a bank any time in the near future?" Hirasawa's mental state might have been questionable, but he wasn't stupid.

I asked Takada what possible explanation there was for this postcard. "Mental retardation," he said. I nodded.

I then asked how a mentally retarded man could carry out a crime as complex and calculated as the Teikoku murders. He said Hirasawa was something of a Jekyll and Hyde, a scientific genius by day and an imbecile by night. It was, to be sure, one of the more interesting theories I'd heard.

Throughout the interview, my interpreter told me that whenever I pressed Takada for details he became tense and difficult with her. Often his answers contradicted one another, and she politely asked him if he meant something else than what he had just answered. She also said that he made numerous asides to her about his support and endorsement of the Metropolitan Police.

As we concluded it was clear that, regardless of Takada's assertions, on one point he remained certain and firm: He had witnessed Hirasawa's confession, had sat in the interrogation room with Hajime Takagi, the procurator who had secured the confession, and had watched Hirasawa calmly admit that he had committed the murders.

Hajime Takagi was my next appointment. Tomizawa, my interpreter, and I travelled together to Takagi's office on the Ginza. The *Yomiuri* had a good personal relationship with Takagi, and I was certain this was the reason he agreed to see me since he had already spoken numerous times with the Japanese press about the Teikoku story. Accordingly, Tomizawa was accompanying me.

Takagi had set terms to the interview. Nothing, but nothing of what would be discussed could appear in the *Yomiuri* newspapers. Tomizawa had to promise that he would take no notes, nor use mine. Further, Tomizawa had to agree not to release anything of this interview to *any* of the Japanese media. A strange request, I thought, but I no longer questioned Japanese behavior.

Takagi's office was unexpectedly austere for a former District Procurator who enjoyed a very successful private law practice. Few things, least of all office space, were inexpensive on the Ginza. Takagi, I learned, was known for his modesty and lack of ostentation. We sat in comfortable but unassuming chairs, and green tea was set before us as I plugged in the tape recorder.

Silver haired, bespectacled, and thin, Takagi sat forward with his legs crossed and his hands clasped on his knees. For a man who exacted such strict terms for an interview, he seemed surprisingly agreeable. At first I sensed a trace of discomfort in his voice, and as we proceeded he frequently shifted in his seat and slipped his hands under his legs.

As a student at Tokyo University, Takagi said, he was involved

with law studies and the swimming club. He graduated with Jirō
Fujita, who later became Chief of Detectives for the MPB at roughly
the same time Takagi became a procurator in the Tokyo District
Court. In 1948, Takagi's office was located next to Hibiya Park in
a two-story building that resembled a military barracks, and he was
working in his office one afternoon when he heard of a tragic case
of food poisoning at the Teikoku Bank. Two hours later, when the
police informed him that what had been thought to be food poisoning was actually mass murder, he went directly to the scene. He
was kept informed of police progress at almost every step of the
investigation.

However, Takagi did not enter the investigation until months
later. Forty-eight hours after an arrest was made, he took custody
of the suspect for interrogation. I asked if, during the months prior
to the arrest, he had formed any impression of what type of person
the killer might be. "The investigation was not conducted on presumption or assumption," he answered, pulling back in his chair.
"It was done on the basis of all the evidence. We were trying to find
the point where all the evidence led." He made a point of empha-
sizing that he had never formed any preconception of the Teikoku
murderer.

However, Takagi continued, when Hirasawa was brought in,
Takagi did not think the crime fit the artist's character. The former
procurator remembered being maybe "forty percent sure that Hirasawa was involved." I asked what changed his mind, hoping that
he might reveal a concrete connection between Hirasawa and the
crime, something which no one had yet been able to show me.

Takagi didn't let me down. Hirasawa said he'd lost Dr. Shigeru
Matsui's namecard after someone had picked his pocket, Takagi
explained, then Hirasawa admitted that the story was untrue. The
artist couldn't say what had happened to the card. Hirasawa also
said that Matsui had written an address with a fountain pen on the
back of the card the doctor gave to him. Matsui, Takagi pointed
out, told the police that he never carried a fountain pen.

As for the money found in Hirasawa's possession, Hirasawa

named several people who had given it to him, but the people he named were either dead or unable to be located except for one—who denied he ever gave money to Hirasawa. Takagi also learned of the dinner table photograph episode with Inspector Igii, and he said that this contributed to his "very near absolute certainty" that the painter was the wanted man.

The police, however, remained divided on Hirasawa's guilt, and as a result the investigation ground to a virtual standstill. Chief Fujita asked Takagi for assistance in sorting through the investigators' reasons for their belief in Hirasawa's guilt or innocence. Takagi said he reshuffled the investigators into different sections and ordered them each to look at the evidence from a different perspective. It was a move that gave the police investigation fresh momentum. Hirasawa, however, was now in the custody of the Procuracy.

In the meantime, Takagi consulted Yoshio Yamada, Hirasawa's lawyer, and outlined the suspicions against his client. "If all these matters can be cleared," Takagi told him, "then we'll let Hirasawa go. If you or his family can help explain things, then please do."

Back in the interrogation room, Takagi got Hirasawa to admit having debunked people of money and, on one occasion, of jewels. The Procuracy was going to call for a charge of fraud, Takagi said, but opted to wait to see what else the painter might confess. Little by little Hirasawa began to say things about having performed the Teikoku crime. Pieces spilled out, Takagi said, until finally, on September 28, 1948, Hirasawa said he was the murderer. For the Procuracy, his confession itself was the concrete connection.

I asked Takagi why it had been necessary to have a journalist witness the confession.

Takagi looked very confused. "We never had a journalist witness the confession."

Now I was confused. I asked if he was absolutely sure.

"We never had *anyone* witness the confession," he replied.

I made a note, and continued along the same line of questioning. I asked if he knew of a Mr. Shuji Takada.

"I have never heard of him," he answered.

I made another note. If I hadn't met and interviewed Takada myself, I might have doubted now whether he even existed. As for whether Takada had actually witnessed Hirasawa's confession, I was now utterly confused. I should believe Takagi, I thought, but I also had no reason to disbelieve Takada.

Takagi mused a moment over something, and the determination on his face made it clear he was stalking some hidden memory. Soon his eyes brightened, and he held a finger in the air. He said he did recall a tall, heavyset American journalist who came to see Hirasawa *soon after* the confession. Hober-something or other.

"Earnest Hoberecht?"

"Yes," he remembered. According to Takagi, Hoberecht was the only journalist who came, and—Takagi emphasized—the American came strictly for an interview with Hirasawa. There was no witness to the confession.

I mentioned the name of Hideo Naruchi. Suddenly Takagi began tapping his finger peremptorily on the table and, speaking in time to the tapping, told me that Naruchi "was never an official of the principal investigation." Though he had never met Naruchi, the former procurator said that Naruchi was only part of the second division, the part of the investigating force which kept track of evidence and collated it along with members from the namecard division, the methodology division, and the other sections of the MPB. Takagi rapped the table with his fist on the last word and sat back in his chair.

He had made his point dramatically enough for me to lose my place in my questions. I tried to find it again but couldn't, and as the silence awkwardly widened, I felt I had to think up some sort of question, even if only as a stall tactic. We'd arrived twenty minutes late for this interview, and I didn't want to keep Takagi waiting again.

While I kept looking for my place, I asked Takagi if he had been in the military during the war.

He said he was inducted into the Army in 1943.

I still hadn't found my place in my list of questions, and so continued with this line to buy more time. I asked where he had served.

"Manchuria," he said.

I looked up. My interpreter had drawn a deep breath, then looked casually away. Tomizawa was listening intently.

I looked innocently down at my notes, and, listening closely, asked Takagi what unit he had been with.

He told me he had been assigned to general infantry and that he had also spent some time in other parts of China.

I asked if he'd known about Ishii and the 731 Regiment, and if he had known they were in that neighborhood.

While he was in Manchuria, Takagi said, he'd heard about a "special squad" that had been sent "to research and develop toxic chemicals and other substances for weaponry." He knew no names at the time, nor any specifics, and said that not until years later when the MPB was investigating these people did he come to learn of General Shirō Ishii and the 731 Regiment.

Takagi had never discussed the 731 Regiment with the Japanese press, and no procurator had ever acknowledged the investigation of 731 personnel before this. I understood why Tomizawa was now shifting in his seat, trying to conceal his anticipation.

I found my place in my questions, but decided to let Takagi continue. He described how, when he heard the police were investigating a special group of former soldiers who had been in Manchuria during the war, he had wondered if they were the same Army unit he had heard about when he was stationed there. He discovered that indeed they were, and then closely followed the MPB's investigation of these former members of the 731 Regiment.

I asked how the lead had been discovered.

Detective Kyoshi Suzuki, now dead, turned up the lead, but Takagi also said that he never found out exactly how Suzuki had gotten hold of it.

My interpreter seemed tense. I asked her if she was having trouble, and she looked at me, hesitated, and said, "I think I'll be okay."

140

During his time in Manchuria, Takagi continued, he had contracted typhus.

I asked if he thought 731's activities might have been responsible for the disease.

Again, his finger started slowly tapping. Flatly, emphatically, and with a smile, Takagi answered, "There is no such fact that Ishii and 731 were ever connected with diseases and epidemics."

TOKYO, 6 May 1947, cable from Commander In Chief Far East (CINCFE), to War Department, Washington, D.C.

Experiments were known to and described by three Japanese and confirmed tacitly by Ishii; field trials against the Chinese. . .took place on at least three occasions; scope of program indicated. . .that four hundred kilograms of dried anthrax organisms destroyed in Pingfan (Manchuria) in August 1945. . .Reluctant statements by Ishii indicate he had superiors (possible general staff) who knew and authorized the program. Ishii states that if guaranteed immunity from "war crimes" in documentary form for himself, superiors, and subordinates, he can describe program in detail. Ishii claims to have extensive high-level knowledge including strategic and tactical use of biological warfare (BW) on defense and offense, backed by some research on best BW agents to employ by geographical areas of Far East, and the use of BW in cold climates. . . .

TOKYO, 18 November 1976, Washington Post wire:

Japanese scientists killed at least 3,000 prisoners during World War II through bacteriological warfare experiments and escaped prosecution by sharing their findings with American occupation forces, a Japanese television documentary has alleged.

At a high-security camp in Manchuria . . .the scientists allegedly killed the prisoners by infecting them with plague, cholera, anthrax, and typhoid.

Five former members of the unit told television reporter Haruko Yoshinaga they were promised complete protection in return for cooperation with U.S. authorities.

(Yoshinaga's) hour-long expose was recently aired by the Tokyo Broadcasting System, the largest commercial network here.

Yoshinaga travelled throughout Japan to track down 20 former members of the wartime unit which had the code title "731." "They trembled, shook, some were so shocked they couldn't speak. As I stood next to one man who is now a health center official I could hear his heart pounding."

(Unit commander General) Ishii studied in the Soviet Union and Europe, specialized in pathology and bacteriology and alerted the army command to the possibilities of bacteriological warfare in the early 1930s.

One witness told Yoshinaga that on August 9-10, 1945, the remaining prisoners were poisoned after refusing to commit suicide. He described feeling "unreal" as he carried and dragged away the bodies to be burned.

Another former officer told Yoshinaga: "The spirit of 731 still exists, and we can be proud of that."

TOKYO, 7 April 1982, UPI wire:

The Japanese government has confirmed the existence of a secret World War II Imperial Army unit that allegedly killed more than 3,000 people. . .in chemical and biological experiments.

The atrocities were committed by the Imperial Army's unit No. 731 stationed in Harbin. Also called Ishii Troops after its commander, Lt. Gen. Shirō Ishii, the unit has been blamed. . .for killing more than 3,000 persons who were used as human guinea pigs.

"There is no such fact. . . ." I made a note, and I asked how long the police had continued to investigate 731 members.

Takagi emphasized that the police stayed on the trail of the 731 Regiment up to the point of Hirasawa's arrest.

If this was true, then it disproved the Society's theory that GHQ stopped the investigation of 731 to protect the secrecy of the Legal Section's deal with Ishii. The only way that the Society's theory could still be true was if GHQ had interceded, coincidentally, at the very time that Hirasawa was arrested. I asked if GHQ interfered with the investigation in any way.

Takagi's eyes brightened. No, he said, GHQ had in fact "co-operated."

He referred, I was certain, to the Public Safety Division's help in clearing reporters out of the MPB's way. With the flat denial he had just issued on Ishii, I didn't think the 731 discussion would yield much more information, so I returned to my original questions, asking his thoughts on why Hirasawa had not been executed. Takagi maintained that the first Minister of Justice to receive Hirasawa's case set a bad precedent by not ordering the execution immediately.

Our agreed time for the interview had expired. I thanked him for his indulgence and started putting my things away. Takagi and Tomizawa rose and talked as they walked toward the door. The interview was officially over, but one of Takagi's unexplained answers was troubling me. As I put on my coat, I whispered to my interpreter to please ask Takagi casually, on her way out, how GHQ had "cooperated." Possibly there was something more to this than I had originally thought.

I waited in the corridor, after saying goodbye to Takagi and watched my interpreter speak to him as Tomizawa stood with them. When Takagi spoke, the look on Tomizawa's face told me that something serious had just happened. Then Takagi went into his office, closing his door behind him, and the two of them joined me in the hall. My interpreter was trying to stay calm.

"He said GHQ let him talk to Ishii," she told me.

"What?!"

"GHQ let him talk to Ishii," she repeated.

Tomizawa was squirming. He said that not Takagi, not the police, not *anyone* had ever before admitted that Ishii himself had been directly involved in the Teikoku investigation. Tomizawa knew he had a major story, and he also knew he couldn't write it. His personal relationship forbade it.

I myself was having a hard time staying calm. I was also having a hard time believing that the Americans, who were deathly afraid of any leak that might expose their deal with the 731 Regiment, would allow any 731 member to talk about his activities. I wanted to go back and beat on Takagi's door and plead for another fifteen minutes until my interpreter told me that, on her way out, Takagi had said he would answer any further questions I might have, if *she* would return with me to interpret. Apparently she had quite unconsciously charmed him. I asked her what she had on her schedule for the next four days.

Later that afternoon I telephoned Takagi and spoke with him through my interpreter. He had a busy week planned, but he agreed to meet me for a second interview in several days.

The Jimbōcho area in downtown Tokyo was overrun by two kinds of stores, sporting goods and books. The well-read athlete was smart to make his home there. In a different direction, away from the city's center, stretched the usual run of shops selling electronic goods, martial arts equipment, cameras, and coffee. Up a side street I found the four-story building that houses the Pacific-Asia Resource Center (PARC), a political awareness group that monitors grassroots activities throughout the Far East and also serves as a general clearinghouse for information. The information I wanted from PARC was what one of its members, Ichiyo Muto, could tell me about his childhood in Manchuria.

Muto described how he had spent his early years of grade school in Japanese-occupied Manchuria during the 1930s. His father was a senior official in the local government established by the Imperial Army after the Manchurian Incident. The winters had always been hard and long but at least they were fairly predictable. Sometime in the mid-1930s, when Muto was nine or ten years old, a very stern and tough-looking man came to the Muto family household. The man wore a military uniform and wanted to speak to Muto's father. After the visit Muto learned that the visitor was a great and feared man.

Then the same man came to Muto's house a second, and final, time. Again he was in uniform, and again he wanted to speak to Muto's father. This time Muto learned that the man had recently come to Manchuria to conduct research on epidemic prevention. He and his 731 Regiment would be working in the area, the man said, though he wouldn't say exactly where his installation would be. Muto's father had listened to Colonel Ishii's assurances that he and his personnel had the public welfare always in mind, and he promised to help the government and the people in any way that the 731 Regiment could.

Soon afterward, Muto remembered, sudden outbreaks of strange diseases ravaged the countryside. Throughout the spring, summer, and fall these seemed sporadic, but in the winter they became regular and vicious. Muto recalled January and February—the coldest months—as the worst times. He walked to school past many houses surrounded by barbed wire and with men in white insulated suits. He watched them carrying out the dead. Sometimes these men came into the schoolhouse and warned everyone to stay away from whatever new fence they were constructing to prevent infected rats from escaping contaminated areas.

The newspapers and the radio stations, Muto remembered, constantly sang praises of Colonel Ishii for having come so fortuitously to Manchuria at a time when the people desperately needed him and his expert knowledge. Ishii and his people not only could help fight the battles against the diseases, but could also explain their mysterious origins. They had come, Ishii said, from the outer provinces, like nearby Siberia. Animals indigenous to the area carried the germs; hunters shot and trapped the animals and brought them back to the farms, where the diseases spread because the infected corpses lay around and the rats fed on them; then the rats became contaminated, and the fleas in turn got contaminated; finally the fleas bit people, and the diseases intensified until they reached epidemic proportions.

Muto said that Ishii was widely and frequently quoted by the press, which had declared him the champion in the campaign against these killer diseases. This went on until early 1944, when Muto's father was transferred back to Japan. It wasn't until the early 1950s, Muto told me, that he heard a different version of what had been happening in Manchuria.

Muto spoke quietly as we talked about possible connections the 731 Regiment had to the Teikoku killings. He said he disagreed with the theory that saw the crime as a political statement, exploiting Japanese feudal behavior. Still, he did not totally reject it because the crime was not without an indirect political effect, he maintained. It was the first of a series of mysterious incidents that indicated something quite extraordinary was happening in Japan.

Muto alluded to three other incidents that occurred during the Occupation in a span of two-and-a-half months, none of which was ever solved. In the summer of 1949, the body of Sadanori Shimoyama, the president of the Japanese National Railroads (JNR) was found mangled almost beyond recognition on the railroad tracks. Two days earlier he had dismissed 37,000 JNR workers in the first segment of a planned 102,000-man layoff. His body was so disfigured that the police could not determine conclusively if he was dead before or after the train had run over him. In mid-July, a locomotive with no one aboard rammed into Mitaka station, killing six people. Its throttle had been tied down to the floor. No one was ever charged in the case, but rumors were spread that labor unions were behind it. One month later, a passenger train derailed near Matsukawa in northern Japan in what was clearly an act of sabotage. Three people died and dozens were injured. Twenty union members were accused and tried for the crime but after twenty years of legal battles were exonerated.

In each incident, as in the Teikoku crime, it was widely reported that the evidence and possible motives suggested GHQ involvement.

"In the early part of the Occupation the U.S. wanted to democratize Japan, which was good," Muto continued. "But late in 1947 there's a big change in the mood of the Occupation. By 1948 it's clear that something is happening, but only in 1949 do we know what it is. The Occupation was no more interested in democracy. It wanted an anti-communist state. In 1948 when the Teigin crime happened, there were already efforts being made against the communist presence in Japan. In 1949 it was openly apparent. The Teigin crime, then, was in this respect a harbinger of mysterious incidents that would follow."

The Occupation got off to bad start because it had done little homework on Japan, its culture and people. But the most damaging oversight of the Occupation was its refusal to focus on rebuilding Japan's shattered economy. The Americans saw their mission in Japan as political, not economic, and failed to understand the crucial link between government and economy. The Occupation also suffered from internal divisiveness. One side, the "China crowd," wanted to transform Nippon into the ideal democracy, while the "Japan crowd" was committed to founding an anti-communist bulwark. From the outset the American Occupation officials couldn't agree on goals.

Contradicting policies evolved as the Occupation tried to convince the Japanese that if their country had embraced democracy in some form before the war, the Japanese would never have been pitched into World War II. But with the economy still in ruins and inflation ravaging the country, the Japanese had little interest in what the Americans called "democratization." By late 1947 the Occupation learned that democracy could not easily be imported and transplanted; it had to emerge indigenously. A plan for retrenchment was devised and put into effect, its main goal being the rehabilitation and restoration of Japan's national economy. But though the Occupation's retrenchment succeeded, it could not do so without reversing major Occupation policies which had been in effect since the Americans' arrival. The Japanese public in postwar Japan had a hard time understanding what their conquerors wanted to achieve.

147

Given that the Teikoku crime and its postwar context often evoke polemics, Muto's assessment of the affair's political significance as a mere harbinger of other mysterious incidents was refreshing. I'd come to believe the major obstacle to retrieving the facts has always been the politics that people have attached to the case. The Society believes Hirasawa was clearly a victim of Occupation policy. Those who believe Hirasawa is guilty maintain that the outcry over 731 involvement in the crime has been nothing but communist-inspired propaganda. Despite having good reason to condemn the 731 Regiment at any chance, Muto spoke guardedly about the possible involvement of 731 people in the Teikoku killings.

"I don't doubt that they were," Muto told me, "but I don't know for sure. Who's to say? *Nobody* knows for certain all the things Ishii was doing."

I asked Muto if he accepted robbery as the motive of the crime. He shook his head. "If it was robbery then the Teikoku crime was not a Japanese crime at all. Bank robberies at that time were very, very rare. They still are. Bank robbery is a western crime."

Japanese police and judiciary records from the Occupation period didn't list bank robbery separately from other forms of larceny, so statistics to substantiate Muto's statement don't exist. However, according to at least a dozen other people—both Japanese and American—who lived and worked in Japan during the Occupation, bank robbery was an indisputably unusual crime.

I walked back through Jimbōcho and continued to think about Muto's last remark. If the motive in the Teikoku crime was robbery, then a Japanese man had committed a foreign crime, a western crime. Moreover, he had committed it poorly, leaving behind more money than he had stolen. The motive for murder in the Teigin incident was far more easily explained than the motive for robbery, but murder as the principal crime was far more difficult to prove.

148

When I met with former Procurator Takagi for a second interview, he was as pleasant as he had been the first time. His secretary politely excused herself from the room, leaving Takagi, my interpreter, and me alone. Tomizawa did not accompany me this time because I thought that Takagi might speak more freely without a member of the Japanese press present.

I started my tape recorder, and we spent the next thirty minutes discussing how Takagi had come to meet General Shirō Ishii.

In late spring of 1948, about four or five months after the Teikoku murders, Takagi went to the home of the chief of the Mejiro police station with about ten MPB detectives. The chief lived in a building adjacent to the Mejiro station, headquarters for the Teikoku investigation. No one from GHQ was present at this meeting, Takagi told me, and this was the only meeting Takagi attended.

He couldn't account for how Ishii had been secured because all arrangements had been made by the police. Everything had been done "unofficially," Takagi recalled, which meant no record of this meeting existed.

For an hour the ten detectives, including Chief Jirō Fujita, stood around Ishii, who sat on a chair in the middle of them as they asked him about a photograph that one detective had brought with him. The photograph pictured approximately twenty men, all of whom were affiliated with the 731 Regiment, and most of whom were known to Ishii. Takagi never found out where the photograph came from or how the police acquired it. Again he explained that he had attended the meeting "as an observer."

Ishii had a square jaw and a stubborn look but, in the end, proved a cooperative man. The detectives questioned him about each man in the photo, asking if any had ever worked with cyanide and a neutralizing substance. To the best of Takagi's memory, Ishii stated at the beginning that his 731 Regiment had certainly been working with cyanide and neutralizers, but that nothing had been perfected.

From having interrogated "hundreds" of people, Takagi said he had developed a strong ability to sense what kind of person he was questioning. Throughout the Ishii interrogation, which Takagi continued to characterize as only "a meeting," he had the strong feeling that Ishii was a good, helpful man.

By the time of this "meeting," the Japanese police had long known about the Imperial Army poison school and how the Teikoku killings most likely involved one of that school's graduates. Yet the photograph of the twenty 731 suspects was never shown to witnesses or survivors of the crime because, Takagi said, "There wasn't enough suspicion against 731 to show the photograph to the survivors." Takagi must have been struck by the contradiction of this comment, because he quickly added, "We also didn't want this part of the investigation known, of course, so we'd have only shown the photograph if one particular member seemed a probable suspect. But none of them ever really became a suspect."

Memorandum of Chief Fujita's meeting with Byron Engle, Eugene Hattori, and other PSD officials: ". . .Request made this information be kept secret for fear of prosecution by War Crimes Tribunal. . . ."

Suddenly Takagi's finger began tapping again as he explained that it was the investigation's poison division and methodology division that together concluded the Imperial Army must be involved. The two divisions checked out the Imperial Army and soon discovered a special unit in Manchuria that matched the description they were seeking.

I wasn't sure why Takagi chose to tell me this with no prefacing remarks. It seemed he wanted to emphasize that, from the outset of the investigation, the police had investigated many likely leads in good faith. The Ishii interrogation, however, did not make the investigation look competent and aboveboard, but rather made it more suspect. If the police had knowledge of and access to Ishii, a known expert with poisons and leader of the infamous 731 Regiment, and if they allowed him to walk away after only one meeting, how could they convict Hirasawa, whose capacity to execute such a complex crime they could never prove?

I then asked Takagi about the strange nature of Hirasawa's confession. I wanted to know why his explanation had made no sense during each of the first fifty-nine interrogations, but then suddenly had fallen logically and incontrovertibly into place during the sixtieth, sixty-first, and sixty-second sessions.

Takagi explained that during the first forty-eight hours that Hirasawa was in police custody, Detective Tamigorō Igii had interrogated the artist, but afterward, when the Procurator's Office took over, Takagi himself interrogated Hirasawa, who, Takagi reminded me, confessed gradually until the sixtieth interrogation, when he told the whole story. The sixty-first and sixty-second interrogations were conducted by Takagi's boss, Idei, who was kept fully informed of Takagi's progress and who wanted personally to confirm Takagi's interrogations. However, as was true of almost every part of the Teikoku crime and investigation, there was a question about Idei's interrogations of Hirasawa.

When I told Takagi that the Society To Save Hirasawa had checked the logbooks of Kosuge prison, where Hirasawa was kept at the time of these final interrogations, and that they had found no record of Idei's visits on the alleged dates, Takagi maintained that not every detail of the investigation could feasibly be recorded. He also said that the prison guard had probably forgotten to log Idei's visits.

Takagi knew the validity of the artist's confession had been debated for years, so I asked him to comment on the controversy.

He began by discussing the legal procedure for detaining a suspect. Whenever the Procuracy requested a detention warrant, a judge had to review the request as well as question the suspect to determine if detention was warranted. In the Hirasawa investigation Justice Shirō Ishizaki had issued all the detention warrants. Takagi repeated that Hirasawa had confessed of his own free will, and as proof Takagi told me that Hirasawa, after confessing to both Idei and to Takagi, also confessed to Justice Ishizaki. This had never before been revealed, and ten weeks later, when Hirasawa went to trial, the presiding judge was none other than Justice Shirō Ishizaki.

I asked Takagi if, after having access to all the information from the investigation and the many interrogations of Hirasawa, he might have any doubts about Hirasawa's guilt.

"People should have all the correct information on this case." he told me. "The Japanese mass media have all said that maybe Mr. Hirasawa is not guilty, but the police and the Justice Ministry are convinced. If you read all the interrogation documents, you'll know automatically he's guilty. I think the public should know the facts, and not the misleading information from the mass media."

Later that night I replayed the tape in my room, listening again to what Takagi had told me. While the revelations he had shared added new and crucial information to the case, they also spurred several critical and unanswered questions. I wondered why Ishii had not been further detained by either the police or the Procuracy, and why he had not been summoned for subsequent interrogation. The survivors never saw the photograph because there wasn't enough suspicion against the 731 people to warrant showing it to them, yet other suspects, who were far less qualified for carrying off the Teikoku crime, were brought personally before the survivors. One possible reason was that the MPB wanted to keep the 731 investigation a secret because if the twenty men in the photograph knew they were under suspicion, they would go into deeper hiding. Still, that seemed weak.

There was a larger consideration—GHQ's involvement. In light of what Takagi said, no longer could anyone claim that GHQ stopped the police investigation of 731 in order to protect the American deal with Ishii, or so it seemed. GHQ had "cooperated" by giving Ishii himself to the MPB for questioning. The move was as much an enigma as the Teikoku crime itself. Even the slightest security leak could expose the 731 deal, so why had GHQ taken such a tremendous risk by allowing ten Japanese policemen to question the man who was the very center of the cover-up?

Of course, whether the helpful General Ishii answered truthfully remains a question. If Takagi's memory was right, Ishii had said that 731 had experimented with, but had not perfected any poison. Either Ishii had lied, or the documents from the Archives had. The memorandum on Chief Fujita's meeting of March 12, 1948, said the Fujita told PSD advisors of the MPB's discovery of a "secret army chemical lab where experiments were perfected in the use of poisons" which were later used "successfully on humans in Manchuria."

"The police checked out the army and found a unit in Manchuria," Takagi had said. How had they "found" this unit? In 1948 not one shred of physical evidence, not one item of record, existed on the 731 Regiment. Ishii and SCAP's Legal Section had seen to that to ensure the secrecy of their deal. Maybe former members of 731 tipped the police, but official confirmation about 731 could only have come from official Imperial Army records, which at that time were in the possession of U.S. Army Intelligence. With the image and reputation of the United States so perilously at risk, the Legal Section would never have let anyone near anything about 731 unless that person was thoroughly, implicitly trusted. GHQ and the MPB perhaps were no strangers to a good personal relationship.

Two days later I was on the Japanese National Railroads, headed north to meet three Society members who would accompany me on a trip to Miyagi Prison in Sendai, where Hirasawa had been held for the last thirty years. We had reservations for the bullet train, which would cover the approximately three hundred miles in under two hours.

At every station waves of people poured into the JNR train, which was already full. People crushed up against each other. I could hardly breathe, and was surprised that nobody protested being bumped and jostled. I watched people trying to find their places again in their papers and magazines, which they held above their heads to read because there was no room for even a piece of paper between the bodies.

When I got off at Ikebukuro station, the elevated platforms were just another swarm of bodies moving in one huge mass. I found the three Society members and, after making our connection to Omiya station, we found our seats on the bullet train to Sendai amid commuters and skiers headed out of Tokyo.

My chances of getting into the prison to see Hirasawa were slim, and that was being optimistic. A year earlier, the Justice Ministry had decided that Hirasawa would no longer be available for interviews. The Ministry also stated that only members of Hirasawa's immediate family, or Society members who had had extensive contact with the artist prior to the Ministry's decision, could continue to see him at the prison. I didn't qualify for either of these categories, but Katsuo Shinmura, a member of Japan's House of Representatives, was going to go with us to the prison and try to convince the prison officials to let me see Hirasawa. Shinmura had been familiar with the Hirasawa case for a long time, having become involved with the Society through his efforts to abolish the death penalty in Japan.

At the appointed hour and minute, the train pulled into Sendai station. I had pictured Sendai as a small city, more reminiscent of the Orient than of the West, less commercial and far less modern than Tokyo. To my surprise Sendai was a major city, the Tokyo of the north, every bit as huge and trafficked and skyscraped and neoned.

Takehiko, Tsunekawa, Mitsumatsu, and I left the station and walked out into icy winds that seemed to slice right through us. After a long walk, we checked into our rooms for the night.

At breakfast the next morning I met Shinmura, a friendly and inquisitive man. Shinmura was going to tell the authorities that I was a Society member from the United States who'd come all the way across the world to pay respects to Hirasawa. It was a bright, clear, and cold morning with few people on the roads, and we made good time to the gates of Miyagi Prison.

The prison compound lay across from a cluster of private homes where laundry was hanging in the yards and where a woman was pushing a pram up the street. Immediately inside the gates was the guard house, a white box made of glass and concrete. Deeper inside lay a paved courtyard adjoining a small parking lot, to the right of which two brown steel doors, each about twenty feet high, barred entrance into the cell blocks. At the far end of the courtyard was the administration building, where Takehiko and Shinmura went as soon as we finished filling out forms requesting to visit Hirasawa.

Tsunekawa, who translated for me, Mitsumatsu, and I headed toward the waiting room. In the middle of the room was a bent and feeble heater that tried unsuccessfully to give off warmth. There were two benches and a wooden table. On one wall hung a color poster of a smiling woman in decolletage, circa 1900. Several other visitors sat waiting in the room.

Twenty minutes passed as we watched the others who were waiting for permission to enter the prison. Finally, a guard yanked the door open.

Outside, Takehiko and Shinmura were walking to the detention center in the distance. The guard came up to us and spoke very quickly. Mitsumatsu jumped up, and cried, "Okay!" He shook my hand heartily, then paused.

The guard spoke again, and Mitsumatsu's enthusiasm disappeared. He had misunderstood. I had been denied permission. No reason had been given for the prison officials' decision.

Although I hadn't expected to be able to meet Hirasawa, I was nevertheless disappointed. I knew Hirasawa lived in a cell roughly twenty yards square, divided in half by a wall panel. On one side was his bed and wash stand, with tatami mats on the floor, on the other side was his atelier, where he kept his paints, easels, and brushes. His daily routine consisted of a nurse taking his blood pressure and pulse in the morning. When he was younger he would take a walk in the afternoon if he felt up to it. Lately, I was told, he spent most of his time sitting on his bed because, at ninety-three, he was too weak to move around very much. From his window he could see the detention center wall. He used to be fond of corned beef and asparagus, but now he can't eat anything more exotic than boiled rice and eggs.

It would have been interesting to hear his voice, which Take-hiko said was barely louder than a whisper. I wanted to see what this man looked like now, since photographs of him were prohibited years ago by the authorities. I wanted to ask him which he thought was the harder to bear—the death sentence he had been handed or the life sentence he had served. I also wanted to hear him explain why, if he was innocent, he had confessed. But I had travelled to Sendai to be turned away. I was to hear nothing.

Before coming to Tokyo I'd exchanged letters with Richard Hughes, an Australian journalist who was convinced of Hirasawa's guilt. In his columns, which were as opinionated as they were lively, he always maintained the image of a maverick. He had followed the Teikoku investigation through his source and friend, Inspector Tamigorō Igii.

Hughes had written the most extensive piece on the crime in English (about five pages), and I had hoped to meet him. In his version of the events he had omitted several points, such as the problems with the confession, and I hoped that since he had discussed the investigation with Igii, he could tell me why he thought those points were not worth mentioning.

Hughes, however, died a year before I came.

I met with one of Hughes' old friends, Bob Horiguchi, who shared Hughes' opinions on the crime. Horiguchi was friendly and talkative. In the course of a long conversation he said several interesting things. One in particular struck me.

"If you apply Japanese standards to the Teikoku crime, then it's all routine."

On Monday, January 26, 1948, Sadamichi Hirasawa left the company of his son-in-law some time shortly after two o'clock in the afternoon. The prosecution maintained that he went to the nearest station and caught the 2:25 train to Ikebukuro, where he arrived at 2:50 and walked to the Teikoku Bank. By 3:15, the prosecution claimed, he was introducing himself as Dr. Jirō Yamaguchi at the side door of the bank.

The defense claimed that it was impossible for Hirasawa, then fifty-six years old, to have walked from Ikebukuro station to the Teikoku Bank in just twenty-five minutes. Hirasawa's attorney submitted that the crowds and the sleet on that Monday made it virtually impossible for even a young healthy man to cover the long distance in so short a time.

Thirty-seven years later, at 2:33 in the afternoon, I arrived at Ikebukuro station to meet Takehiko, Mitsumatsu, and several other Society members. We were going to walk from Ikebukuro station to the Teikoku Bank and time it, to see just how quickly one could cover the distance on foot.

The bank itself had closed not long after the crime, and though the building still stood, the years had effected definite changes. The roads were no longer dirt roads as they had been in 1948. All of them were paved now, and the weather was also different today.

Clear and cold, not dark and sleeting. Still, the most significant element—the distance from the train station to the bank—remained unchanged, as did the layout of the neighborhood.

Mitsumatsu wore a shoulder bag that was the same shape and size as the one the killer had carried with him. In the bag were bottles and pipettes, approximately the same size and weight as those that had been used in the crime. Carrying the bag was necessary in order to duplicate as much as possible the conditions in which Hirasawa was said to have walked this distance. Mitsumatsu was picked to simulate Hirasawa's role because he was nearest the age Hirasawa had been in 1948.

Takehiko held the stopwatch. We grouped together in the middle of the platform with Mitsumatsu at the head. A young man agreed to run ahead of us by ten to fifteen yards with maps. His job was to make sure we took the correct turns along the way. The Society had reenacted Hirasawa's alleged walk several times, so I looked forward to confirming or refuting for myself a central contention in the case against the artist. At 2:50 Takehiko started the watch, and we departed.

It took us three minutes to clear the crowds at the station and get outside to the street. We walked through the middle of the shopping district that surrounded the station. An electronic billboard with "Coca Cola" displayed on it stood about seventy feet above a McDonald's restaurant. The young man stayed on the sidewalk and held a finger on the map. As we walked in silence, my mind reviewed the flood of information I'd gathered. I was still trying to make some order of all the conflicting stories. Random pieces of information jumped in my thoughts.

Television reporter: Don't you think the fact that Hirasawa has not been executed is strange?

Justice Shirō Ishizaki, who heard Hirasawa's confession and later presided at Hirasawa's trial: There must be some reason. I don't know why.

We turned down a busy street where men with jackhammers blasted the sidewalk and wheelbarrows blocked some traffic. Mitsumatsu held the shoulder bag tightly.

Two nights ago I found that a senior Japanese police investigator published an article saying Hirasawa was framed, but no action was forthcoming. Only silence from the Justice Ministry. A casual dismissal of another complaint.

We left the busy shopping district and found ourselves among homes and parks in tighter streets. The young man had stopped ahead and was looking back and forth from one street to another.

MPB sergeant Hideo Naruchi, who said he was a senior investigator of the Teikoku crime, had retired from the police and written an article for a fairly prestigious journal called Nippon Magazine. *The title of the article was "Sadamichi Hirasawa Is Not the Culprit." Naruchi said that Chief of Detectives Jirō Fujita requested him to track and interview about one hundred people once connected with the 731 Regiment. Naruchi wrote that Chief Fujita had warned him to keep this investigation secret because GHQ had these people in custody under a special arrangement. Fujita insisted that under no circumstances was the press to get word of Naruchi's activities.*

This jibed with Takagi's statement that GHQ cooperated. It also confirmed the existence of some sort of special relationship between GHQ and the police.

Naruchi described late night meetings under bridges, in seedy bars, with 731 people. Almost all of them said the same thing. "It's a professional job, especially with the sixty-second timing between doses." Several told him of one doctor who had been working in Manchuria specifically on cyanide experiments for use in mass assassination.

Naruchi began to put together a composite of the principal suspect: fifty-one years old, about five feet two inches or five feet three inches tall, black spots on his face, pale complexion, gray hair, gentlemanly composure with the appearance of being an intellectual; earliest known whereabouts, May 1943, working in an Army hospital in Japan. In September 1944 he was ordered to Manchuria but returned before surrender because of drug addiction, which Naruchi found was common among 731 personnel as a means of living through the daily murders and atrocities. After returning to Japan, the doctor disappeared.

Of the one hundred suspects Naruchi questioned, many said that this man was the likely killer. Naruchi searched extensively but never found him.

A policeman who had investigated the crime had publicly announced Hirasawa was innocent and that the 731 Regiment had been involved in the investigation, and most likely committed the crime. Didn't anyone in the Justice Ministry find that interesting, or odd?

The young man led us up a side street for about thirty yards, then stopped. We've taken the wrong turn, he said, and reversed course. Mitsumatsu said he thought we had gone the wrong way but had not been sure. Takehiko decided that we would go back and then proceed in the other direction.

We returned to the point of the original error and took the right course. I noted a delay of some fifty seconds.

Tetsuzo Kojina, Justice Minister when the Supreme Court upheld Hirasawa's death sentence: I never signed Hirasawa's execution into effect because the orders for it never came to me.

We passed by old wooden houses, all tightly pushed together. We were on a street so narrow that we barely fit walking four abreast. The young man kept a brisk pace ahead, as Mitsumatsu and I followed closely behind him. The others brought up the rear at a distance of about twenty yards.

We took a sharp left, then a right, went straight for less than a minute, then cut sideways again. We were walking a maze, but this was the route Hirasawa said he took. It was two minutes past three o'clock.

Kunio Nakaga, Justice Minister, 1963: I was willing to sign the execution into effect, but the differences of opinion among the survivors prevented me.

Inside one of the houses we passed, someone was playing "Suite Judy Blue Eyes" by Crosby, Stills, and Nash on the stereo. For a minute I felt transported, displaced, back in America. Then my eyes fell on the colorful paper decorations that hung from the telephone lines and lampposts. Three weeks into January, and Japan was still in the middle of a special New Year celebration. The Japanese calculate their year based on when the Emperor began his reign. Hirohito, the current emperor, took his position in 1925; thus what was 1985 in the Christian world was the year 60 in Japan. There were five cycles, each one twelve years long, totalling sixty years, and this was the first time in the history of Japan that an emperor had reigned long enough to complete all five cycles. People were still calling out "Happy New Year" to each other and decorations festooned both homes and shops alike.

We were back on the direct and proper route, proceeding in a calm, orderly manner. But I noticed the young man running back toward us again.

Hajime Takagi, the former procurator, and Riichi Takeuchi, the former journalist, said that Naruchi was never a member of the principal investigation but just a minor character. Naruchi himself, the Society, and Kazuhiko Nagoya, the Yomiuri columnist, said that Naruchi certainly was involved with the principal investigation. It would probably never be determined who was right, but one thing was clear: Among the 731 doctors who Naruchi interviewed was Yukimasa Yagisawa, whose name also appears on a GHQ list of doctors working with the U.S. Army in December 1947. Yagisawa had been the 731 research director in charge of botanical disease experiments such as fungal injections; after his stint with Ishii and then with the Legal Section, Yagisawa went on to become editor of a journal on pharmaceuticals, specializing in antibiotics. Yagisawa died sometime in 1980 or 1981. Furthermore, Naruchi also knew about the 731 Regiment's sister units, Detachment 100 and Detachment 1644.

If Naruchi was not part of the secret investigation, how did he know the names of the 731 doctors and the identity of the sister units? And how did he know that GHQ gave the police these doctors?

Mitsumatsu, Takehiko, and the young man consulted each other as to where we were. We had taken more than a dozen turns in the span of thirteen minutes, had walked past homes that looked older than Hirasawa, had nodded to all sorts of people who had gazed out at us from windows, and had cut through a complex path that, according to the maps, the prosecution, and Hirasawa's confession, was the most direct route from the station to the bank. My head hurt from the walk, from the facts, from the confusion.

The Society and columnist Nagoya quoted Naruchi from an article in Bungei Shunju as having said that GHQ had stopped the Teikoku investigation. In this same article Naruchi wrote that GHQ did not interfere at all. I expected Naruchi to offer as proof the fact that he was given access to 731 doctors. But no, that would have been too logical. Naruchi instead cited what he considered proof of GHQ's assistance. It was the memo by Jack Munroe of the Public Safety Division, stating that PSD was checking up on every Lt. Parker ever assigned to Japan. Which meant nothing more than that the PSD helped the police check out a lead. GHQ had no reason to

*stop the Parker investigation. They did, however, have every reason
to stop the 731 investigation.*

Mitsumatsu guessed we should take the right fork in the street,
and I wondered if it was even worth checking my watch any more.
We were passing through tiny markets that separated the private
homes, then we walked alongside a wall that had barbed wire on
top of it. The signs were not clear about which street was which.
We had maps, and we were getting lost. Which meant that Hirasawa
had to rehearse this walk to memorize the route. Which meant
risking exposure to people in the neighborhood who took note of
every stranger who passed, as they were now taking note of us.

At the last stop we made, I checked the young man's map and
saw that he had drawn a line through all the tortuous streets to
trace the most direct route possible from the station to the bank. I
decided that if Hirasawa was guilty, then he in fact was a genius—
just for figuring out this route. We had taken so many turns by now
that if the group had left me there alone, I would still be wandering
in that neighborhood.

*Tetsuro Morikawa, Takehiko's father, was responsible for get-
ting Naruchi to write the article. Morikawa had tracked Naruchi
for years until finding him. The former policeman was reluctant at
first to write anything, but Morikawa insisted.*

*Naruchi never appeared at Hirasawa's trial because he was never
called to testify. The defense had no knowledge of his activities in
the investigation. Indeed, the defense knew nothing at all about the
731 investigation, thereby missing a critical opportunity to discredit
the MPB's case against Hirasawa. Naruchi never volunteered to be
a witness because that would have been a disgraceful exhibition of
lese-majeste. The codes of honor. Which is why Morikawa had a
hard time convincing Naruchi to publish what he knew about the
crime and investigation.*

The article led to harsh censure, most notably from Naruchi's own family. After Naruchi's death in the mid-nineteen seventies, Morikawa asked the former detective's family if Naruchi had left behind any papers or records. They said they had burned whatever documents they had found so that no more articles could be written. Such articles, in their view, betrayed professional ethics and sullied the Naruchi family name.

Naruchi was a detective who, if not directly involved in the principal investigation, knew some intimate details about it, and had published those details. Each was an indictment of the MPB's case against Hirasawa.

I asked the Society officials what reason the Justice Ministry gave for not acting on the revelations in Naruchi's article. The Society didn't know. They said the Ministry just ignored it, and none of them had asked why.

Hajime Takagi had read Naruchi's piece; he wasn't impressed. Masami Tomizawa of the Yomiuri told me that the Justice Ministry ignored the article because it had not specifically mentioned the name of the doctor that Naruchi had tracked.

Things, however, became even more confusing. Naruchi, as Tomizawa correctly said, did not name the doctor, but Tetsuro Morikawa did. In several articles and books, Morikawa named the doctor as one Saburo Suwa.

Naruchi knew about Suwa weeks after the Teikoku crime had been committed. He also knew Dr. Suwa had died sometime in 1949. Fear of a libel suit would not have been a concern for Naruchi, because a libel suit would have resulted in what the article directly or indirectly had intended—a reopening of the case to investigate Dr. Suwa's alleged connection. Indeed Saburo Suwa had been named many times, if not by Naruchi, then by Morikawa quoting Naruchi in appeal after appeal to the Justice Ministry.

Why did everyone want to steer clear of this case?

We grouped together again as Mitsumatsu and our young guide tried to decide in which direction to continue. We followed a narrow street all the way to *Yamanote-dori,* a four-lane boulevard where we stopped for the traffic light. My interpreter told me that the was not here in 1948, but the road was. Hirasawa would have only had to wait at most half-a-minute to cross. When we got to the other side, the street rose in a gentle incline.

Naruchi offered his own theory on why Hirasawa couldn't explain the source of his money: Korsakoff's disease.

Naruchi said he had discovered that Hirasawa suffered from this rare psychological disorder which, according to Naruchi, produced fits of compulsive lying in those it afflicted.

It was an interesting theory, but Korsakoff's disease is a form of brain damage generally produced by intense alcoholism, on the scale of a fifth of whiskey a day for a minimum of ten years. Symptoms include disorientation, confusion, nerve inflammation and impulsive behavior. Compulsive lying is not a specific symptom of the disease, but confabulation—the use of plausible guesses to fill memory gaps—commonly accompanies the memory disorder associated with Korsakoff's disease. Severe damage to the central cortex, such as a blow to the head, can also cause this rare disease, regardless of the person's alcohol intake.

There was no evidence that Hirasawa was an alcoholic in 1948. His mental state, both then and now, had been questioned, but no one could say whether Hirasawa ever sustained the sort of cerebral cortex damage that could bring on this disease. Maybe he had been struck on the head long ago; maybe he hadn't. There was, of course, no record.

We stopped again, and I shook my head. The young Society member told me that the bank was "about thirty meters straight ahead." I asked why we had stopped, and he said we had to walk past Mr. Aida's house, which meant finding the exact road Hirasawa allegedly took.

As part of the ruse, the killer had told the bank employees that

165

dysentery had been diagnosed at the home of a Mr. Aida, who lived in the neighborhood. Not only was Aida an actual person, but dysentery had indeed struck at his home that day. In his confession Hirasawa said that he passed Aida's house while walking to the bank, saw an American jeep out front, and learned that two Army doctors were inside treating someone for dysentery. Thus he was able to exploit this fact when carrying out his crime.

I asked the young Society member who was acting as my interpreter where Aida's house was in relation to where we now stood.

"About three blocks to the right."

"Can you see it from here?"

"No. We must walk there."

"Wait, that doesn't make any sense."

Takaji Kobayashi, Justice Minister, 1970: Hirasawa is now over seventy years old. No one should be executed at such an age. He should be released.

"Wait!" I repeated.

My interpreter turned to me, puzzled. The group walked on. It was already 3:20.

"It's three blocks to the house?" I asked.

"About that. We must turn left after three blocks."

"And then what?"

"The house is in the middle of the next block."

"And how do we get to the bank?"

"We pass the house, then turn left again."

"And come *back* three blocks?"

"*Hai.*"

"So it's a detour of about seven blocks total?"

"*Hai.*"

"And we can't see the house from here?"

"*Hai.*"

166

"And from where we are now, it's a straight line of about thirty meters to the bank?"

My interpreter nodded.

"Why would Hirasawa have taken a detour of seven blocks for something he can't even see from here, when all he had to do was keep walking straight, and he's already there at the bank?"

My interpreter didn't understand.

I told him again that it didn't make any sense to me.

Hirasawa said that he had just happened upon Aida's house and discovered the dysentery case by chance. He also said he had taken this route which we had walked and were about to complete. There was no evident reason why anyone about to commit a meticulously timed, premeditated murder would make a seven-block detour for something he can't see, when he *can* see the bank straight ahead of him. The only plausible explanation for such a deviation from his course would be that Hirasawa already knew the Army jeep and the doctors were at Aida's house for dysentery treatment. But if he already knew this, then he had no need to make a detour to see it. This point of the confession wasn't just inconsistent; it was ridiculous. Hadn't anyone remembered that the dysentery ruse had been used in the rehearsals?

"This is what Hirasawa said he did," my young interpreter told me. " We must catch up."

Mitsuo Setouchi, Justice Minister, 1974: Hirasawa is now over seventy, and no one that old should be executed. . . .

We walked three blocks ahead and turned left, then continued until we stopped in front of a set of small, red-brick buildings. Aida's house was no longer standing. A new building had been constructed on the ground where Aida's house had stood.

Mitsumatsu pointed to one building and said it used to be Aida's house. Takehiko pointed to another one and said no, this was Aida's house.

A television docudrama on the Teikoku crime had problems while filming. The actor playing the role of the killer could not manipulate the medicine dropper. He held it from above by the rubber bubble, letting it dangle. This was the same way I would hold it. This was also the same way Hirasawa said he held it. Several actors tried to work the dropper but, like the original actor, failed to manage it in such a way that accurate measurements of liquid could be drawn. A physician was consulted, and he demonstrated the proper technique: The dropper was laid diagonally across his open palm so that the bubble could be grasped by his thumb and index finger; his hand closed on the dropper, which was then held somewhat like a dagger. This was also the way survivors remembered the killer using the pipette.

It was 3:24. Mitsumatsu and Takehiko looked at both brick buildings and talked to each other. After a moment they agreed that the one Takehiko had pointed out was Aida's former house. Across the street lay a vacant lot. We walked to the end of the block, then cut back toward the bank, which we approached from the rear.

"I am 100 percent sure of Hirasawa's guilt. . . ." Tamigorō Igii, Detective, Tokyo Metropolitan Police Board.

Ever since we crossed *Yamanote-dori,* the road had been steadily rising. On January 26, 1948, with sleet and rain, the drainage would have all flowed back Hirasawa's way.

Inspector Igii, hidden in the doorway of his house, told TV reporters who wanted to interview him: "It's very impolite for you to come. I have nothing but bad memories from Teigin."

I could see the Nagasaki Shinto Shrine across from the bank.

Kenichi Asano argued in his book that the Japanese press behaved irresponsibly when reporting crime. Tomizawa knew Asano. The two of them once covered the same murder case. Tomizawa claimed that Asano had gathered all his information solely from the defense attorney and never from the police. Tomizawa said, "Asano's too young to write a book about crime reporting." Everybody here knew everybody else. Everybody discredited everybody. Everybody wanted to know the truth, but nobody wanted to tell it.

Finally we arrived at where the Teikoku Bank had stood. Different owners had changed the look of the building over the years but the basic structure was still there. The wooden fence had disappeared years ago, and had been replaced by an iron gate. The tall, wild trees had also been replaced. Now smaller, younger trees and neatly-shaped shrubbery stood around a cool, quiet fountain. What had been wooden panels at the front of the bank were now automatic sliding glass doors, and what had been dirt roads on each side of the bank were now paved streets with painted crosswalks.

My watch read 3:26. It had taken us thirty-six minutes to walk from the station to the bank, with some delays.

Riichi Takeuchi had said that GHQ did not censor the Yomiuri on the investigation. The GHQ documents from the Archives said otherwise. Not a major contradiction but another point that kept bothering me.

Mitsumatsu walked through the iron gate and headed for the glass doors. With an electric hum the doors parted, and a stout, elderly man inside bowed to Mitsumatsu as he entered.

"It's now a real estate office," Takehiko told my interpreter. "After the bank closed, a Sumo wrestler bought the building and changed it into a restaurant. It did not do well. He sold it. I don't remember what happened to it after that."

I nodded, and headed for the gate.

Seiryo Okuno, Justice Minister in 1975: Hirasawa has not yet paid for his crime. He should not be released.

Inside I met Mitsumatsu and the stout, elderly gentleman, who now owned the building. He had bought it twelve years ago, and had put it through some major changes.

He had removed the back half of the original building and then turned the open space into an exquisite garden. Later he installed a small aviary, where he kept exotic birds. Inside the building, he repositioned walls to create more open space, and he also raised the ceilings. Sofas, chairs, cabinets, and several aquariums filled the large room. On the floor were artworks, bonsai trees, and three magnificently plumed birds in elaborate cages.

Business had been very good for him, he told us. Someday, however, he hoped to move into the building next door, raze this one, and construct a religious shrine on this land.

In 1948, after the mass murder, the building was first offered for sale. The present owner told us that he could have bought it then, but waited because the memory of the killings was still too repulsive, too vivid. I checked my watch and noticed that exactly thirty-seven years ago, at this exact hour, sixteen people were dead or dying on the very floor on which I now stood.

It's a western crime, bank robbery. It's a western crime.

Three nights ago I had asked Takehiko if he agreed, and he had said yes. I asked what his theory was on the motive for the crime. He reiterated his father's interpretation that the Army Chemical Corps may well have wanted to verify some of Ishii's work, meaning that the crime itself was something of an experiment.

The theory had sounded farfetched to me at first, but I learned that two other significant Japanese figures, Seichō Matsumoto and Saburo Ienaga, supported this same theory.

Matsumoto was a Japanese mystery writer, famous in Japan for his stories that blame the Occupation for many of Japan's problems.

He had been regarded as an extremist, but when the U.S. Army's deal with the 731 Regiment became known, and as Japan emerged in the 1970s as a nationalistic power, Matsumoto's views were no longer so easily dismissed.

Ienaga was a venerated Japanese historian, known for his many scholarly volumes. Ienaga repeated to me this same theory, which he had also postulated in his book, The Pacific War, *a lengthy and well-documented historical account dealing in part with Ishii and the 731 Regiment.*

As proof of the theory, Takehiko's father mentioned a man named Shintani whom he met and befriended after the Occupation. Shintani had worked for American intelligence operations during the Occupation. He told Takehiko's father that sometime in 1947 an American intelligence officer asked him to assist in an experiment on disease prevention, in which he would play the role of a doctor. Either the alleged experiment was never conducted or someone else was used, because Shintani never heard from the officer again, but the solicitation had been made.

Shintani's testimony would have been explosive had it been included in an appeal to the Justice Ministry, but it never was used. Maybe Shintani had invented the whole story. Maybe Morikawa had. The claim remained unsubstantiated and, like so much else in the Teikoku affair, unverified.

We spent approximately twenty minutes with the owner of the former Teikoku Bank building. He did not know we were coming that day, but treated us courteously, as though we were invited guests. He inquired about Hirasawa and commented that thirty years in prison was certainly a long time. Although he voiced no opinion about Hirasawa's innocence or guilt, he did express his wishes for Hirasawa's release. Many Japanese shared the same sentiment. They didn't really think much about the Teikoku affair, but felt that even if guilty, Hirasawa had served his time and should not be executed.

Mitsumatsu and the owner exchanged namecards, then bowed once again to each other, and we went back outside to where Takehiko, the convicted artist's adopted son and heir, waited for us.

Hirasawa's wife divorced him in 1952. His daughters entirely dissociated themselves from him once his conviction was upheld. The society in which he had raised his daughters had also shaped and dictated their actions. No matter how suspect the case against Hirasawa was, it was the only thing for them to do in the light of such dishonor. And when they abandoned their father, no one thought less of them, least of all Hirasawa himself.

We grouped together once again, as Takehiko said he wanted to visit a second-hand bookstore nearby. Its owner had sent a note to Tetsuro Morikawa, who had died before he could answer. In the note the man said he thought he could help the Society with some information.

We walked in the opposite direction from which we had come, taking less than five minutes to get to the bookstore. In the back we met the owner, a pleasant man in simple clothes, who took us up a rear staircase to his apartment. We removed our shoes and put on slippers, then stepped through the narrow, bright kitchen and onto the tatami mats of the next room.

Everyone his age who lived in the area, he said, still remembered what they were doing on January 26, 1948. He had been at work in the store downstairs, taking note of the time because he wanted to get to the Teikoku Bank and make a deposit before it closed for the day at 3:00 P.M. Business at the bookstore had been good that Monday, so good that he had lost track of the hour until it was almost closing time at the bank. Still there would be time, he thought, because a friend of his worked at the Teikoku Bank as a clerk and his friend had often let him in to make transactions after the bank had formally closed for business.

He went out into the cold rain and took a shortcut that brought

172

him around the rear of the bank, on the incline. That day the mud and the runoff from the rainfall were terrible. His memory had faded on many things, but he vividly recalled sinking into the mud beyond his ankles and even up to his shins, especially on the last muddy stretch of road on the incline behind the bank.

He knocked on the side door of the bank and asked for his friend but was told that everyone was very busy totalling receipts and deposits and that no more transactions could be made that day. He told us that by taking the shortcut he had arrived at the bank at about 3:05. Wet and disappointed he went back to the store. Sometime after he left, the killer appeared at the same side door.

If the Society had had the support of Hirasawa's daughters instead of their silence, then the Society's appeals for the artist's release would have carried some added weight. Of course, the Justice Ministry would probably have acted no differently on his case. Still, their endorsement could only have helped the Society, and, certainly to westerners, it seemed suspect that they would not want to help their own father.

The two older daughters still lived in Japan, but refused any association with the Society. The youngest of the daughters married an American not long after Hirasawa's conviction, and then moved to the States. In 1982 or 1983 (again, no Society official could remember for certain) Hirasawa received a letter from his youngest daughter. It was the first communication he had received from any of his children since 1952. She wrote that she had been thinking about him and that she hoped he was well. She did not include any return address, but Hirasawa recalled that she had mentioned in the letter that she was still enjoying life in America.

I asked if anyone had saved the envelope to check the postmark. Takehiko and Mitsumatsu looked at each other, then back at me, and Takehiko said, with great chagrin, no. Hirasawa, they thought, threw the envelope away.

Takehiko and Mitsumatsu were especially interested in the bookstore owner's remark about the deep mud, and about the bank's rear area, through which Hirasawa was said to have passed. Takehiko pointed out that mud as deep as this man remembered would have covered the boots of anyone who had approached the bank from the rear. The Teikoku killer had worn rubber boots that Monday, and if he had walked to the bank as Hirasawa's confession had said, his boots and perhaps his pants as well would have been coated with mud.

I asked how much of the killer's legs had been covered by his boots.

Takehiko reached into the shoulder bag he was carrying and pulled out a burnt-orange rubber boot, a duplicate, he said, of the type Hirasawa said he had worn. It rose to about mid-shin.

No survivor, not even Miss Akuzawa who gave the killer slippers that afternoon, had mentioned any trace of mud, but it was safe to assume that there couldn't have been much mud on his boots, otherwise no one would have been able to notice the color. Takehiko said that the extent of the mud had never been mentioned before and he believed this was a significant piece of evidence. Mitsumatsu asked the gentleman if he would write an official statement to be used in an appeal.

Two sons of Hidehiko Nishimura, a clerk killed in the Teikoku Bank: There's no proof that Hirasawa is the criminal. He has been in prison so long. We doubt that he is the killer. If he is, though, we could never forgive him.

The bookstore owner wrote down everything he had just told us, and then signed it. Takehiko thanked him and then we excused ourselves, put our shoes back on, and went back outside.

"There's a file in Japan you'll never see."

174

As we were planning our return trip to Ikebukuro station I was trying to rationalize this circuitous, yet supposedly most direct route we had taken to the bank. I was trying to reason why any killer on his way to a crime would risk getting lost as we had (and we had maps) and then just happen to stumble three blocks out of his way, the entire time risking being recognized by people in the neighborhood. Wouldn't he have had to rehearse the tortuous route prior to the day of the crime? And didn't people in the neighborhood take special notice of strangers, as they had when we had walked past the windows of their homes?

Hirasawa had left his son-in-law's house wearing none of the clothing that the survivors remembered the killer had worn. When and where did he find the time and the place to change clothes, and still get to the bank so soon after three o'clock that afternoon?

As I stood thinking, I was looking at something in front of me but not focusing. Suddenly my vision cleared.

I was looking at a JNR station not more than seventy yards away from the bank, and more than that, it was a straight walk. I looked at the bank, I looked at the station, and I pulled the arm of my interpreter.

"What station is that?" I asked.

"Shiinamachi station."

"Does the train that passes through it go to Ikebukuro station?"

"Yes."

"Did it go there in 1948?"

"Yes."

"Then why would Hirasawa walk the long and confusing route we took, when he could take the train directly here?"

"We do not know, but this is what Hirasawa said he did."

"If you apply Japanese standards to it, then it's all routine." Horiguchi was right.

Mitsumatsu didn't know why the killer would not have travelled to Shiinamachi station, only seventy yards from the Teikoku Bank, rather than getting off at Ikebukuro station and taking the labyrinthine walk from there to the bank. Neither did Takehiko. I had to admit the supreme farce of it all, and I had fallen into it: Why had I taken this part of Hirasawa's confession seriously, when every other part of it sounded either simply incredible or simply contrived? And why hadn't the Society, which had retraced Hirasawa's alleged footsteps from Ikebukuro station with this annual trek for years, asked why Hirasawa didn't go the Shiinamachi station? Had they really ignored the obvious, or had they not seen it?

Haumichi Nomura was a fish farmer who in 1964 suddenly came forward and stated that he had bought paintings from Hirasawa sometime near the end of January 1948. He had kept silent for sixteen years, he said, because his daughter was having an illicit relationship with Hirasawa at the time of the murders, and Nomura wanted no embarrassing publicity. In light of Nomura's testimony, the Justice Ministry ordered a hearing to determine if Nomura's statement warranted a retrial for Hirasawa.

One night before the hearing, Nomura got a phone call from an anonymous man who casually asked Nomura if he remembered a case not long ago when a witness was about to testify, then suddenly disappeared, for good. The caller cautioned Nomura against suffering the same fate, and suggested that he change his mind about testifying.

At the hearing Nomura stepped forward and said that he never bought any paintings from Hirasawa, that his previous statement was a lie. The judge instantly charged Nomura and a stunned Morikawa with perjury.

That was the Society's version. The Justice Ministry's version was that the hearing had flushed out two conspiring liars. I found both versions equally credible. Of course, there was no supporting evidence for Nomura's original story and no record of the threatening phone call, and my research had shown me that the manu-

facture of evidence, whether to aid the defense or the prosecution, was not uncommon in Japan.

We started to walk back to Ikebukuro, and Takehiko started the stopwatch. I was still laughing at myself for simply, and wrongly, presuming that logic was something I could pack in my suitcase and take with me, that it was transportable and transferable from culture to culture.

The Teikoku incident, I decided, was built upon cultural ciphers. It spoke its own logic, its own language.

Endo, the Society's attorney, was having the GHQ documents translated into Japanese to determine the import of the revelations that I had found in the Archives and brought with me to Tokyo. The task of translating that many pages would take as long as six weeks, he told me. Endo and the Society had two possible strategies in this thirtieth year after the Supreme Court's 1955 ruling that upheld Hirasawa's conviction and death sentence. One strategy was to file an appeal for Hirasawa's release, based solely on Japan's Human Rights Protection Law which implied that if a death row convict was not executed within thirty years of his death sentence, then he must be released from prison and given his freedom. The second strategy was to file an appeal for Hirasawa's retrial, based solely on the discovery and introduction of new evidence, specifically those revelations contained in the GHQ documents from America. The first appeal was based on the passing of time, the second was based on the passing of fact. Both were now matters of public record.

I did not know which course of action Endo and the Society would choose, and my time in Japan was ending in only a few more days.

The return trip from the bank to Ikebukuro station, with no detours, diversions, or wrong turns, took thirty minutes and twenty-eight seconds. For whatever it was worth, I made a note.

Several days later I left Japan and returned to Washington, where I mulled over all the information I had gathered. There must be some logical or cultural grid over which I could lay the pieces of the Teikoku affair and make sense of it all.

The month in Japan had deepened my understanding of the Teikoku crime's cultural context, and Takagi's revelation of his meeting with Ishii had cast new and disturbing light on GHQ's involvement in the investigation. Chief Fujita and most of the other Japanese police who had been involved with the Teikoku case were dead now, and former Inspector Igii was unwilling to talk, so the only possible way to find out any other firsthand information about the 1948 investigation was to return to the American principals.

I tried Eugene Hattori again because I wanted to know what he'd say about the March 11, 1948 meeting in which he, Engle, other PSD officers, and Chief Fujita discussed the former Imperial Army unit that "was sent into Manchuria (and) used (prussic acid) on humans and animals successfully."

He replied: "I have no knowledge of that."

Byron Engle, former Administrator-in-Charge of the Occupation's Public Safety Division, was seventy-four, retired, and living comfortably in Bethesda, Maryland when I met him.

Henry Eaton and Arthur Kimberling, Engle's former PSD colleagues, had died years ago.

I found Jack Munroe, former PSD investigator, living in Ocala, Florida. I spoke with both Engle and Munroe, and neither recalled much about the Teikoku crime except that it was, in their words, "extraordinary." They did, however, remember Jirō Fujita and the MPB rather well. Engle, whom I interviewed at greater length, said the Japanese police were "inherently good investigators." Munroe agreed. Engle had nothing but high compliments for Fujita and the investigative talents of the Japanese police during the time the PSD was operating.

Both Engle and Munroe told me that the PSD never had any evidence that the Japanese police abused or tortured prisoners for confessions, either before or during the Occupation. Engle pointed to the communist countries, saying that their police forces were notorious for such tactics. He acknowledged that there may have been reports of Japanese police abuse, but that none had been substantiated. He also admitted that his memory may not be totally reliable.

The records I found in the Archives, however, told a different story. The SCAP (Supreme Commander for the Allied Powers) "Monograph on Police Reform" outlined the extent of Japan's abusive police system. Because the Meiji Constitution either had "no proscriptions of such activities, or the proscriptions had been easily subverted," the Monograph stressed the following measures for countering some old practices:

> 1. elimination of authority to detain persons for unlimited periods and to exercise summary court jurisdiction.
>
> 2. elimination of power to arrest without a warrant.
>
> 3. requirement of immediate advice of charges against arrested individual.
>
> 4. requirement that an arrestee be advised of his right to talk privately with counsel.
>
> 5. guarantee of privacy in a home except after due legal process.
>
> 6. *elimination of torture, of illegal detention, of the use of the Third Degree, of extorted confessions, and of unnecessary secrecy.*

7. *outlawing conviction where a confession was the only proof against the accused.*

8. requirement that police make certain that a suspect was aware of his rights, including provision that he might not be compelled to testify against himself. (emphasis added)

The Monograph further observed:

In a land where persons had not been able to move freely and where the neighborhood associations made apprehension of suspects easy, the police had never experienced great need for perfecting techniques to uncover and prepare conclusive evidence of guilt. Retraining thus became a necessity if the new reforms were to be effective in preserving law and order.

Engle discounted the Monograph on Police Reforms, and said it was probably compiled by "a nonprofessional." A curious choice of words, I thought, since it implied that only a "professional" could define and comment on obvious abuses of authority.

Exactly who compiled the Monograph was not clear from the report, so Engle's point might have been valid, were it not for further records from his own department that resoundingly contradicted him.

One hundred forty-four declassified documents, which I secured from the National Archives through the Freedom of Information Act after my return from Japan, revealed a great deal about the level of police competence during the Occupation. They related to the investigation of the death of Japanese National Railroads (JNR) president Sadanori Shimoyama, one of Japan's few unsolved cases.

When Shimoyama's body was discovered in pieces along a railroad track outside of Tokyo in July of 1949, the Japanese police began an immediate and reportedly extensive investigation. As in the Teikoku case, the autopsies performed on the body led the coroners to conflicting conclusions. There was admittedly little for the doctors to work with. The head had been smashed, and no brains were left to examine. Tokyo University Hospital maintained that Shimoyama had been run over *after* death, implying that he had been murdered. Keiō University Hospital ruled Shimoyama's death a suicide because the coroner there found no sign of foul play. At the top of the list of items in dispute was Shimoyama's bloodless corpse, save for a discharge from the right testicle. As the coroners debated explanations for the mysterious condition of the body, the Tokyo police fell into a state of confusion.

The PSD was notified of Shimoyama's death after his body was identified, and an investigator was promptly assigned to the case in an advisory role.

On July 11, 1949, five days after the body was discovered, the PSD investigator filed a Confidential report, in which he stated:

> Due to poor and incompetent manner in which (Metropolitan Police Department) is conducting this investigation, information has only been forthcoming in response to questions put by the (PSD) investigator. Elementary procedures have been overlooked and simple routine investigation requirements left undone.

Four days later a PSD administrator filed a memorandum and similarly noted:

> From investigation conducted to date it is quite apparent that the police are slow in gathering routine police information. . . . Whether Shimoyama was murdered or committed suicide should not stop the police in gathering every bit of information possible.

In another Confidential report written on July 19 the PSD investigator remarked how the police ignored a critically valuable lead:

> MAKAJI, Taneyoshi, according to reports, visited the

181

home of SHIMOYAMA, at 8:00 A.M., July 6th (only hours after discovery of the body), at which time he made a request of the brother of SHIMOYAMA, to issue a statement as being that of SHIMOYAMA, himself, declaring his suicide as "I, SHIMOYAMA, am taking my life, with the intent of promoting better relationship between Capital and labor in their current strife," or words to that effect. No further details were offered by (police inspector) Togawa, another example of the incomplete investigations made by the Metropolitan Police Department.

Dozens of other documents revealed that the police had to be prodded to check many leads in the Shimoyama case. Both Engle and Munroe had said the PSD rarely got directly involved in Japanese investigations because the police were working on "hundreds" of cases at any one time, and there were only a handful of PSD investigators available. The PSD's police branch devoted full attention to the Shimoyama case because it was so politically charged. The Occupation's economic retrenchment plan had recently gone into effect, and only days before his death, Shimoyama had announced wholesale firings of union employees. Hostile labor unions made the atmosphere throughout Japan dangerously volatile.

However, one last note from another Confidential report revealed more about the police force's investigative shortcomings, as well as about the relationship between the PSD and the Japanese police. It read, in part:

To date, the police have avoided as much as possible, direct questioning of important witnesses and in this manner important testimony is being held up that would probably clarify this case. However, direct investigation by the (PSD) investigator has been avoided to date to avoid possible interpretation of (PSD) interference by MPD who are jealous of their responsibility.

It was also evident from these documents that the PSD investigators assisted and advised the MPB as much as possible during the Shimoyama investigation. At first, the Japanese police leaned toward the murder theory, then they switched to the suicide theory. Despite many attempts, including those by the PSD, the case has never been conclusively resolved.

Nonetheless, the documents had significant relevance to the Teikoku investigation as well. Police incompetence in both instances helped to obscure, and even to lose, important pieces of evidence in both cases.

Engle and Munroe had also said that the PSD did not have evidence that the Japanese police were abusing suspects. This may have been true, but other GHQ documents I found said that somebody else did. The National Archives' Modern Military Field Branch released a comprehensive report to me which the Attorney-General's Office and Japan's Civil Liberties Bureau had compiled in 1951 and had delivered to the Occupation's Legal Section.

> Cases where human rights were infringed by members of the Police Service personnel (from 1948 to end of December, 1950)
> . . .cases relating to acts of violence, cruelty, and forced confession.

24 April 1948
Confession was forced through   Advice was given.
infliction of torture.

30 September 1948
Confession was forced by means of   Passed unnoticed.
threats.

10 February 1949
Through infliction of violence   Warning was given.
confession was forcibly demanded.

14 July 1948
Same as above.   Passed unnoticed.

29 March 1949
Same as above.   Advice was given.

25 May 1949
Same as above.   Passed unnoticed.

11 July 1949
Inquiry was made of a woman   Advice was given.
who was kept undressed
throughout inquiry.

28 May 1949
Confession was forced by   Advice was given.
means of torture.

21 October 1949
Confession was demanded   Passed unnoticed.
through acts of violence.

27 September 1949
Confession was forced by   Passed unnoticed.
means of torture.

2 February 1950
Confession was forced through   Making decision was suspended.
threats.

7 April 1950
Through violence and infliction   Passed unnoticed.
of injury, confession was forced.

10 May 1950
Confession was forced by means   Making decision was suspended.
of torture.

—1950
As the person was subjected to   Passed unnoticed.
cruel investigation, he committed
suicide later.

3 April 1950
In making investigation, threats   Passed unnoticed.
were used, and photographs were
taken.

8 January 1950
The police committed acts of cruelty to a woman on the excuse of making a search of her person.

The case was settled in accordance with advice.

18 September 1950
Confession was forced through violence and infliction of injury.

Under investigation.

27 August 1950
Same as above.

The case was settled administratively in accordance with advice.

7-8 March 1950
Confession was forced by way of insulting investigation.

Under investigation

2 October 1950
Confession was forced through torture.

Advice given.

25 October 1950
Same as above.

Under investigation.

11 July 1950
Same as above.

Ditto.

17 October 1950
Same as above.

Ditto.

16 June 1950
As investigation was severe, the person committed suicide after his return home.

Passed unnoticed.

6 May 1950
During investigation, coercion and abuse were employed to force confession.

Passed unnoticed.

4 July 1950
Confession was forced by giving mental and physical pain during investigation lasting deep into the night.

Advice given.

30 August 1950
Taking advantage of the feeble   Passed unnoticed.
mind of the person, the police
forced him to make false
confession. . . .

The report contained nearly eight hundred incidents of police violence. In only fewer than ten cases were the allegations unsubstantiated.

The Civil Liberties Bureau was founded in Japan in February 1948, only one month following the Teikoku killings, and for the whole year recorded a total of less than twenty cases of human rights violations. However, as the Japanese people began to understand what civil liberties were, the number of reports increased at an alarming rate. In 1949 the Bureau handled 5,076 cases, and by June the number of reported cases averaged one thousand a month. Every year the Japanese police headed the list of civil liberties violators.

Engle, however, held that his program to retrain Japanese policemen in "democratic methods" was a success, mainly because the program was directly tied, as any successful social program must be, to "the political, social, economic, and cultural conditions of the country." Precisely which conditions Engle meant, feudal or democratic, remained unclear. As for the success Engle spoke of, it was certainly not immediately evident. Documented violations of suspects' civil rights by MPB officers continued after the last Japanese policeman finished the retraining program "some time around 1950." Again, Engle could not recall exactly.

On May 4, 1951, after hearing testimony by a U.S. Army eyewitness to a gruesome police attack, George M. Koshi, a Legal Section lawyer who was highly respected by his Japanese counterparts as well as by his American employers, wrote a memo on the subject of police violations in Japan. Koshi noted that the situation was bad and getting worse. The latest figures he cited indicated that as much as eighty percent of the total violations reported to the Civil Liberties Bureau involved Japanese police officials. Koshi recounted several detailed cases, characterizing each as one more "example of typical police brutality in which the police official completely identifies himself with the most vicious type of ruffian in the execution of his supposed duty of maintaining peace and order. It is, indeed, regrettable that such a feudalistic practice still exists in present day Japan."

In 1962, on the strength of having retrained one hundred thousand Japanese policemen in two months' time, Byron Engle was named the head of the Office of Public Safety (OPS), which was established to train and equip police forces of foreign governments. Engle also worked with, or for, the CIA.

According to A.J. Langguth's book *Hidden Terrors*, Engle was "recruited by the CIA after it was established in 1947," and therefore allowed OPS operations in Latin America to provide cover for illegal CIA activity, such as advice on torturing political dissidents. Langguth documented how various OPS advisors were sometimes implicated in the tortures.

The Office of Public Safety, it should be noted, was dissolved in the early 1970s after a Senate investigation disclosed, among other things, that OPS police advisors were not, as they claimed, teaching Latin American policemen how to defuse terrorist bombs, but rather how to make them.

Philip Agee, the former CIA agent who wrote *Inside the Company,* laughed when Langguth suggested that Engle might *not* be CIA. Alexis Johnson, who was instrumental in Engle's appointment to the top position at OPS, told me that Engle's "CIA connections were minimal." Johnson knew that Engle's CIA background might not look good to some people who would need to confirm Engle's selection, but he was willing to take that chance.

In his conversation with me, Engle denied working for the CIA and denounced Langguth and his book as "propagandist." Engle, it should be noted, also told Langguth that he had never known of the existence of a certain Argentinian terrorist group that later killed an OPS advisor. Langguth had proved that official OPS reports about the terrorist group were filed every month.

It was evident that the prewar police practices in Japan changed little during the Occupation period. In 1948 the Civil Liberties Bureau had issued a statement publicly charging Hajime Takagi with violating Hirasawa's rights. Takagi, in turn, thirty-seven years later, had supplied me with the most significant and damaging revelation about the Teikoku investigation since the crime occurred. But Takagi's revelation of the "meeting" with Ishii was not yet public knowledge. Confusion, intrigue, and contradiction still surrounded the Teikoku affair as Sadamichi Hirasawa, the death row artist, sat in prison, awaiting his ninety-fourth birthday.

On March 14, 1985, the Society to Save Hirasawa filed their seventeenth appeal for a retrial based on the GHQ documents. On April 5, Makoto Endo, the Society's attorney, entered an appeal with the Tokyo District Court claiming that, after thirty years, Hirasawa's death sentence had expired.

PART III
Flowering of the Bamboo

For more than half a century Tokyo has been famous as a strange and exotic place. It was once the world's third largest city and is a fascinating blend of Oriental and Occidental cultures. Early in '45 five crushing B-29 raids smashed fifty-one percent of the city into ruins, but not even incendiary bombs were able to rob Tokyo of its distinctive charm. There are still plenty of interesting places to see.

> Promotional flyer from "G.I. Tours" distributed by the 8th Army Special Services to Occupation Personnel.

On January 26, 1948, *somebody* dressed as a health official walked into the Shiinamachi branch of the Teikoku Bank sometime after three P.M. and distributed liquid from two bottles marked "First Drug" and "Second Drug" in English to all sixteen people inside. Twelve died.

The police concluded that the methodology used was so elaborate and technical that only an expert could have committed the crime. An official report, dated June 26, 1948, and discovered by Shigeo Motoike of the *Yomiuri Shimbun,* states the following:

FROM: The Criminal Affairs Division Chief, The Metropolitan Police Department

TO: Public Safety Division, The General Headquarters of the Allied Powers

It is noted that the suspect was very confident about the relationship with the amount of poison and its effect. Especially, his behavior showed he prepared everything in order such as 2 cc size pipette to be used to put 2 drops of solution from a 120 cc bottle into each person's tea cup beforehand to kill 16 people. We do not believe that it was coincidental that everything worked well. It must have been with careful calculation. Otherwise, there would have been some kind of failure, or the suspect would have left if he was not sure of the amount to be used.

Secondly, it is noted that the suspect was very confident about the timing effect of the poison.

He prepared the first drug and the second drug for those to take.

The first drug is suspected to be a poison and the second one must have been a harmless liquid such as water.

The reason for the above assumption is that the suspect dealt the first drug with great care and the amount was small and strong. But the second one did not seem to have any strong taste and he dealt with it without any concern. At Teigin, he prepared this in a big bottle and laid it at the foot of the desk. He poured the liquid directly from the bottle into cups without using a pipette and even made some people drink two cups. . . . The suspect told people "this is a counteragent so you do not have to take it".

He allowed one minute between the first and second drug. This one minute was extremely important because he had all the people who had swallowed poison under his control and the poison was starting to take effect on individuals at varying degrees depending on their body size during this minute. If he left these people free at that time, it would have been dangerous for him because some might have gone out of the room to ask for help, right after swallowing the poison. He calculated that "it is OK" after everyone took the first medicine, one minute later, then the second one. . . .

Thirdly, it is the way he made them swallow. . . . He stuck his tongue out and showed them how to swallow it at once. This is the most effective way to take a stimulant hydrocyanic solution without throwing up. Especially, the way he made them trust him by taking medicine himself is quite professional and it shows he has some kind of experience in handling the poison.

The stolen money, including the check, totalled approximately one hundred eighty thousand yen. The amount left behind in stacked bills on a desk was three hundred thousand yen.

The same police report of 26 June 1948 describes the killer based on survivors' statements:

. . .he was around 40 to 54 or 55 years old.

Most people said around 50. On the other hand, when we consider the calmness, speech and behavior, healthy skin and handwriting of the suspect, that age seems right. And so if a suspect appears to be in his thirties or sixties, he is not the right suspect.

* Height . . . 158 cm - 161 cm

Most witnesses noticed the height of the suspect as between 158 cm - 168 cm. The majority said it was around 158 cm - 161 cm. And so if the height of a person is less than 151 cm or over 170 cm, he is unlikely to be a suspect.

* Weight . . . medium

Most witnesses said he is of medium build. Only one person said he is a little fat. So we can safely assume that the suspect is of medium weight or a little bit thinner than normal.

* Face . . . He is handsome. . . . There are slight differences of opinion as to the shape of his chin, mouth and nose.

His color was pale then, but we do not know his coloration now. We excluded a stain on his cheek and a scar on his chin on purpose to avoid too much dependence on them, but if these characteristics were found, he is a possible suspect.

* Hair ... White hair mixed with black. At that time he had a short haircut and mixed white hair, but we do not know now. Considering a possible disguise, he might look different now....

Sadamichi Hirasawa said he was the man.

Dr. Shigeru Matsui's namecard had been used in the November 1947 rehearsal of the technique used in the Teikoku crime. Hirasawa had exchanged cards with Matsui in July 1947, but when Detective Tamigorō Igii asked Hirasawa for Matsui's card, the artist could not produce it. Later, he behaved suspiciously as Igii questioned him about the Teikoku killings.

Igii investigated Hirasawa and discovered he had little money before the crime, but soon afterward had cash reserves roughly matching the total amount stolen from the Teikoku Bank. Hirasawa could never satisfactorily explain the sources of the cash.

Igii maintained that Hirasawa was, in January, desperate for cash to cover gambling debts and to support his mistresses, who were never identified. According to Igii, the robbery had originated as the plot of a mystery Hirasawa intended to write, until the would-be author got the idea of actually carrying out the plan.

Hirasawa's alibi was never corroborated. Neither was Igii's claim.

After sixty-two interrogations in thirty-five days, Hirasawa confessed.

Hirasawa's confession was detailed and specific, and on the surface sounded convincing. However, 'it also had some serious inconsistencies.

Hirasawa said he walked from Ikebukuro station to the Teikoku Bank. The prosecution claimed he left the station at 2:50 P.M. and arrived at the bank by 3:15. On a clear day, accompanied by people who had taken the route before, and using maps, I walked from Ikebukuro station to where the Teikoku Bank used to stand. It took me thirty minutes and, unlike Hirasawa, I didn't have to stop to change clothes. Hirasawa said it took him twenty-five minutes to make the same walk in sleet, mud, and rain. No one asked him why he hadn't taken the train one more stop to Shiinamachi station less than seventy yards from the bank.

The March 11, 1948, document summarizing the meeting between Chief Fujita and several members of the PSD reveals a more serious contradiction.

The police were positive the crime required expertise in toxicology, and such expertise convincingly appeared to have come from former members of a secret poison school where techniques of mass poisoning were perfected through successful experiments on animals, and humans. We also know from the document that certain former members of this school were acting as police informants, and were afraid of public exposure which would lead assuredly to a war crimes investigation and trial. More interestingly, the document noted that the school's experiments involved prussic acid, a cyanide-base compound which, Fujita said in this meeting, "was the poison used in the Teikoku Bank." Five months later Sadamichi Hirasawa was accused of killing with potassium cyanide, the poison he admitted using in the Teikoku murders. Unless you know a few things about toxicology and history, the inconsistency seems insignificant.

It was lost on me until I talked to a pharmacologist, who listened carefully as I outlined what happened inside the Teikoku

Bank. The salient point, he said, was the survivors' recollection of "a white, chalky substance" at the bottom of the murky liquid inside the bottle marked First Drug. The survivors remembered that the killer skimmed the top of the solution for his own dose, then plunged the dropper to the bottom, into the precipitate, for the doses he gave everyone else. A difference of procedure that could mean life or death, and did.

Several methods of precipitation exist, and each one must be precisely computed to complete the process thoroughly. Potassium cyanide can be precipitated by introducing any high volume of alcohol—such as acetone or ethyl alcohol—into a mixture of water and a highly concentrated solution of potassium cyanide. Most of the poison crystals will thus go to the bottom, but not all, unless the person handling the substances has been careful enough to neutralize the tiny poison crystals that float on top of the liquid. In the hands of an expert, a small dose of the liquid may not be lethal (hence the few drops on his tongue for the tactical demonstration). He will also know that a certain amount of potassium cyanide can be inactivated inside the body and that all that's necessary to kill a human is around fifty milligrams. The symptoms are burning of the throat and a feeling of weakness, the same symptoms reported by survivors of the Teikoku poisoning. If the solution is weak, some will survive.

Whatever the solution was, at least one minute elapsed before any signs showed. This fact alone indicates the solution the killer used was borderline. That four survived confirms it. Hirasawa said in his confession that he had taken 15.9 grams of potassium cyanide and mixed it in 80 cc of water, and from that mixture he gave each person a 5 cc dose. These amounts work out to an approximately one gram dose of potassium cyanide per person. Anyone taking this much potassium cyanide would be dead, in the words of the experts, before he hit the floor. One gram of potassium cyanide is a larger amount than that found in a suicide capsule.

The above principles apply to prussic acid, save for one critical difference. Any form of cyanide is deadly since it blocks the body's ability to use oxygen, but the toxicity of prussic acid is higher than that of potassium cyanide. The liquid left after precipitating prussic acid is potentially lethal even in a minuscule dose. Which means that anybody using prussic acid has to be even that much more experienced, and practiced.

Apply Japanese standards to the Teikoku crime, Bob Horiguchi said, and it's all routine.

During the prewar and wartime years, when the militarists invoked the name of the Emperor to secure their power, Japan's police became the civilian agents of military aggression and suppression. Edicts like the 1925 "Law Against Dangerous Thoughts" made it illegal to espouse anything that could be interpreted even remotely as a threat to the Emperor. This law led to the creation of the Thought Section of the Criminal Affairs Bureau, whose job it was to ensure that anyone thinking dangerous thoughts was properly dealt with. Though opinion is divided on how extensive were the human rights violations committed by the Thought Section, there is little difference of opinion over the terror the *Tokko*, or Special Higher Police, wreaked on the Japanese. Their brutality was surpassed only by that of the *Kempei Tai*, or military police. Random beheadings and rapes were the signatures of the *Kempei Tai*, as documented by historians, victims, witnesses, and the IMT.

Also, Japan's procuracy and judiciary, remodelled in 1889 on the Continental system in which the accused bore a good part of the burden of proof, had been subverted during the war years. The Continental system itself was as likely to release a suspect as to bind him over for trial. But as the militarists fanned the fires of Emperor worship, so the agents of the Emperor stood more firm and immovable. In the Meiji Constitution of 1889 it was written that the courts would exercise the law "in the name of the Emperor." With that, the Minister of Justice came to be regarded as a member of the Imperial family, and beneath him was the hierarchy of judges, prosecutors, and policemen. In this system, a mistake by one agent was perceived as a mistake by all, and the system would brook no errors. Anyone who was responsible for the hierarchy's losing face might not be promoted for years, or might even be demoted. Thus, a judge might collude with a prosecutor or merely disregard egregiously flimsy evidence when a case came to trial, all to preserve the integrity, as it were, of the system. Accordingly, appeals against a verdict were useless.

Chalmers Johnson noted that one of the important differences between the Continental (semi-accusatorial) system and the Anglo-American (adversarial) system is the former's focus in criminal cases on the questions of "Who did it, and why?" as opposed to the latter's focus on "How do we know who did it?" When "Who did it, and why?" are the priority questions in a court structured in favor of the judiciary and prosecution, the accused is pressured for an answer, and guilt or innocence is determined on his answer's plausibility. Taking no chances, prosecutors were known to script logical confessions so that plausibility was assured. However, the more elaborate or complex the crime, such as the Teikoku murder-robbery, the harder it was to script a consistent confession.

With the outbreak of war, the *kensatsu fassho* as they called it, or fascism of the procuracy, prevailed. After the war, the Occupation authorities tried to stop the widespread injustices of the Japanese legal system. The new Provisional Codes of Criminal Procedure, enacted with the new Constitution on May 3, 1947, stipulated that a warrant (hitherto unknown) for arrest had to be issued before a suspect could be detained. The suspect had to be immediately informed of why he'd been arrested and advised of his right to counsel. He had forty-eight hours to clear himself; failing that, the prosecutor had to take custody of him and within twenty-four hours either release him or get a warrant for detention from a judge.

This warrant was good for ten days, renewable one time. Total legal detention time was twenty-three days, after which the suspect was to be released in the absence of formal charges filed. The Japanese judiciary fought hard to extend the detention time, but this point was one of the few on which SCAP fought back with firm resolve.

In his book Johnson described the impact of these new codes:

> These safeguards sound good on paper. . .(and though) 23 days. . .is not as long as was possible under the old law. . .it is a long enough time for most procurators merely to have adapted their procedures to it. There are other safeguards. . .but there are also escape clauses, provisions that sound very much like the old procedure—for example, judges are allowed to take secret testimony from witnesses prior to trial when the likelihood exists that such testimony would be contradicted in open court. Many of the clauses that the American drafters thought they were allowing in the new code in order to deal with highly unusual situations turned out, in fact, to establish new—old—norms.

On January 1, 1949, the Provisional Codes of Criminal Procedure, with minor changes, became the final codes. However, the Japanese police and procuracy, which had been trained in semi-accusatorial principles, had difficulty interpreting the new codes, which were based in SCAP's own words on the "Anglo-Saxon concept of presumption of innocence until guilt was established by regular court action." No monitoring system was established. The police and procuracy were expected to police themselves.

Another of SCAP's major moves was the controversial, wholesale purge in 1946 of all Japanese public service personnel who were suspected of "ultra-nationalist sentiment." Even the remotest suspicion of warmongering cost people their jobs. The purges, however, were only partially effective and never achieved the immediate effect

SCAP wanted, which was to neutralize the elements that might rekindle Japan's war sentiments.

Hirasawa's chance for a fair trial was almost nonexistent because SCAP's purges didn't extend to judges. One of Hirasawa's more unfortunate distinctions is that he was the last man to go to trial under the old Imperial code, and before prewar judges.

The Occupation instantly dissolved the Special Higher Police and the Thought Section, but Byron Engle's massive retraining for the nation's police force wasn't to happen for another four years. Accordingly, when the Teikoku crime occurred the policemen who investigated it were those who had survived the purges or who had been hired in the last two years. Their basic procedures were still those of prewar and wartime days. It's generally accepted among Japanese and American experts and observers that the Japanese police didn't begin responding to democratic reforms until a decade after the Occupation ended.

To be fair, the judicial and police systems during the Occupation were at a disadvantage. There existed no precedents to assist the judges and procurators in interpreting the new criminal codes. In the absence of a clear supervisory system, the police were unsure about how to proceed. Everyone simply reverted to established procedures, and with good reason: The new codes were confusing and old ways die hard.

There was more than just the old ways, however, propelling the case against Hirasawa toward either a confession or an indictment. The Attorney General's Office and the Civil Liberties Bureau attacked the basis on which the warrant for Hirasawa's arrest was issued, saying that it was unconstitutional. Igii's remark also fell under severe criticism because of its attack on Hirasawa's reputation. The more that civil liberties officials pressed the police to account for Igii's remark, the more police dodged the question. Had Hirasawa been released, the police and procuracy could have been held liable under the new State Redress Law and the Criminal Indemnity Law. The first law would apply if the state was proved to have willfully or negligently damaged Hirasawa's civil rights. Not only would an unprecedented public apology be required, but also financial compensation.

In the second law, which applied after a trial, a not-guilty verdict would have required the same compensation. Both laws had only recently come into effect, and Hirasawa's case was the first to test them. Moreover, after eyewitnesses cleared Hirasawa, the Civil Liberties Bureau announced that as soon as Hirasawa was released, a full investigation would be launched of police and procuracy conduct in the case. All judicial and investigative authorities would have had to explain their actions. It was a demand that had been unheard of in the history of the Japanese judiciary. The only way to avoid answering both the new laws and the inquiry was to net a confession and a guilty verdict. In Hirasawa's case, the police and procurators got both.

At the heart of the Teikoku mystery lies the complex question of motive: the killer's, the Tokyo Metropolitan Police Board's, and GHQ's.

In their investigation of the Teigin incident, the Japanese police misinterpreted the killer's motive. Robbery is an insufficient motive in this case for two reasons: First, more money was left than was taken; second, robbery fails to account for the ruthlessly sociopathic methodology.

The police accurately saw parallel behavior between Hirasawa's self-confessed ruses to bilk people and the deception practiced by the Teikoku killer. But the police failed to see that Hirasawa's dissemblings had never required any scientific expertise. When Hirasawa's sudden wealth became known, the police investigated the artist, believing robbery to be the primary motive.

It was characteristic of the police to base investigations on a round-up of usual suspects, detaining only those who lacked an alibi. In his book *Conspiracy at Matsukawa,* Chalmers Johnson explained the efficiency of such a formula, and also revealed its flaw:

> It does not seem likely that the police made many mistakes—they knew their own society too well—but it is equally undeniable that they launched most investigations on the basis of a hypothesis as to motive. Whenever this hypothesis turned out to be wrong, disaster usually resulted: false confessions were elicited or manufactured, and the police stuck to them through thick and thin. To do otherwise would have seriously damaged their prestige. The only real change in the postwar world was that confessions had to be reinforced with physical evidence. Too often, it appears, this evidence was collected with the confession in mind; and evidence that contradicted it was either discarded or ignored.

In solving the Teikoku murder-robbery, the police were faced with accounting for two motives for the same crime, and they pursued the easier one. The more difficult was murder, and neither motive alone was fully adequate to explain the crime. If the sole motive was robbery, then why was any money left, and if the sole motive was murder, why was any money taken?

Perhaps the key to understanding the Teikoku crime is to imagine what would have happened had no one survived.

One explanation for the crime that would satisfy both motives is that a former 731 member or poison school graduate decided to use his wartime expertise to commit the perfect bank robbery. At the Teikoku Bank the police had originally suspected food poisoning, and had no one survived, they might never have investigated further. As it was, no precedent for this methodology existed in Japan, and so the police were completely baffled. Further, if there had been no survivors, the killer would have been free to commit the same crime again because both his identity and his methodology would have gone undetected. Maybe this hadn't been designed as a singular incident. Thieves seldom quit after one job and the Teikoku robbery-murder might have been only the first in a planned series of bank robberies. It's important to remember that the autopsies of the victims were unable to conclusively identify the poison. An expert poisoner would know that a certain amount of cyanide would be neutralized in the body and pass unnoticed, hence the low dose used by the killer.

It's not only possible but likely that the killer suffered abdominal pains shortly after taking the sample dose. Prussic acid and potassium cyanide, even in the smallest amounts, cause stomach pain, dizziness, nausea and vomiting, if not death. Maybe the killer intended to take all the money, but began suffering the effects of his own poison and had to leave before finishing the job.

Seichō Matsumoto has a different theory on motive. In his view an experimental BW unit of the U.S. Army recruited the 731 poisoners to test and confirm the techniques the poisoners had developed during the war. Matsumoto further alleges that the Teikoku crime was a test not only of the methodology for mass assassination, but also of a new type of poison which would be untraceable in an autopsy. The U.S. Army was an accomplice in murder.

A third interpretation of motive also views the Teikoku crime as a test-run, but not under GHQ's direction. Defeated soldiers often suffer depression and alienation after their return from war to civilian life. Furthermore, in this case, a conquering power occupied a bombed and gutted homeland. Three years after the Occupation began, poverty, starvation, and disease were still rampant. A resentful 731 man, embittered by the miserable living conditions and unable to apply his wartime expertise in the peacetime world, might have vented his anger and frustration through an original, ritualistic act of terror. By identifying himself with the Occupation, he was able to exploit the American symbols of power as well as the Japanese feudal submission to authority to make what could have been the first in a planned series of personal political statements. Had no one survived, he would have remained as untraceable as the poison he used, because coroners would have only been able to speculate on the cause of death. In a letter as skillfully crafted as the methodology the killer could have claimed credit for the act without exposing himself or his tactics. He would have been free to continue striking at will. In this interpretation, a bank was chosen as the target to emphasize the killer's intent: Money wasn't accidentally but deliberately left behind because terror, not robbery, was the motive.

Exactly who committed the murders will probably remain a point of conjecture. However, certain facts are documented. The police were investigating former members of 731, and with good reason, because the police knew that 731 had developed the methodology of the crime. As early as 1946, both the Tokyo police and the Occupation authorities also knew something about the Imperial Army's poisoning activities. The following exchange between the American prosecuting attorney David N. Sutton and the President of the Court during a session of the International Military Tribunal in Tokyo actually made these activities a matter of record:

> 29 August 1946
> Sutton: The enemy's TAMA Detachment (731 affiliate) carried off their (Chinese) civilian captives to the medical laboratory, where the reactions to poisonous serum was tested. This detachment was one of the most secret organizations. The number of persons slaughtered by this detachment cannot be ascertained.
>
> The President: Are you going to give us any further evidence of these alleged laboratory tests for reactions to poisonous serums? This is something entirely new, we haven't heard before. Are you going to leave it at that?
>
> Sutton: We do not at this time anticipate introducing additional evidence on that subject.

The defense rejected Sutton's claim, saying that the TAMA

Detachment might have actually been carrying out a civilian inoculation program. The Soviets, however, enacted their own war crimes trial of 731 members in Khabarovsk in late 1949. Their transcript provides further evidence of poisoning experiments conducted by Detachment 100, another 731 affiliate. The Soviet prosecutor questions Hirazakura Zensaku, a Detachment 100 researcher:

21 October 1949
Question: What do you know about Detachment 100 of the Japanese Imperial Kwantung Army?

Answer: As a bacteriological experimental detachment, Detachment 100 was staffed with researchers—bacteriologists, chemists and veterinaries, who were completely occupied in developing various types of germs and strong poisons; research was conducted on methods for the wholesale poisoning of both people and animals with these poisons. For this purpose the personnel of this detachment conducted experiments on animals and human beings.

In the 535-page trial summary, published under the laborious title, *"Materials on the Trial of Former Servicemen of the Japanese Army Charged With Manufacturing and Employing Bacteriological Weapons"* (1950, Foreign Languages Publishing House), this is the only mention in any detail of the poisoning experiments.

Because of the special interest the U.S. Army had in Ishii, we know that Occupation authorities didn't act in either 1946 or 1949 when the BW issue was raised outside of G-2 Intelligence circles. However, a close look at how the Khabarovsk trial came about tells us more about how much GHQ knew and the extent of their fears of being discovered—points relevant to the Teikoku investigation.

The Soviets declared war on Japan per the Potsdam Agreement, crossed the border into Manchuria on August 8, 1945, and captured an unspecified number of 731 personnel, a dozen of whom eventually were tried in the USSR for war crimes. After Japan's surrender, Soviet interrogators gradually got their prisoners to reveal what had been going on at these various "Water Prophylaxis" stations. The Soviets then tried to get further information from GHQ on Ishii and his BW activities, about which the prisoners apparently knew a great deal. GHQ equivocated, saying that no evidence existed of such activities and that because the charges involved Chinese victims of alleged Japanese war crimes, the Russians should mind their own business. The Soviets charged that Russian soldiers and citizens were strongly believed to have been victims too, and pressed GHQ for access to any information concerning the 731 Regiment. GHQ sidestepped as much as possible, but the Soviets just wouldn't go away.

On January 15, 1947, at nine A.M. in the War Ministry Building in Tokyo, Col. Leon Smirnov of the Russian Prosecution Section at the IMT met with several U. S. Army officers and asked to interrogate Ishii and two of his senior doctors. This came as a surprise since GHQ wasn't aware the Soviets knew that Ishii was already in U. S. custody. GHQ denied the request on the firm advice of the War Department in Washington, but the Soviets were not to be stopped. Suspecting that something serious was about to happen— or already had—the Russian prosecutors threatened to force the entire BW issue into the IMT, putting Ishii and company on trial before the world if the Americans didn't cooperate with Soviet private requests.

It was all GHQ needed to prod Ishii, who himself had been sidestepping his American interrogators. For a year he'd supplied parts of his BW knowledge, but nothing about its full extent nor of the human experiments. With the Soviets so interested in Ishii, claiming they had testimony from some of his former personnel about extensive human experiments, the American officers went back to Ishii for another round of interrogations.

At that point Ishii started hinting that, if granted complete immunity, he would divulge scientific data on bacteriological warfare confirmed through human experiments. Ishii may have felt that

206

his only hope lay with the Americans, since news that the Soviets were after him seemed to work. The Russian interrogators might not have been as accommodating as the Americans.

Meanwhile, Maj. Gen. Charles A. Willoughby, MacArthur's chief of intelligence, alerted the Chief of Staff in Washington to what was happening. In a memo dated 27 March 1947 Willoughby wrote:

> 1. This has to do with Russian request for transfer of the former Japanese expert in BW.
> 2. The U.S. has primary interest, has already interrogated this man and his information is held by the U.S. Chemical Corps classified as TOP SECRET.
> 3. The Russian has made several attempts to get at this man. We have stalled. He now hopes to make his point by suddenly claiming the Japanese expert as a major war criminal.

Three days later Willoughby wrote another memo to Chief of Staff on the same subject.

> 1. (War Department) interrogated Japs last year.
> 2. Their product is "Top Secret".
> 3. We were warned not to let the Russians in on this.
> 4. They have been at us for months.
> 5. We stalled: Failing in this, the Russ now approaches this via War Crimes Theory.
> 6. This is a clear-cut fake; a trumped-up method to get their hands on these people and take them away. They were in the war five days.
> 7. This is quite clear to the War Department. . .the same position must be taken in letter to (Soviet member at Allied Council Lt. Gen.) Derevyanko.

The reply from Washington, in State-War-Navy Coordinating

Committee cable 351/1, reveals the U. S. concerns and strategies which later become integral to the Teikoku investigation. In his article in the *Bulletin of Concerned Asian Scholars,* John Powell quoted and examined the main points of the cable:

(Russian access to Ishii) might be granted as an "amiable gesture," provided certain precautions were taken. First, the Japanese were to be reinterviewed by the most competent U.S. personnel available. If such interviews brought out any new or significant information, the Japanese were to be instructed not to reveal that information to the Soviet questioners. And last, the Japanese were to be told to make no mention to the Soviet authorities that they had ever been interviewed by the U. S. investigators.

It appears, however, that the "amiable gesture" was never made, because Gen. Derevyanko soon received a letter to the effect that Willoughby prescribed. Paranoia or a simple change of heart might have been the reason, but on this and the surrounding series of events the truth remains vague. According to the Soviets, their prosecutors personally delivered written testimony from two 731 people, who told ghastly details of human experiments along with overwhelming and consistent figures on bacilli production, to senior American prosecutor Joseph Keenan, who simply pocketed the information and never did anything with it. The American prosecutors, whether on orders from above or acting on their own, maintained that the evidence wasn't enough to warrant an investigation.

The Soviets, twice thwarted by the Americans, announced a grandstand trial in Siberia. However, when the trial got underway in the city of Khabarovsk, GHQ got two lucky breaks. First was a simple but stupid mistake by the Soviets—they didn't invite any western press to cover the trial. News of it trickled into Japan, but SCAP censorship took care of the Japanese papers, and the foreign press never picked up on the story. Second, the Cold War made it very easy for GHQ to denounce the Khabarovsk trial as, in the words of MacArthur's diplomatic chief William Sebald, "a smoke screen" for not responding to Allied calls upon the USSR to account for several thousand Japanese soldiers still held prisoner.

Smoke screen or no, the Khabarovsk trial elicited a wealth of information, largely technical, and too frighteningly consistent to have been invented. Moreover, all of it tallied with information GHQ got from Ishii and his top people. Soviet prosecutors repeatedly proclaimed the trial was done in the name of humanity "here in the most humane court in the world." The transcript is rife with probing questions that reveal a covetous and determined Soviet scientific interest—reminiscent of GHQ's interest—in Japan's BW progress. And though the prosecutors uncovered a vast program (one installation alone could produce eight tons of bacteria a month), they got none of the more specific information, such as how long a man can live after being injected with mouse brain suspension. The ultimate humanity of the trial is, at the very least, arguable, so GHQ's dismissal of Khabarovsk as sheer propaganda is not without some validity.

With the beginning of the Cold War, the Americans wanted to keep Ishii's BW findings and techniques away from the Russians at all costs. Russian cross-examination of Ishii at the Military Tribunal would certainly divulge that data to the world, which is why U. S. authorities, from soldiers to physicians, staunchly opposed putting Ishii on trial. There was also the possibility a Russian investigation might reveal that American POWs had been used in Ishii's experiments. In Russian hands that revelation would have been dynamite.

It is conceivable that the man who killed twelve people in the Teikoku Bank was not a former member of the 731 poison school, but the evidence indicates that at the very minimum he either knew or had access to somebody who was, if only to have borrowed equipment and have been briefed on the secret method of poisoning.

When the 731 installations and those of the affiliates were destroyed at the end of World War II as Ishii and his personnel retreated, they smuggled equipment home with them because such expensive, sophisticated equipment was unavailable on the civilian market. Furthermore, Japan's BW program was not limited to mainland China and Manchuria. The Imperial Army's Water Prophylaxis stations engaging in similar, though less extensive, activities were spread throughout the Far East, including Java, where Dr. Shigeru Matsui was stationed. Thousands of Japanese military personnel worked at these special installations during the war, so there was no lack of suspects.

Dr. Matsui himself was likely a link to something more than namecards. Given his medical and military background and experience, coupled with the fact his own card turned up in one of the rehearsal attempts, Matsui must have known more than he told the police during the investigation. A man seeking prussic acid in Matsui's name shortly before the crime, the death of more than two hundred people at Matsui's hands, whether by accident or by designed experiment, and the extent of Matsui's involvement with bacteriology and poisons went unexplained. Yet, he was the man whose information led to the arrest of Hirasawa.

Still, out of the blurred and slanted memories, the wash of time, the dirty deals, the declassified documents, and the conversations with central and peripheral actors in the drama, the truth about what happened emerges, if only in pieces.

The police were digging up as much hard evidence as possible while secretly investigating former 731 personnel to learn more about their wartime activities and special knowledge of poisoning. Some police informants were, by their own admission, candidates for war crimes trials. Why the police found it necessary to oblige these people is only the first of several questions that involve the dark aspects of the Occupation.

Exactly who knew what, and when, within SCAP are significant questions that will likely go unanswered forever, because on those matters as many memories fail as at any other juncture in the Teikoku affair. However, the March 11, 1948, documents detailing the Fujita-PSD meeting about the secret poison laboratory show that the police knew of 731's existence, and so, therefore, did the PSD. It seems unlikely that the Public Safety Division knew much about the Legal Section's deal with Ishii, but the PSD wasn't entirely unaware of the goings-on either. PSD worked closely with SCAP's Counter-Intelligence Corps (CIC), whose 8th Army counterparts (G-2) had been involved with the Legal Section in the Ishii deal. Even sensitive information was often shared between these groups, but evidently anything on 731 was jealously guarded.

No surviving PSD member recalled anything about a secret deal, but when I asked Engle if he had passed on the information about war criminals to war crime investigators, he referred me to his March 4, 1948 memo, which recorded Chief Fujita's request for the PSD to secure any available information regarding poisoners in the Japanese military, and which concluded with the carefully worded line, "It is believed that these persons were highly trained in preparation of various poisons and that a SCAP section is investigating them for possible war crimes."

It's unclear whether Fujita said this or whether Engle penned it as his own observation, but in any case both the date and the wording of this memo are important. If the line reported what Fujita had told Engle, Fujita must have known that some SCAP section, which we know to be the Legal Section, was investigating alleged war criminals, who we know to be 731 personnel. The implication then would be that the PSD had no foreknowledge of 731 or its deal with Ishii. If Engle wrote this concluding line, however, then he must have known about the Legal Section's investigation of the poisoners, and he chose such careful wording to protect himself and the PSD from any future claims of either knowledge of, or involvement in the SCAP investigation or the Legal Section's deal with Ishii. The deal with Ishii was almost a year old by the time of this memo. Perhaps Engle intended to relay Fujita's request to the Legal Section to preserve his relationship with the MPB Chief of Detectives.

We know that in March 1948, the MPB was under extreme public pressure to solve the Teikoku murder-robbery, that the police were the target of public ridicule for their ineptitude, and that the investigation was virtually stalled in the absence of any firm leads. We also know that MPB detectives were already investigating 731 personnel, and that Sergeant Hideo Naruchi had already interrogated at least one 731 doctor working for the U. S. Army. Because the Legal Section of SCAP had granted immunity not only to Ishii, but also to all former 731 personnel a full year earlier, the MPB had no leverage in their interrogation of 731 suspects. The police could hardly threaten to expose them if they didn't cooperate, since the Legal Section had guaranteed them both secrecy and protection. Hence, the MPB also had to honor the secrecy. This may also explain why the MPB asked the PSD to censor the *Yomiuri* reporters.

It seems inconceivable that Fujita could have been unaware of the constraints under which his men were forced to operate in their pursuit of 731 suspects. What other stipulations the MPB might have been forced to honor is a matter of speculation, but the memo implies that the informers were not totally helpful. Otherwise, why ask the PSD for further information on them? The MPB must certainly have been restricted to asking only certain types of questions. There is the possibility that, after accepting the condition for secrecy, the MPB was given free rein on its questions but the 731 informers withheld information, moving Fujita to request further information from the PSD.

Only a few months after the March 1948 meeting, in late May or June, Fujita gained access to Ishii himself, the coveted and protected man already working for the U.S. Army. Procurator Hajime Takagi, Hirasawa's interrogator, was at that meeting, which he disclosed publicly for the first time as proof that GHQ actually cooperated with the police investigation.

However, the meeting with Ishii raises some serious questions. It was reasonable to think GHQ would stop anything that might expose the Ishii deal and all its sensitive and damning details. Why then did they allow the MPB access to Ishii in connection with the Teikoku investigation? Didn't this pose a direct threat to their secret?

Ishii reportedly answered every question, but how truthfully or how completely is, at the very least, suspect. This was the same man who had butchered thousands with scalpels, hypodermics, and bubonic plague bombs. When the Legal Section once contemplated the same "amiable gesture" for the Russians, Ishii and his people were to be strictly instructed on what to say, and what not to say. Bearing in mind the paranoia, the secrecy, and the high stakes surrounding the deal with Ishii, it's safe to assume he was similarly instructed before going to the meeting with Takagi, Fujita, and the other policemen. He didn't need any coaching, however, on how to stonewall. He had been successfully stonewalling his American interrogators for over a year. A one-hour session was, by comparison, only a minor challenge. What Takagi called an act of "cooperation" was in fact a smoothly orchestrated obstruction of the police investigation of 731 members by the Legal Section of SCAP or by whoever granted the access to Ishii.

From the evidence they uncovered, the MPB believed there was direct or indirect 731 involvement in the crime. The training, equipment, language, and expertise were virtually identical to those developed at the Imperial Army poison school. Yet with the man who was the founder and leader of the 731 Regiment, the police got only one sixty-minute session, and the photograph of twenty former 731 members which they showed him was never shown to the survivors and other witnesses. According to Takagi, Ishii had no idea who could have committed such a crime. Maybe that was true.

One can only speculate on why Fujita didn't further pursue other specific 731 suspects after talking with Ishii. Maybe Ishii's performance convinced him that a 731 man may not have been involved. Or maybe Fujita, who knew of at least part of some sort of deal between 731 and the U.S. Army, was beginning to realize

213

the dangerous ground his investigation was on. Fujita knew that the 731 informants had to be protected from the IMT. He also knew that the Imperial Army had conducted poisoning experiments on humans in Manchuria and Korea during the war. He knew that publicity would expose these people and their crimes. Did the meeting with Ishii reveal or suggest the scope of these crimes were much larger than he ever imagined? Did the absolute secrecy GHQ demanded about Ishii imply to him that what was at risk was the complete disgrace of his country and his Emperor? Could Fujita have known through intelligence circles that the Emperor's signature was on the 731 charter, and that one of the staff officers at the Operations Division of 731 was a Lt. Col. Miyata, who was none other than Prince Takeda himself of the Imperial family? In the absence of a full investigation of the 731 Regiment, the truth may never be known.

A frightening replay of the Teikoku investigation, but on a grander scale, was the investigation of the Matsukawa derailing in 1949—twenty accused, eight forced confessions, suppression and manufacture of evidence by the prosecution, and police fumblings (not one officer could remember who had discovered the only two pieces of material evidence in the case). It took fifteen years and five trials, two in the Supreme Court, but the Matsukawa defendants were acquitted. To this day, the case remains unsolved.

Unlike the Matsukawa incident, which ultimately proved that democracy, civil liberties, and criminal justice had actually taken root in Japan, the Teikoku affair has not been granted similar judicial review. Moreover, the facts that have survived the confused affair serve as a reminder that Japan's fabulous success is not without its dark side.

Retrials have been rare but not impossible. Yukio Saito was on death row for twenty-four years, filing appeal after appeal, claiming he had been framed for the murder of a Japanese family. In 1984 he finally won a retrial, and was found innocent. The judge ruled that the confession had been obtained under questionable circumstances, and suggested that the police had faked the bloodstains on his clothes the day after the crime. However, though the closed door of retrial has been opening, Hirasawa's chances for winning one may not have improved because the Teigin incident is more than just a bank crime.

With so many ties to the 731 Regiment, the Teikoku affair is still a political bombshell, especially as long as the Emperor is alive. The question remains whether the Emperor willingly signed the 731 charter, or signed it under pressure from the military leaders. It would seem that few Japanese want to know the answer, for although General MacArthur had Emperor Hirohito publicly renounce his divinity, the Emperor still retains a powerfully symbolic status in Japan. The full details of Ishii's and his colleagues' experiments, including whatever facts may be relevant to the Teikoku crime, remain buried in the U.S. Army's chemical warfare lab at Fort Detrick, Maryland. Some of the facts might still be buried in Japan, and there is no telling what a reopening of the Hirasawa case might reveal.

On April 28, 1985, the Justice Ministry moved Hirasawa from his prison in Sendai to the Medical Prison in Tokyo. At first the reasons for the move were vague, but a few days later the Ministry announced its surprising intention to question Hirasawa in person at a closed-door hearing in connection with his appeal based on the expiry of the death sentence. On May 9, 1985 the Ministry questioned Hirasawa, who maintained, as he has since recanting his confession in October 1948, that he was innocent and had been coerced into confessing. The Ministry retired to deliberate.

Observers said the move was strictly an empty gesture, and that the Ministry had no intention of letting him go. In their opinion, the Ministry hopes Hirasawa will die in the Medical Prison so that detractors will not be able to say the Ministry failed to provide for Hirasawa's weakening condition.

At present, no official Japanese agency is investigating the Teikoku crime. Even if one was, there are few people to interview.

Wayne Ely or Eddy was never found, despite the Society's and my efforts.

Lt. Paul E. J. Parker's last known address was in France in 1951.

Dr. Shigeru Matsui died twenty or thirty years ago, depending on who you ask.

Chief Jirō Fujita also died twenty or thirty years ago.

Hajime Takagi's opinions are all on record already, as are Tetsuro Morikawa's and those of his son, Takehiko.

The same applies to Riichi Takeuchi and Masako Takeuchi, nee Murata.

Former detective Tamigorō Igii has also stopped talking about the Teigin incident. After arresting Hirasawa he founded the Baritsu Chapter of the Baker Street Irregulars—a club for devotees of Sherlock Holmes.

Shirō Ishii returned to Japan, lived to an old age, and died of cancer.

Jack Munroe died of a stroke in 1984.

Eugene Hattori, the Japanese-American, still refuses to talk.

Byron Engle is retired, lives near Washington, D.C., and works as a consultant.

Two of Hirasawa's daughters are living in Japan, and one is believed to be living somewhere in the United States.

216

On May 30, 1985, claiming that the statute of limitations on a death sentence applied only to fugitives who had never been tried for their crime, the Justice Ministry rejected Hirasawa's appeal. The Society announced that it would press on with Hirasawa's seventeenth appeal for a retrial based on the GHQ documents. Hirasawa may die at any time, but his story will not die with him. As Hirasawa's adopted son, Takehiko dedicates his life to clearing Hirasawa's honor. Because Japanese law provides for posthumous appeals by members of the convict's immediate family, Takehiko and the Society have pledged to continue their efforts should the artist die in disgrace. Appeals may eventually succeed in vindicating Hirasawa; however they will not likely explain what happened on January 26, 1948. There will probably never be an answer to the Teikoku mystery unless someone can roll away the black mists surrounding the 731 Regiment. The likelihood of that happening is perhaps as remote and improbable as a fateful and chance meeting between a doctor and an artist on a train ferry sailing from Hokkaidō to Honshū some thirty-eight summers ago.

APPENDIX

Memorandum dated July 21, 1943, from Combined H.Q., Eastern India D.I.S. No. 310, Re: The Flowering of the Bamboo.

Memorandum dated January 27, 1948, from Director of Criminal Department, Metropolitan Police Board to Chiefs of All Police Stations, Re: Instructions Regarding Case of Killing Members of the Teikoku Bank.

Public Safety Division (SCAP) Memorandum for the Record dated February 20, 1948, Re: Teikoku Bank Robbery Investigation.

Memorandum dated February 24, 1948, from Johnson F. Munroe, Investigator, Public Safety Division, to Byron Engle, Administrator-in-Charge, Police Branch, Public Safety Division, Re: Teikoku Bank Robbery Investigation.

Memorandum dated March 4, 1948, from Byron Engle, Administrator-in-Charge, Police Branch, Public Safety Division, Re: Teikoku Bank Robbery Investigation.

Notes Taken on Conference With Chief of Detectives Jiro Fujita dated March 11, 1948, Re: Tokyo Murder-Bank Robbery Case.

Memorandum dated March 11, 1948, from Johnson F. Munroe, Investigator, Public Safety Division to H.S. Eaton, Chief Administrator, Police Branch, Public Safety Division, Re: Teikoku Bank Robbery Case.

Memorandum For File dated March 12, 1948, from Johnson F. Munroe, Investigator, Public Safety Division, Re: Teikoku Bank Case Investigation.

Cases Where Human Rights Were Infringed by Members of the Police Service Personnel (From 1948 to end of December, 1950), Civil Liberties Bureau, Attorney-General's Office. (extracts)

Memorandum dated May 1947, from U.S. War Department, War Crimes Office, Judge Advocate General's Office, Re: Interrogation of Certain Japanese by Russian Prosecutor. (extracts)

Notes dated July 6, 1949, from Public Safety Division, Re: Shimoyama death.

Combined H.Q. Eastern India D.I.S. No. 310
Copy No. 144 - July 43

The Flowering of the Bamboo. From the Southern CHIN HILLS has come a
report that a plague of rats seriously damaged TAUNGYA (shifting hill
cultivation) crops last year. This apparently insignificant statement may provide a guidance on the availability of bamboo for con-
structional purposes in the ARAKAN during the next year or two.

For some reason, for which there appears to be no satisfactory
explanation, a plague of rats occurs on the ARAKAN YOMAHS at the time
of the flowering of the bamboo.

The bamboo has a life period of about 25 years. At the end of
this time, it blooms, dies and rots, and new shoots spring from the
roots of the old plants. The new shoots grow to maturity in 3 or 4 years,
during which period the quality and supply of bamboo are far below
normal.

The flowering of the bamboo occurs over a wide tract and spreads
very rapidly to neighbouring areas, so that in succeeding localities
there is a periodic dearth of this useful plant.

The bamboo last flowered in the LEMRO-KALADAN areas in 1919. The
accompanying plague of rats attacked the paddy crops in the fields of
MINBYA and MYOHAUNG, as well as in the TAUNGYAS, causing economic dis-
tress in the areas affected.

It is reasonable to assume that the flowering of the bamboo which
is suspected of having started in the KANPETLET area, on the Eastern
ranges of the ARAKAN YOMAHS, will spread to the Western ranges within
a year. If this occurs, there will be a shortage of high grade bamboo
suitable for temporary bridges in some of the localities of the upper
LEMRO-KALADAN areas, if not throughout the whole tract.

Issued at 0830 hrs 21st July 1943.

TO   : Chiefs of All Police Stations

FROM   : Director of Criminal Dept., MPB.
           Director of Police Affairs Dept., MPB.

SUBJECT: Instructions Regarding Case of Killing Members of
          Teikoku Bank.

      You are already informed by telegram that on the afternoon
of Jan. 26 the sixteen members of Shiinamachi Branch, Teikoku
Bank, located within the jurisdiction of Mejiro Police station,
were asked by a man who called himself a member of Sanitary
Section of Tokyo Metropolitan office to swallow a liquid poison
he brought which he said was a preventive against dysentery,
to be taken by them according to an order issued by the Occupation Forces, that ten of the sixteen victims were killed
by the poison on the spot and two at the hospital, and the
other four are given medical aid but that their fate is
still to be seen.

      This crime, which was committed at the closing hour of
the bank and in the assumed name of the Occupation Forces,
killing many lives at one time and attempting to rob much
money of the establishment, is one of the rarest and boldest
crimes ever seen in the history of crimes. In view of the
tremendous repercussion being shown by the public with regard
to this case, we must, through cooperation of all our police,
make greatest possible efforts for apprehending the offender.

      For this reason, you are asked to recognize the extraordi-
nary importance of the case and, giving complete instructions
to your subordinate officers in accordance with the following
and positively guiding and supervising effective use of the
rules of investigation, make immediate report to the investigation headquarters whenever you get any data for furthering
investigation and that with special care not to let the
secret escape.

1. Date and time of the crime: 15 minutes around 3.30 p.m.,
        January 26 (Monday), 1948.

2. Place of the crime: Within Shiinamachi Branch of Teikoku
        Bank, #39 1-chome, Nagasaki, Toshima-ku, Tokyo.

This establishment, formerly Fujita Pawn-shop and consisting of one building with a godown, is situated between the business and residential quarters in front of Nagasaki shrine about 60 meters northeast of Shiinamachi station on Seibu Agricultural Line (formerly called Musashino Line).

3. Victims:

Ueda Takejiro (43), now being under treatment,
#812, Oguchi-Machi, Ota-ku.

Watanabe Yoshiyasu (43), died
758 Oizumi-machi, Itabashi-ku.

Nishimura Hidehiko, (36), died
10 2-chome, Shin Ogawa-machi, Ushigome Shinjuku-ku.

Shirai Shoichi, (29), died
519 3-chome, Asagaya, Suginami-ku.

Sawata Yoshi (22), died
449, Fujisawa , Fujisawa-mura, Irima-gun, Saitama Pref.

Tanaka Tokukazu, (19), being under treatment
793 2-chome, Kami-Ochiai, Shinjuku-ku.

Akiyama Miyako, (23), died
c/o Akiyama Kunosuke, 13 1-chome, Nagasaki, Toshima-ku

Uchida Hideko, (23), died
5, Kita Toyotama, Nerima-ku

Akuzawa Yoshiko, (19), being under treatment
c/o Akuzawa Shobei,
#14 1-chome, Nagasaki, Toshima-ku

Kato Teruko, (16), died
1,713 2-chome, Ikebukuro, Toshima-ku

Takeuchi Sutejiro, (49), died
170, Horikiri-cho, Katsushika-ku

Takizawa Tatsuo, (46), (servant)
His wife Ryu (49), his daughter Takako aged 19
and son Yoshihiro aged 8. All of them died.

4. Offender:

Name and address: Unknown. He said he was medical member
of Sanitary section, Tokyo Metropolitan office and of Welfare
Dpt., Welfare Ministry, and had a title of Doctor of
medicine.

Description: Aged between 44 and 50, about 5 ft. 3 in.
in height, rather thin, with oval face, high nose,
pale complexion, hair cut short or rather long and
grizzled.

Appearance: Dressed in a lounge suit (brown, figured
weave, not new); with an overcoat or spring-coat
in arm; wearing brown rubber shoes (not certain; a
white cloth band on left arm (which had on it the
mark of Tokyo Metropolitan office (𝕆) in
red, and under the mark was written in black and
good hand "Disinfecting member" or "Disease
Preventive Doctor".

Articles possessed by the offender: A metal box, about
3 cm x 15 cm in size, such as often carried by
doctors (he took the poison out of this box); one
small and one medium-sized glass medicine bottles
(holding poison).

Characteristics: About two brown spots 1.5 cm long on
the left cheer (not scars of burns or boils, but
such as often seen on the skin of an old man).
A handsome man; well composed and looking like an
intelligent man.

5. Brief account of the case:

The victims opened their business as usual at 0930 hrs.,
and after Ushiyama, Senji, their chief, went home with
stomachache about 1400 hrs., continued at their work till
1500 hours, when they closed the front door and began wind-
ing up the remaining affairs for the day.

At approximately 1530 hrs. the offender made his sudden
appearance at the side-entrance and showing his name-card
(printed with his false title, as described above) to
Akuzawa Yoshiko, one of the victims, expressed his wish
to see the chief. So the latter showed him into the
office-room, and Yoshida Takejiro, the assistant chief,
had a talk with him.

According to the statement of the offender, there
have cropped up a number of dysentery cases among those
who drink the water of a public well in front of Aida's,
and have been reported to It. Porton (or something sounding
like that) as well as to the Japanese police. So a disinfecting team of the Allied Forces was coming, he said.

He himself was dispatched by the Lt. in advance of the said team to make an investigation, as a result of which he found that an inmate of the house of a dysentery sufferer had visited their office on the day. In accordance, everything in the office, including the books, papers, bank-notes, etc., must receive a disinfecting process, for which nothing should be carried out till the arrival of the disinfecting team, he declared.

When Yoshida said to him; "How can you have got the knowledge so soon, I wonder?" the offender said in reply: "In truth, the doctor who made an inspection of the sufferer has made a direct report to the Occupation authorities."

"The disinfecting team will soon be here," continued the villain," and in the meanwhile you all must take this medicine given us by the Occupation authorities. This is a medicine so powerful and effective as to make you absolutely immune from dysentery if you take it.". So saying, he took some phials, large and small, out of his medicine-chest (a metal chest for a medical practitioner, as described above).

All the victims, wholly unsuspicious of the fiendish intention of the offender, whose perfect composure and plausible explanations as well as his arm-band of Tokyo Metropolitan office having satisfied them to lay full credit in his words, formed a circle around him--a circle of poor victims sixteen in all.

Then the devil opened his mouth and said: "This medicine will injure the enamel of your teeth, and so I will show you how you must swallow it. Do as I am going to show you. There are two kinds of medicine. Take the second about a minute after you take the first. Be sure to drink it within a minute, or you will get a bad effect."

After such explanations he poured into the victims' cups some liquid medicine, transparent and otherwise, out of the small phials with a fountain-pen filler, a filler each. Then he took a cup of his own in his hand, and, saying, "This is how to drink," gulped its contents by dripping them drop by drop on to his tongue, which he had put out in the form of a shovel. So the poor victims, without exception, gulped the fatal water following the devil's example.

The liquid in question had a burning taste, and the victims got a feeling as if they had taken some strong whisky. After about a minute, the tricky villain again showed them how to drink the second medicine, and again the poor innocents followed his example, not suspecting in the least that they were actually killing themselves.

The devil had the audacity to advise them to rinse out their mouths so as not to injure their teeth, and they went to have some water at the tap several yards off in the

- 5 -

passage. Just about this time they felt themselves suddenly
overwhelmed with torpor, and fell one by one in the office-
room, passage, matted room, etc., sinking into a complete
comatose state. As a natural conclusion, nobody knows--but
the devil and God--what the offender did after his victims
fell senseless.

SOME RULES FOR C.I. AGENTS TO ACT UPON:

(1) Send warnings without delay to banks, post-offices,
and other places where large sums of money is handled, not
to fall easy victims to some similar attempts. Institute
at the same time a close investigation as to whether such
attempts have been made in the past.

(2) Make an immediate inquiry as to where the offender's
name-card was printed, carrying your search into every corner
of the Metropolis where some printer of name-cards may have
printed same such items.

(3) Make an immediate inquiry as to whether there lives
some suspicious person at all similar to the descriptions
given of the fiendish offender, within the area you are
assigned to cover. Pay a special attention to bank employees,
disinfecting officials and their assistants, health officials
and their men, physicians, druggists, and those who have some
record of having been employed in the sanitary work of the
Occupation authorities.

(4) Examine any person, at all suspicious, more strictly
than ever, paying a special attention to his name-card, phials,
and medicine-chest made of metal.

(5) Try and catch some clue concerning those who may have
some business or other connections with the bank in question.

(6) Ransack your memory and memoranda for some person
with criminal records (especially, fraud), at all resembling
the devilish offender described, either in his features or
in his peculiar way of committing crimes.

(7) Carry out a secret surveillance over the daily habits
and characteristic features of the Metropolitan health officials
and such others as are engaged in sanitary works in the
Metropolis.

N.B. Your speedy written report is impatiently expected at
the Investigation Headquarters as soon as your task is
completed.

PUBLIC SAFETY DIVISION

20 February 1948

MEMORANDUM FOR RECORD:

SUBJECT: Teikoku Bank Robbery Investigation

1. At 1000 hours on February 19 was called in conference with Mr. Eaton and Mr. Miyakawa, Liaison Justice Ministry, and Sgt. Naruchi, Second CID Section, assigned to special team investigating the Teikoku Bank Robbery, First Branch. Information from citizens, Phone Number Ginsa 57-0439. They requested the Public Safety Division to assist in locating a Lt. Hornet and Lt. Parker. Both have been associated with the typhus disinfecting teams in the Tokyo area. Lt. Hornet is believed to have been associated with the Toshima Team in Oji and Matsushika Wards of Tokyo and Parker with the Ebara Ward Disinfecting Team. Sgt. Naruchi stated that on 14 November 1947 the suspect went to Yasuda Bank, Ebara Branch, Shinagawa Ku, Hiratsuka Machi, 3 Chome 722 and told the employees, "I came here with Lt. Parker in a jeep because a new typhus case happened in this vicinity." He produced some liquid which he told the employees was preventive medicine for typhus control and directed them to drink it. They did so, suffering no ill effects.

2. On 26 January 1948 a man believed to be the same individual appeared at the Teikoku Bank, Shina-Machi Branch, Toshima Ku, and stated, "I came here because there have been many dysentary cases in this vicinity." "Lt. Hornet will be here very soon." "You must take this medicine for prevention." Sixteen employees drank the liquid simultaneously that he produced. Twelve died immediately.

3. The Japanese Police desire any information, names, and addresses of Japanese individuals either connected with or having knowledge of the disinfecting work done by either of the above Lieutenants, particularly interpreters or individuals in the group who speak English. The Police advise elimination of individuals below the age of 30 or above the age of 60.

4. The Japanese Police have heard a rumor that one of the Lieutenants was connected with the Asakusa Cavalry Division.

5. Action to Date: Mr. Eaton contacted Mr. Allen of the Tokyo MG Team Sanitation Control who advised Mr. Eaton that ten low-ranking medical officers were used by the above MG Team in typhus epidemic control activities in 1946. There are at present no military personnel employed by the MG Team in such work. Disinfecting work, however, is being carried out by Japanese employees of the ward officers in Tokyo.

6. Mr. Eaton contacted by phone Ex-Officer, Public Health and Welfare, named Deville. No such teams are working for the Public Health and Welfare. Mr. Eaton also contacted by phone Lt. Gibbons, Hq and Service Group, Repair and Utilities Officer, who stated that they had some men engaged in rodent control but no one by the name of Parker or Hornet.

7. Engle contacted Captain H. F. Schwartz, Rm 2, 26-6205, Hhpothec Bank, AG Section, GHQ, and checked the files to ascertain the names of any lieutenants or Captains by the name of Parker or Hornet who have been assigned in Japan. No one by the name of Hornet appeared in the files. Unfortunately, records of Lt. Parker, who had departed from this theatre of which there are about a half dozen, do not contain information as to their previous assignments. Listed below are the names of military officers with names similar to the above and their present assignments.

Lt. McDonald L. Parker - 218 Station Hosp. - Arrived Theatre
                                    October 1947.

1st Lt. James L. Parker - 347 Trans. Harbor, Craft Co., 8th Amm.

Captain James R. Parker, Inf. - 35 Inf., 25 Div.

2nd Lt. John G. Parker, FA - 99th FA Bn, 1st Cav Div.

Loriner A. Parker, 1st Lt. - 41 Troop Carrier, Mito Tachikawa

1st Lt. Evan J. Parker   - 11 fa Bn. 24 Div.

Capt Edw. A. Parker, TC   - 347 Trans., Harbor Craft, Yokohama

1st Lt. Eugene A. Parker   - Team Com

2nd Lt. Wm. C. Parker   - 99 Fa Bn., 1 Cav.

1 Lt. CA Wm. R. Parker   - 753 AAG Bn, 8th Army

Lt. Jack Horner   - 8th Inf., Engineers, Camp Drake

Lt. Marion Homer   - Tokyo, QM Depot - Departed July from
                                                              U. S.

Capt. Roland L. Homer,   - Capt. Eng.-599 QN Bn, Eng. Base Depot

24 February 1948

MEMORANDUM

TO: Byron Engle, AIC, Police Branch, PSD

FROM: Johnson F. Munroe, Investigator

SUBJECT: Teikoku Bank Robbery Investigation

     1. Further investigation conducted on 21 February 1948 at the Office of Major Sam A. Plemmons, Medical Section, GHQ, Dai Ichi Building, disclosed that First Lt. Paul E. J. Parker, MC, O-1745607, 24th Corps (Korea) was assigned to the Tokyo Area on several cases between 30 June 1946 and June 1947 to assist in various health control activities. The dates of these TDY periods are not reflected in the records of the GHQ Medical Section. It was stated, however, that the above referred official undoubtedly was the "Lt. Parker," who was assigned on a typhus control team in Oji Ward with the Tokyo MG in March 1947.

     2. Medical Section had no record to establish that a Lt. Hornet was ever assigned in this theatre from June 1946 and records do reflect that a Captain J. Hartnett, MC, O-428958, was in this theatre from June 1946 until April 1947 and that his MOS indicated public health work. It was stated that Captain Hartnett who came to this theatre as a First Lieutenant was assigned as a Medical Officer to FEAF.

     3. Investigation conducted on 24 February 1948 at the Office of Lt. Col. P. G. Fleetwood, Personnel Officer, FEAF, Meiji Building, developed that the above referred Captain Hartnett was assigned to duty in Guam. During his entire stay in this theatre he was never engaged in any work in the Tokyo area. It was suggested, however, that his name may have been known to some Japanese prisoners of war in Guam who later were repatriated in Japan.

JOHNSON F. MUNROE
Police Investigator

4 March 1948

MEMORANDUM

SUBJECT: Teikoku Bank Robbery Investigation

1. On 3 March Mr. Harry Kobayashi, Liaison for the MPB, related a request from Mr. Fujita, Chief of Detectives of the MPB, that the investigators of the PSD attempt to secure any information available pertaining to a group of former Japanese military personnel that were sent to Korea as poisoners during the war. It is believed that these persons were highly trained in preparation of various poisons and that a SCAP Section is investigating them for possible war crimes.

BYRON ENGLE
Administrator in Charge
Police Branch

Notes Taken on Conference With Chief of Detectives Jiro Fujitta
Re; Tokyo Murder-Bank Robbery Case.   Notes taken by Harold Mulbar, March 11'48.

- -

Present at Conference;   Mr. Byron Engle,
                            Lieut. Eugene H. Hattori,
                            Mr. Andrew Jackson,
                            Mr. Johnsen F. Munroe and
                            Mr. Harold Mulbar.

In brief Mr. Fujitta reported as follows;

(1) Y 1,280,000 has been appropriated to cover two months expense to investigate
    this case.

(2) It may sound like a joke." Japanese people with gray hair were rushing to barber
    shops to have their hair dyed because of being stopped so many times by police
    for questioning in connection with this case.

(3) Have new lead they hope will be productive of results. Checking former
    personnel who worked in the laboratory (Japanese Army) in Chiba experimenting
    with prussic acid to be used as poison during the war. A corp was sent into
    Manchuria that used this poison on humans and animals successfully. Request
    made this information be kept secret for fear of prosecution by War Crimes
    Tribunal. Japanese Army issued pamhlet on this subject that was issued to
    Japanese Army personnel. Modus operandi of the criminal who murdered the
    twelve people in this bank by the use of prussic poison was very similar to
    that as the training that developed from the Arsenal laboratory.
    Information obtained by a detective who visited the bank reports that even
    in the language of the bank robber-murderer it is indicative that he was trained
    in this laboratory. As example he mentions " First Drug" and Second Drug" in
    English that leads the police to believe that it is someone trained in the
    Arsenal Laboratory that was experimenting with prussic acid to be used in
    warfare.
(4) The police further believe that they are on the right trail because the murderer
    drank from the same bottle that the employees in the bank drank from knowing
    that due to fatt that the poison had been precipitated and he could safely drink
    from the fluid that was on top of the bottle.

(5) Told of the experiemtnts in precipitation with prussic acid using oil from
    Palm Tree's.

(6) Further evidence that lead the police to be believe that the murderer was schooled
    at this arsenal laboratory is because of the equipment he had with him that
    answers description of equipment used at the laboratory. (At the close of the
    war when the laboratory was chosed most of the employees took equipment home etc.

(7) Mr. Fujitta stated that information as to personnel who were at the lab when
    it was in operation was being obtained from Former Major Nonoyama and former
    Col. Yokoyama.
(8) Mr. Fujitta complained that he was having conisderable dificulty with the press
    who were interfereing with the investigation and sought the cooperation from
    this section in this matter. He complained particularly about the Yomiuri Press.

GENERAL HEADQUARTERS
SUPREME COMMANDER FOR THE ALLIED POWERS
Civil Intelligence Section, G-2
PUBLIC SAFETY DIVISION

APO 500
11 March 1948

MEMORANDUM

SUBJECT: Teikoku Bank Robbery Case

TO: Mr. H. S. Eaton, Chief Administrator, Police Branch

    1. Interference by Japanese newspaper reporters with
the police investigation of the Teikoku Bank Robbery case,
as reported by Jiro Fujita, Chief of Detectives, Tokyo
Metropolitan Police earlier on 11 March 1948 was discussed
informally by Byron Engle, Administrator in Charge, Police
Branch, and this investigator; at 1100 hours this date with
Major D. C. Imboden, OIC, Press and Publications Section.

    2. In response to suggestions of PSD representatives,
Major Imboden approved Mr. Fujita's projected press conference for the purpose of discussing the Teikoku case with
Japanese newspaper executives in order that the problems
created by interference of news reporters might be fully
explained to the newsmen and for the purpose of soliciting
the co-operation of the newspapers in halting such reported
practices as reporters' following suspects in the case and
shadowing police investigators working on the case as well
as reporters representing themselves to be detectives in
order to secure news matter. Major Imboden advised Mr.
Engle at 1300 hours this date that telegraphic advice had
been dispatched to all Japanese newspapers not to interfere
with the police investigation in the Teikoku case or
indulge in such practices as have been ascribed to the
Tokyo reporters by Mr. Fujita.

    3. Major Imboden also stated he would communicate
personally with the publisher of the Yomiuri Shimbun in
Tokyo and advise him to have his reporters removed
immediately from their reported watch on the homes of
persons working or secretly assisting in the investigation.
He also said he would discuss the matter with Allied
censorship authorities exercising control of Japanese publications and request the censors co-operate in stopping
publication of any article containing any reference to the
police investigation of a Japanese Army Poison School being
connected with the Teikoku case; further he will request
the censors to screen all articles pertaining to the Teikoku
case on the basis of whether publication of the article
will hinder apprehension of the culprit.

                          JOHNSON F. MUNROE
                          Police Investigator

APO 500
12 March 1948

MEMORANDUM FOR FILE:

SUBJECT: Teikoku Bank Case Investigation

1. Progress of Japanese Police in investigating the
Teikoku bank robbery-murders and problems created by Japan-
ese newspaper reporters in shadowing police investigators
assigned to the case or "tailing" persons under suspicion
were reported in a conference 11 March 1948 by Jiro Fujita,
Chief of Tokyo Detectives. Present at the conference were:
Byron Engle, AIC, Police Branch; Harold Mulbar, Administrator;
Lt. Eugene H. Hattori, Liaison, and Investigators Andrew
Jackson and Johnson F. Munroe.

2. Mr. Fujita requested the assistance of PSD in
halting such interference on the part of newspaper reporters
as he reported, particularly since the police are now working on a lead which he stated appears to be the best uncovered
so far in the Teikoku Bank Case investigation, and publication
of any of the facts pertaining to this phase of the investigation would be a severe hindrance to successful completion
of the inquiry. Briefly, the lead involves investigation of
all personnel who attended or were employed during the war
years on a secret army chemical laboratory at Tsudanuma,
Chiba-Ken, where experiments were perfected in the use of
poisons, including prussic acid, the poison used by the
Teikoku Bank robber. Techniques for administering this acid,
which were developed at the laboratory, were published in an
army pamphlet for the guidance of soldier-students, Fujita
said, and the method used by the Teikoku robber was identical
to that outlined in the pamphlet. Further evidence indicating to the police that the murderer was schooled at the
Tsudanuma Laboratory was seen in the equipment used by the
murderer which was identical to that used at the laboratory,
he said, as well as his use during the robbery of identical
phrases as appear in the pamphlet. A group of army people
trained at this laboratory were sent into Manchuria to practice the techniques learned at the laboratory on human beings
as well as animals, according to information developed by the
police, and because of their fear of being involved in a war
crimes trial, individuals acquainted with the facts pertaining

to the secret laboratory are proving reticent about discussing it with the police. However, the secret assistance of two former army officers connected with it (Colonel Yokoyama and Major Nonoyama) has been obtained by the Teikoku Bank case investigators, and it is anticipated that their help in the matter will prove invaluable if kept secret.

3. However, the fact that these former Army Officers are assisting the police has leaked to certain newspaper reporters, Fujita said, and the home of Major Nonoyama is being kept under surveillance of reporters representing the YOMIURI SHIMBUN, a Tokyo daily. Fujita said police fear that their sources of information will be cut off if news of the inquiry into the poison laboratory is published now while their investigation is still in progress. For this reason he requested advice and assistance of PSD in insuring that such information would not be published and further to insure that police investigators would not be further hampered by newspapermen following them or shadowing suspects under investigation by the police.

4. Mr. Engle advised him that the matter would be reported to the proper allied authorities exerting control over Japanese newspapers and a report of whatever action was to be taken by Occupation authorities would be given to Mr. Fujita later in the day. Results obtained through discussion of the matter with the Press and Publications Unit of Civil Information and Education Section, GHQ, (See Memo of this investigation dated 11 March 1948) were given to Mr. Fujita at another meeting with him at 1400 hours 11 March 1948 in the PSD conference room.

JOHNSON F. MUNROE
Police Investigator

1 Encl.
Typed Notes on Fujita
Conference prepared by Mr. Mulbar.

Cases where human rights were
infringed by members of the
Police Service personnel (From
1948 to end of December, 1950)

Civil Liberties Bureau,
Attorney-General's Office

	Date	Place	Manner in which human rights were allegedly infringed	Disposition	Remarks
94	11, 6, 1949	Shizuoka-ken	Inquiry was made of a woman who was kept undressed throughout the inquiry.	Advice was given.	
95	28, 5, 1949	Nara-ken	Confession was forced by means of torture.	Advice was given.	
96	, 1949	Chiba-ken	Confession was demanded through acts of violence and infliction of wounds.	The allegation was unfounded.	
97	16, 3, 1949	Saitama-ken	Confession was demanded through threats.	The allegation was unfounded.	
98	6, 9, 1949	Tokyo-to	Confession was forced through violence.	The allegation was unfounded.	
99	23, 8, 1949	Ehime-ken	Confession was forced through coersion and violence.	The allegation was unfounded.	
		Akita-ken	The person was assaulted and wounded after arrest.	Passed unnoticed.	
100	21, 10, 1949	Tokyo-to	Confession was demanded through acts of violence.	Passed unnoticed.	

(3) Cases received in 1950

	Date	Place	Manner in which human rights were allegedly infringed	Disposition	Remarks
101	14, 1, 1950	Akita-ken	Confession was demanded through assault.	The allegation was unfounded.	
102	27, 9, 1949 2, 1950	Yamaguchi-ken	Confession was forced by means of torture.	Passed unnoticed.	
103	12, 12, 1947 13,	Hyogo-ken	After arrest, investigation was made through assault.	Passed unnoticed.	
104	2, 2, 1950	Miyazaki-ken	Confession was forced through threats.	Making decision was suspended.	
105	7, 4, 1950	Yamaguchi-ken	Through violence and infliction of injury, Confession was forced.	Passed unnoticed.	
106	10, 5, 1950	Okayama-ken	Confession was forced by means of torture	Making decision was suspended.	
107	17, 5, 1950	Gumma-ken	After unlawful arrest, the person was subjected to torture and threats for prolonged hours.	The allegation was unfounded.	
108	28, 6, 1950	Tokyo-to	During investigation, the person was assaulted and wounded.	Making decision was suspended	

(3) Cases received in 1950

	Date	Place	Manner in which human rights were allegedly infringed	Disposition	Remarks
85	2, 2, 1950	Fukushima-ken	Even after the elapse of 48 hours allowed for Police detention was made for prison further 6 days without a warrant of detention.	The case has been disposed of administratively on the basis of an advice for disposition.	
86	21, 6, 1950	Fukuoka-ken	A person requiring protection was placed under arrest for protection, but he was detained for 18 days without a writ.	The case was administratively disposed of before an advice for disposition was given.	

4. Cases relating to acts of violence, cruelty and forced confession.

(1) Cases received in 1948

	Date	Place	Manner in which human rights were allegedly infringed	Disposition	Remarks
87	5, 5, 1948	Tokyo-to	Improper physical examination.	Suspended.	
88	24, 4, 1948	Okayama-ken	Confession was forced through infliction of torture.	Advice was given.	
89	30, 9, 1948	Kanagawa-ken	Confession was forced by means of threats.	Passed unnoticed.	

(2) Cases received in 1949

	Date	Place	Manner in which human rights were allegedly infringed	Disposition	Remarks
90	10, 2, 1949	Shizuoka-ken	Through infliction of violence, confession was forcibly demanded.	Warning was given.	
91	14, 7, 1948	Ishikawa-ken	Same as above.	Passed unnoticed.	
92	29, 3, 1949	Kyoto-fu	Same as above.	Advice was given	
93	25, 5, 1949	Hokkaido	Same as above.	Passed unnoticed.	

9	14, 7, 1950	Tokyo-to	On personal feeling, the police used violence and inflicted wounds on the sufferer.	Administrative disposition was advised.
10	, 1950	Tokushima-ken	As the person was subjected to cruel investigation, he committed suicide later.	Passed unnoticed.
11	3, 4, 1950	Kumamoto-ken	In making investigation threats were used, and photographs were taken.	Passed unnoticed.
12	7, 9, 1950	Iwate-ken	From private feeling, the police used violence and inflicted wounds on the sufferer	Passed unnoticed (as the matter is already settled.)
13	1950	Tokyo-to	During investigation the suspected was assaulted and wounded.	Making decision was suspended.
14	18,)11, 1949 19,	Yamanashi-ken	During investigation, the suspected was kicked and wounded.	Passed unnoticed.
115	5, 3, 1950	Tokyo-to	During investigation, the person was subjected to violence and injured.	The matter is already settled administratively. Passed unnoticed.
116	27, 8, 1950	Fukushima-ken	Same as above.	Under investigation
117	18, 9, 1950	Aomori-ken	Confession was forced through violence and infliction of injury	Under investigation.
118	21, 8,) 25, 9,) 1950	Mie-ken	Same as above.	The case was settled administratively in accordance with advice.
119	7,)3, 1950 8,	Fukushima-ken	Confession was forced by way of insulting investigation.	Under investigation.
120	4, 1950	Akita-ken	False confession was forced through torture.	The case is pending in public trial.
121	15, 7, 1950	Niigata-ken	From private feeling the police used violence and inflicted wounds.	In accordance with advice, the case was settled administratively.
122	31, 5, 1950	Fukuoka-ken	False confession was forced through torture.	Under investigation.

- 11 -

23	2, 10, 1950	Okayama-ken	Confession was forced through torture.	Advice was given.
24	1, 7, 1950	Yamanashi-ken	Confession was forced through use of violence.	Under investigation.
25	25, 4, 1950	Ibaragi-ken	Confession was forced through violence and infliction of wounds.	Under investigation.
26	, 1950	Kumamoto-ken	As the person did not comply with summons, the police assaulted him, and when he reported to the office he was induced to make confession through the influence of liquor.	Under investigation.
27	15, 5, 1950	Fukuoka-ken	Confession was forced through use of violence.	Passed unnoticed (as the matter is already disposed of)
28	28,) 1, 1950	Fukuoka-ken	During investigation, the police resorted to violence and inflicted injury.	Under investigation.
29	1, 4, 1950	Kagoshima-ken	From private of feeling, the police under the influence of liquor assaulted and injured him.	Under investigation.
30	25, 10, 1950	Hokkaido	Violence and threats were resorted to during investigation, so the person made false confession.	Ditto
31	11, 7, 1950	Hokkaido	Confession was forced through the use of violence for investigation.	Ditto
32	17, 10, 1950	Same	Same as above.	Ditto
33	11,)12,)12, 1948 13,)	Toyama-ken	Same as above.	Passed unnoticed.
34	9, 9, 1950	Okayama-ken	Being dead drunk, the police destructed articles and committed acts of violence.	The matter was settled in accordance with advice.
35	16, 7, 1950	Gumma-ken	From private feeling the person was taken to the police office and assaulted.	Advice was given.
36	23, 11, 1950	Tochigi-ken	On the road, the person was subjected to violence and was injured.	Under investigation.

19, 4, 1950	Okayama-ken	Coersion was employed during investigation	Under investigation.
8, 9, 1950	Akita-ken	During investigation violence was used to the person who was handcuffed.	Under investigation.
8,10, 1950	Tokyo-to	During investigation the person was assaulted and injured.	Under investigation.
31, 8, 1950	Yamanashi-ken	The person was subjected to violence and injured on the road.	Under investigation.
16, 6, 1950	Fukuoka-ken	As investigation was severe, the person committed suicide after his return home.	Passed unnoticed.
11, 1, 1950	Tokyo-to	During investigation, confession was forced through use of violence.	Passed unnoticed.
5, 5, 1950	Kanagawa-ken	During investigation, the person was subjected to violence.	Passed unnoticed. (The case is already settled)
6, 5, 1950	Tokyo-to	During investigation, coersion and abuse were employed to force confession.	Passed unnoticed.
3, 2, 1950	Toohigi-ken	During investigation, violence was used to force confession.	Passed unnoticed.
15, 5, 1950	Tokyo-to	From personal feeling the police used violence and inflicted injury.	The case was settled in accordance with advice.
4, 7, 1950	Kumamoto-ken	Confession was forced by giving mental and physical pain during investigation lasting deep into the night.	Advice was given.
30, 8, 1950	Hokkaido	Taking advantage of the feeble mind of the person, the police forced him to make false confession by giving coersion.	Passed unnoticed.
8,11, 1950	Yamaguchi-ken	The police treated the person violently on the reason that his attitude was bad during his investigation.	Advice was given.
8, 1, 1950	Tokyo-to	The police committed acts of cruelty to a woman on the excuse of making search on her person.	The case was settled in accordance with advice.
5, 2, 1950	Okayama-ken	The police used violence against the persons who entered without tickets.	Advice was given.
3,12, 1950	Hokkaido	The police committed violence when his request for a drink was rejected at an eating-house.	Under investigation.

~~CONFIDENTIAL~~

WAR CRIMES OFFICE

Judge Advocate General's Office

DECLASSIFIED

By_____ NARS, Date_____

DECLASSIFIED BY ORDER
OF THE SEC ARMY BY TAG
PER

77047 5

See also Nos._____

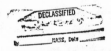

~~CONFIDENTIAL~~

Enclosure 2

~~Top Secret~~   ~~CONFIDENTIAL~~

ENCLOSURE

INTERROGATION OF CERTAIN JAPANESE
BY RUSSIAN PROSECUTOR

THE PROBLEM

1. To formulate a reply to CINCFE's radio C-52423,
date 2 May 1947, (Appendix "A") recommending the retention
of Japanese BW information in Intelligence channels and
that such material not be employed as "war crimes" evidence.

FACTS BEARING ON THE PROBLEM

2. Part 2 of cable cited in paragraph 1 above states
that General Ishii and associates would supply technical
BW information if guaranteed immunity from "war crimes" in
documentary form. Ishii and associates have to date, vol-
untarily supplied and are continuing to supply such information without a documentary guarantee of immunity.

3. Nineteen Japanese BW experts have written a 60 page
report concerning BW research using human subjects. A
twenty page report covering 9 years of research on crop
destruction has been prepared. A report by 10 Japanese
scientists on research in the veterinary field is being
written. A Japanese pathologist is engaged in recovering
and making photomicrographs of selected examples of 8,000
slides of tissues from autopsies of humans and animals
subjected to BW experiments. General Ishii is writing a
treatise embodying his 20 years experience in all phases
of BW.

Directorate for Freedom
of Information & Security Review
Office of the Assistant Secretary of Defense
(Public Affairs)
Room 2C-757, Pentagon, D.C.
8 JUL 1977

DOWNGRADED TO:
CONFIDENTIAL
DECLASSIFY on
Classified by

4. The only information concerning Japanese BW
experiments on humans admitted by the Soviets to be in

~~CONFIDENTIAL~~   - 1 -   Enclosure

their possession they state was obtained by them from two
Japanese prisoners of war. These prisoners of war admitted
to the Soviets that such experiments had been carried out.
They stated, however, that their knowledge of the experiments was gained from observation only and that they could
offer no technical details.

DISCUSSION

5. The value of Japanese BW information.

    a. Data already obtained from Ishii and his
colleagues have proven to be of great value in confirming, supplementing and complementing several
phases of U.S. research in BW, and may suggest new
fields for future research.

    b. This Japanese information is the only known
source of data from scientifically controlled experiments showing the direct effect of BW agents on man.
In the past it has been necessary to evaluate the effects
of BW agents on man from data obtained through animal
experimentation. Such evaluation is inconclusive and
far less complete than results obtained from certain
types of human experimentation.

    c. In addition to the results of human experimenta-
tion much valuable data is available from the Japanese
experiments on animals and food crops. The voluntary
imparting of this BW information may serve as a forerunner for obtaining much additional information in
other fields of research.

6. Desirability of avoiding "war crimes" involvement.

    a. Since it is believed that the USSR possesses
only a small portion of this technical information, and

CONFIDENTIAL   Enclosure

since any "war crimes" trial would completely reveal such data to all nations, it is felt that such publicity must be avoided in interests of defense and security of the U.S. It is believed also that "war crimes" prosecution of Ishii and his associates would serve to stop the flow of much additional information of a technical and scientific nature.

b. It is felt that the use of this information as a basis for "war crimes" evidence would be a grave detriment to Japanese cooperation with the United States occupation forces in Japan.

CONCLUSIONS

7. It is concluded that:

a. Information of Japanese BW experiments will be of great value to the U.S. BW research program.

b. In the interests of national security it would not be advisable to make this information available to other nations as would be the case in the event of a "war crimes" trial of Jap BW experts.

c. The value to U.S. of Japanese BW data is of such importance to national security as to far outweigh the value accruing from "war crimes" prosecution.

d. The BW information obtained from Japanese sources should be retained in intelligence channels and should not be employed as "war crimes" evidence.

RECOMMENDATIONS

8. It is recommended that:

a. SWNCC approve the above Conclusions.

b. After approval by SWNCC, the JCS be requested to transmit the message in Appendix "B" to CINCFE providing they have no objection from the military point of view.

c. All subsequent communications dealing with this phase of the subject ████████████ Top Secret.

APPENDIX "A"

From: CINCFE Tokyo Japan

To: War Department for WDGID (pass to CCMLC) MID pass to
Major General Alden Waitt

Nr: C-52423   6 May 1947

JCS radio W 94446 (Appendix "A" to SWNCC 351/1) SWNCC
351/1 and Doctor Fell's letters via air courier to General
Waitt 29 April and 5 May 1947. This radio is in 5 parts.

Part 1-Statements obtained from Japanese here confirm
statements of USSR prisoners Kawashima and Karasawa contained in
copies of interrogations given US by USSR.

Part 2-Experiments on humans were known to and described
by 3 Japanese and confirmed tacitly by Ishii; field trials
against Chinese Army took place on at least 3 occasions; scope
of program indicated by report of reliable informant Matsuda
that 400 kilograms of dried anthrax organisms destroyed at Pingfan
in August 1945; and research on use of BW against plant life
was carried out. Reluctant statements by Ishii indicate he had
superiors (possibly General Staff) who knew and authorized the
program. Ishii states that if guaranteed immunity from "war
crimes" in documentary form for himself, superiors and subordinates, he can describe program in detail. Ishii claims to have
extensive theoretical high-level knowledge including strategic
and tactical use of BW in defense and offense, backed by some
research on best BW agents to employ by geographical areas of
Far East, and the use of BW in cold climates.

Part 3-A. Statements so far have been obtained by
persuasion, exploitation of Japanese fear of USSR, and desire
to cooperate with US. Large part of data including most of the

   Appendix "A"

valuable technical BW information as to results of human experiments and research in BW for crop destruction probably can be obtained in this manner from low echelon Japanese personnel not believed liable to "war crimes" trials.

B. Additional data, possibly including some statements from Ishii probably can be obtained by informing Japanese involved that information will be retained in intelligence channels and will not be employed as "war crimes" evidence.

C. Complete story, to include plans and theories of Ishii and superiors, probably can be obtained by documentary immunity to Ishii and associates. Ishii also can assist in securing complete cooperation of his former subordinates.

4. None of above influences joint interrogations to be held shortly with USSR under provisions of your radio W-94445.

5. Adoption of method in part 3W above recommended by CINCFE. Request reply soonest.

End

CM IN 912   (May 47)

Appendix "A"

E N C L O S U R E

‾INTERROGATION OF CERTAIN JAPANESE BY RUSSIAN PROSECUTOR

Memorandum by the State Member, SFE

The Department of State cannot approve the proposal in
SFE 188/2 that Colonel Ishii and his associates should be promised that BW information given by them will be retained in
intelligence channels and will not be employed as "war crimes"
evidence. It is believed on the basis of facts brought out in
the subject paper that is is possible that the desired information can be obtained from Colonel Ishii and his assistants without these asssurances, and that it might later be a source of
serious embarrassment to the United States if the assurances
were given. At the same time, every practicable precaution
should be taken to prevent the BW information possessed by
Colonel Ishii from being made generally known in a public trial.
It is therefore recommended that (1) that CINCFE, without making
any commitment to Ishii and the other Japanese involved, continue
to obtain all possible information in the manner heretofore
followed; (2) that information thus obtained be retained in
fact in intelligence channels unless evidence developed at the
International Military Trial presents overwhelming reasons why
this procedure can no longer be followed; and (3) that, even
though no commitment is made, the United States authorities for
security reasons not prosecute war "war crimes" charges against Ishii
and his associates.

It is proposed that paragraph "c" of the "conclusions" of
SFE 188/2 be amended as in Appendix "A" hereof, and that
Appendix "D" of SFE 188/2 be amended as in Appendix "B" hereof,
to accord with the above recommendations.

~~CONFIDENTIAL~~

SFE 188/3   - 1 -   Enclosure

APPENDIX "B"

DISCUSSION

~~CONFIDENTIAL~~

1. The value of Japanese BW information.

a. Data already obtained from Ishii and his colleagues have proven to be of great value in confirming, supplementing and complementing several phases of U.S. research in BW, and may suggest new fields for future research.

b. This Japanese information is the only known source of data from scientifically controlled experiments showing the direct effect of BW agents on man. In the past it has been necessary to evaluate the effects of BW agents on man from data obtained through animal experimentation. Such evaluation is inconclusive and far less complete than results obtained from certain types of human experimentation.

c. In addition to the results of human experimentation much valuable data is available from the Japanese experiments on animals and food crops. The voluntary imparting of this BW information may serve as a forerunner for obtaining much additional information in other fields of research.

2. Desirability of avoiding "war crimes" involvement.

a. Since it is believed that the USSR possesses only a small portion of this technical information, and since any "war crimes" trial would completely reveal such data to all nations, it is felt that such publicity must be avoided in interests of defense and security of the U.S. It is believed also that "war crimes" prosecution of Ishii and his associates would serve to stop the flow of much additional information of a technical and scientific nature.

b. It is felt that the use of this information as a basis for "war crimes" evidence would be a grave detriment to Japanese cooperation with the United States occupation forces in Japan.

c. For all practical purposes an agreement with Ishii and his associates that information given by them on the Japanese BW program will be retained in intelligence channels is equivalent to an agreement that this Government will not prosecute any of those involved in BW activities in which war crimes were committed. Such an understanding would be of great value to the security of the American people because of the information which Ishii and his associates have already furnished and will continue to furnish. However, it should be kept in mind that there is a remote possibility that independent investigation conducted by the Soviets in the Mukden Area may have disclosed evidence that American prisoners of war were used for experimental purposes of a BW nature and that they lost their lives as a result of these experiments, and further, that such evidence may be introduced by the Soviet prosecutors in the course of cross-examination of certain of the major Japanese war criminals now on trial at Tokyo, particularly during the cross-examination of Umezu, Commander of the Kwantung Army from 1939 to 1944 of which army the Ishii BW group was a part. In addition, there is a strong possibility that the Soviet prosecutors will, in the course of cross-examination of Umezu, introduce evidence of experiments conducted on human beings by the Ishii BW group, which experiments do not differ greatly from those for which this Government is now prosecuting German scientists and medical doctors at Nuremberg.

~~CONFIDENTIAL~~

APPENDIX "B"

MESSAGE TO CINCFE

Following Radio in 2 parts.

Part 1. Re URAD C-52425 of 6 May 1947. Recommendation in part 5B and 5 approved. Information obtained from Ishii and associates on BW will be retained in Intelligence channels and will not be employed as "war crimes" evidence.

Part 2. All communications above subject will be classified Top Secret.

~~CONFIDENTIAL~~

- 6 -   Appendix "B"

Rec. 6 July 49 - 1800   Christ̶ ̶t̶o̶t̶o̶t̶ - 335225
Fr. CID, MPD

1. He was run over by tram (after death.)
2. Time last night, time unknown
3. Contents (stomach) nothing
4. Presumably did not e̶a̶t̶ a̶t̶ n̶i̶g̶h̶t̶ a̶n̶d̶ t̶h̶i̶s̶ m̶o̶r̶n̶i̶n̶g̶ lunch and supper
5. ᵐᶦⁿᵒʳ Bruises on hands and right legs - Possibly before death this day murdered
6. Did not bleed much after being run over
7. No brains left to examine
   Cause of death: no sign of dope, narcotic etc
   Examination pending on poisonous drug
              Alcoholic contents pending
              Not murdered by suffocation, strangulation
* Type A blood
   Right testicle bleeding

BIBLIOGRAPHY

BOOKS

Bergamini, David. *Japan's Imperial Conspiracy*. New York: William Morrow, 1971.

Blakemore, Thomas (translator). *The Criminal Code of Japan*. Rutland, Vermont: Charles E. Tuttle, Co., 1954.

The Code of Criminal Procedure. Tokyo: Daigaku Syobo, 1949.

Dando, Shigemitsu. *Japanese Criminal Procedure*. B.J. George, Jr. (translator). South Hackensack, New Jersey: Fred B. Rothman and Company, 1965.

Deacon, Richard. *Kempei Tai: A History of the Japanese Secret Service*. New York: Berkley Publishing Group, 1983.

The Historical Encyclopedia of World War II. New York: Greenwich House, 1984.

Hughes, Richard. *Foreign Devil: Thirty Years of Reporting in the Far East*. London: Deutsche, 1972.

Ienaga, Saburo. *The Pacific War*. New York: Pantheon, 1978.

Japanese Government, Ministry of Justice. *The Code of Criminal Procedure of Japan*. Tokyo: Eibun Horei Sha, 1961.

——. *The Penal Code of Japan*. Tokyo: Eibun Hoirei Sha, 1965.

——. The Supreme Court. *Courts in Japan*. Tokyo: The Supreme Court, 1965.

——. *Outline of Criminal Justice in Japan*. Tokyo: The Supreme Court, 1963.

Johnson, Chalmers A. *Conspiracy at Matsukawa*. Berkeley, California: University of California Press, Ltd., 1972.

Langguth, A.J. *Hidden Terrors*. New York: Pantheon Books, 1978.

Maki, John M. *Court and Constitution in Japan: Selected Supreme Court Decisions, 1948–1960*. Seattle, Washington: University of Washington Press, 1984.

Materials on the Trial of Former Servicemen of the Japanese Army Charged With Manufacturing and Employing Bacteriological Weapons. Moscow: Foreign Languages Publishing House, 1950.

253

Mitchell, Richard H. *Thought Control in Prewar Japan*. Ithaca, New York: Cornell University Press, 1976.

Oppler, Alfred Christian. *Legal Reform in Occupied Japan*. Princeton, New Jersey: Princeton Press, 1976.

Reischauer, Edwin. *The Japanese*. Cambridge, Massachusetts: Harvard University Press, 1977.

Roth, Andrew. *Dilemma in Japan*. Boston: Little, Brown, 1945.

ARTICLES

Fearey, Robert. "The Occupation of Japan — Second Phase," Report to the Institute of Pacific Relations, 1950.

Martin, Edwin M. "The Allied Occupation of Japan," A Study for the Institute of Pacific Relations, 1948.

The Nation, Vol. 234, No. 6. February 13, 1982.

Powell, John W. "A Hidden Chapter in History," *The Bulletin of the Atomic Scientists*. Vol. 37, No. 8. October 1981.

Powell, John W. "Japan's Germ Warfare: The U.S. Cover-up of a War Crime," *The Bulletin of Concerned Asian Scholars*. Vol. 12, October–December, 1980.

Sebald, William and Spinks, C. Nelson. "Japan: Prospects, Options, and Opportunities," A Study for the American Enterprise Institute for Policy Research, March 1967.

OTHER

International Military Tribunal for the Far East. Court House of the Tribunal War Ministry Building. Tokyo, August 29, 1946.

Supreme Commander for the Allied Powers. Selected Archives. United States National Archives. Legal Section. Medical Section. United States Army Surgeon General. United States Chemical Corps. Public Safety Division. 441st Counter-Intelligence Corps. G-2 Intelligence.

"War Crime," *60 Minutes*. transcript, Vol. 14, No. 27. CBS Television Network. April 4, 1982.

INDEX